MAP OF KOREA

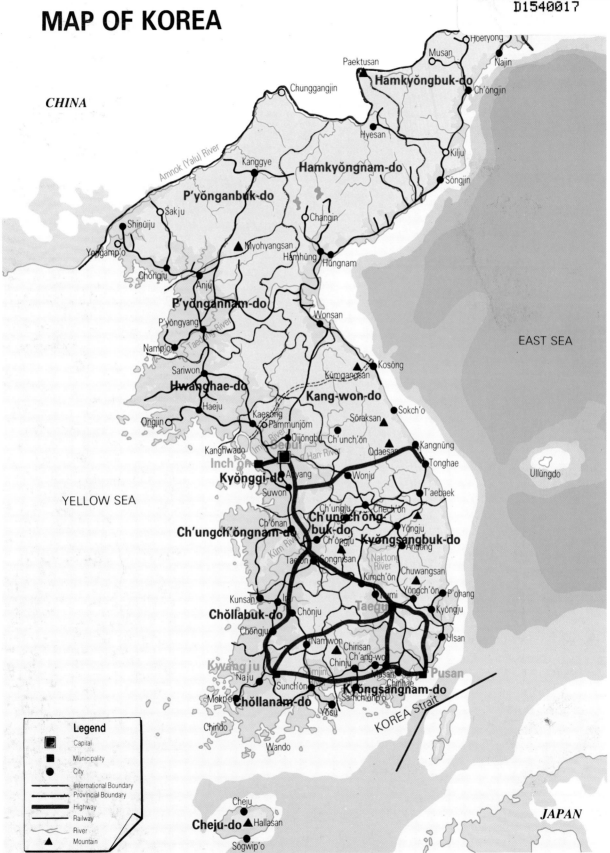

CHINA

Paektusan

Hoeryong
Musan
Najin
Chunggangjin
Hamkyŏngbuk-do
Ch'ŏngjin
Hyesan
Kilju
Kanggye
Hamkyŏngnam-do
Sŏngjin
Amnok (Yalu) River
P'yŏnganbuk-do
Sakju
Changjin
Shinŭiju
Myohyangsan
Hamhŭng
Hŭngnam
Yŏngamp'o
Ch'ŏngju
Anju
P'yŏngannam-do
Wŏnsan
P'yŏngyang
Taedong River
Namp'o
EAST SEA
Sariwon
Kŭmgangsan
Kosŏng
Hwanghae-do
Kang-won-do
Sŏraksan
Sokch'o
Haeju
Kaesŏng
Ongjin
Panmunjŏm
Sŏraksan
Uijŏngbu
Ch'unch'ŏn
Odaesan
Kangnŭng
Kanghwado
Im River
Seoul
Han River
Tonghae
Inch'ŏn
Anyang
Wŏnju
Ullŭngdo
Kyŏnggi-do
Suwon
T'aebaek
YELLOW SEA
Ch'ungju
Check'ŏn
Ch'ŏnan
Ch'ungch'ŏng-buk-do
Ch'ungch'ŏngnam-do
Ch'ŏngju
Yongju
Taejŏn
Songnisan
Kyŏngsangbuk-do
Kŭm River
Chuwangsan
Kimch'ŏn
Naktong River
Andong
Kunsan
Iri
Kumi
Yŏngch'ŏn
P'ohang
Chŏllabuk-do
Chŏnju
Taegu
Kyŏngju
Chŏngju
Ulsan
Namwŏn
Chirisan
Ch'ang-wŏn
Naju
Chinju
Masan
Kwangju
Sŏmjin
Chinhae
Pusan
Sunch'ŏn
Kyŏngsangnam-do
Samch'ŏnp'o
Mokp'o
Chŏllanam-do
Yŏsu
KOREA Strait
Chindo
Wando
Cheju
JAPAN
Cheju-do Hallasan
Sŏgwip'o

Legend

▣	Capital
■	Municipality
●	City
──	International Boundary
──	Provincial Boundary
━━	Highway
──	Railway
~~	River
▲	Mountain

THE MAKING OF
MODERN KOREA

Dr. Yushin Yoo
Murray State University

THE GOLDEN POND PRESS
NEW YORK LOUISVILLE

THIS BOOK IS DEDICATED TO MY PARENTS,
REV. EUL SUL YOO AND SHOON HI CHOI
and
to Christopher & J. J. Yoon

Preface

There has been an overwhelmingly enthusiastic reception for my earlier book, Korea the Beautiful: Treasures of the Hermit Kingdom. Many scholars and general readers have encouraged me to bring out a similar work covering the period from the close of the Second World War to the present day. This book, the Making of Modern Korea is the result.

This work is intended to give scholars, students and general readers an understanding of the uniqueness of Korean culture and an appreciation of its contribution to both Asian and world civilization. The theme of this book is the philosophy of Benefits to All Mankind, which has been the spirit of the nation from its foundation.

I would like to express my gratitude to the Committee on International Studies and Research at Murray State University, for the research grant which allowed me to complete my research for this book during the year 1989-90. I wish also to express my appreciation to Mr. Park Shinil, Korea's Assistant Minister for Overseas Information Service, and to all his staff members. This office provided me with many valuable documents and much assistance in my endeavor.

I am especially grateful to several outstanding professors at Murray State University and want to give particular thanks to Dr. Michael M. Cohen, Dr. Terry Foreman, Dr. Jerry A. Herndon, and Dr. Coy Harmon. They all reviewed this work and gave me many valuable suggestions and criticism. They materially assisted me in improving the book.

Special thanks go to Ms. Maura L. Corley, Ms. Patsy Rains, and Ms. Tina Kennedy who assisted me with various tasks in preparing the manuscript.

Grateful appreciation also goes to all those readers of Korea the Beautiful who telephoned and wrote me to encourage me to continue my work. Without this type of inspiration, this new work would never have been created.

MURRAY, KENTUCKY
JANUARY 1990

Yushin Yoo

THE MAKING OF
MODERN KOREA

U.S. Library of Congress Cataloging in Publication Data
    YOO, YUSHIN
    The Making of Modern Korea

    Includes appendices and indexes
    SUMMARY: An Introduction to the Modern Period of Korea,
    Education, Economics and Social Changes.

    1. Korea-Civilization 2. Korea-History 3. Korea-Education
    4. Korea-Economics 5. Korea-Industrial Revolution
    6. Olympic Games, Seoul 1988.
    I. Title.

    DS 902.4 Y64 1990   915.19   LC 90-80305
    ISBN 0-942091-03-5

Copyright 1990 by Yushin Yoo
1005 Westgate Dr., Murray, Kentucky 42071

Golden Pond Press
16 South Village Ave.
Rockville Center, New York 11570

Golden Pond Press
909 Stoney Kirk Drive
Louisville, Kentucky 40223

Contents

Chronological Table

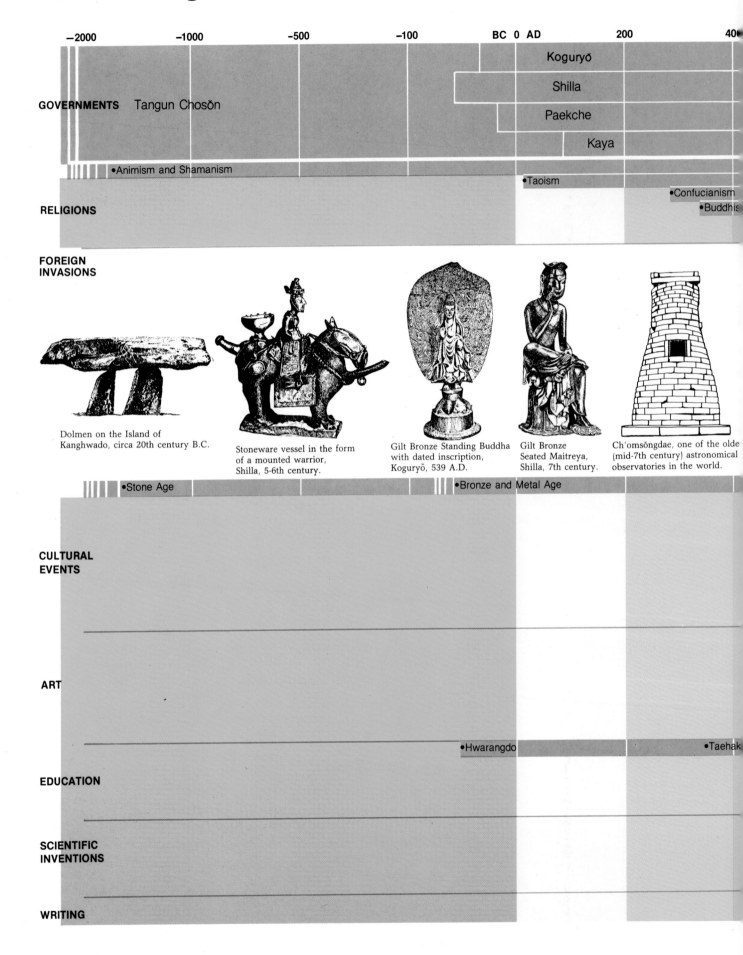

	−2000	−1000	−500	−100	BC 0 AD	200	40
GOVERNMENTS	Tangun Chosŏn				Koguryŏ / Shilla / Paekche / Kaya		
RELIGIONS	•Animism and Shamanism				•Taoism	•Confucianism / •Buddhis	
FOREIGN INVASIONS							

Dolmen on the Island of Kanghwado, circa 20th century B.C.

Stoneware vessel in the form of a mounted warrior, Shilla, 5-6th century.

Gilt Bronze Standing Buddha with dated inscription, Koguryŏ, 539 A.D.

Gilt Bronze Seated Maitreya, Shilla, 7th century.

Ch'omsŏngdae, one of the olde (mid-7th century) astronomical observatories in the world.

CULTURAL EVENTS	•Stone Age				•Bronze and Metal Age		
ART							
EDUCATION					•Hwarangdo	•Taehak	
SCIENTIFIC INVENTIONS							
WRITING							

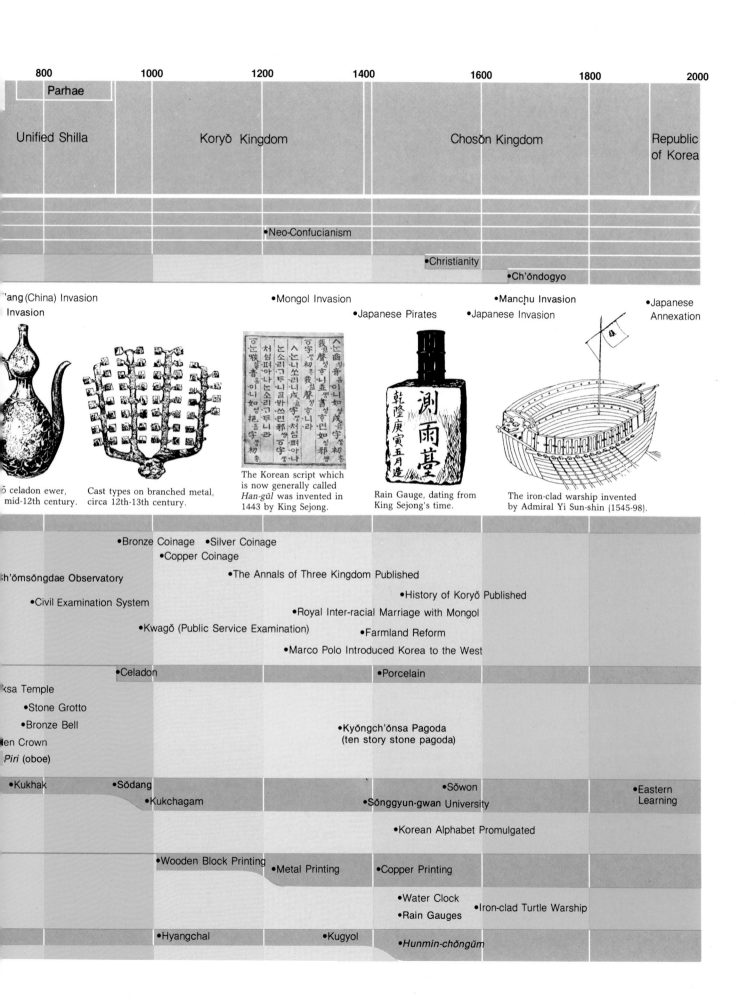

800	1000	1200	1400	1600	1800	2000

Parhae

Unified Shilla | Koryŏ Kingdom | Chosŏn Kingdom | Republic of Korea

•Neo-Confucianism

•Christianity

•Ch'ŏndogyo

'ang (China) Invasion
Invasion

•Mongol Invasion

•Japanese Pirates

•Manchu Invasion

•Japanese Invasion

•Japanese Annexation

ŏ celadon ewer, mid-12th century.

Cast types on branched metal, circa 12th-13th century.

The Korean script which is now generally called *Han-gŭl* was invented in 1443 by King Sejong.

Rain Gauge, dating from King Sejong's time.

The iron-clad warship invented by Admiral Yi Sun-shin (1545-98).

•Bronze Coinage   •Silver Coinage
•Copper Coinage

h'ŏmsŏngdae Observatory

•The Annals of Three Kingdom Published

•History of Koryŏ Published

•Civil Examination System

•Royal Inter-racial Marriage with Mongol

•Kwagŏ (Public Service Examination)

•Farmland Reform

•Marco Polo Introduced Korea to the West

•Celadon

•Porcelain

ksa Temple

•Stone Grotto

•Bronze Bell

en Crown

Piri (oboe)

•Kyŏngch'ŏnsa Pagoda
(ten story stone pagoda)

•Kukhak   •Sŏdang

•Kukchagam

•Sŏwon

•Sŏnggyun-gwan University

•Eastern Learning

•Korean Alphabet Promulgated

•Wooden Block Printing

•Metal Printing

•Copper Printing

•Water Clock

•Iron-clad Turtle Warship

•Rain Gauges

•Hyangchal

•Kugyol

•*Hunmin-chŏngŭm*

CHRONOLOGICAL TABLE

	KOREA	CHINA	JAPAN	THE WEST
B.C.	Paleolithic Age Neolithic Age			
5,000		Bronze Age	Jomon Period	Early Mesopotamia Egyptian Kingdoms
2,000		Shang Dynasty (1766-1122) Chou (1122-256)		
1,000	Bronze Age Ancient Chosŏn	Spring and Autumn Era (770-476) Iron Age		Greek Civilization Founding of Rome (735)
500	Iron Age Puyŏ	Warring States Era (475-221) Chin Dynasty (221-206) Western Han Dynasty (206B.C.-A.D.9)	Bronze Age Yayoi Period	Socrates (469-399) Alexander the Great (356-323) First Punic War (264-241) Second Punic War (219-201)
200	Confederated Kingdoms of Samhan (Three Han States)			Julius Ceasar (101-44)
100	Three Kingdoms: Shilla (57B.C.-A.D.935) Koguryŏ (37B.C.-A.D.668) Paekche (18B.C.-A.D.660)			Birth of Jesus Christ
A.D.	Kaya (42-562)	Hsin Dynasty (8-25) Eastern Han Dynasty (26-221)		
200		Three Kingdoms (220-280) Chin Dynasty (265-420)	Iron Age Tumulus Period	
300				Christianity established as state religion of Roman Empire (392) Roman Empire split in two (395)
400		Northern and Southern Dynasties (420-581)		Anglo-Saxons established in Britain (449)
500		Sui Dynasty (581-618)	Asuka Period (552-645)	Mohammed (570-632)
600	Parhae Kingdom (669-928) Unified Shilla Kingdom (618-935)	T'ang Dynasty (618-906)	Nara Period (645-794)	Hegira (622) and beginning of Islamic era
700			Heian Period (794-1185)	
800				Charles the Great crowned first Holy Roman Emperor (800)
900	Koryŏ Kingdom (918-1392)	Five Dynasties (906-960) Sung Dynasty (960-1279)		
1000				First Crusade (1096-99)
1100			Kamakura Period (1185-1392)	
1200		Yüan Dynasty (1279-1368)		Magna Carta (1215) Marco Polo (1254-1324)
1300	Chosŏn Kingdom (1392-1910)	Ming Dynasty (1368-1644)	Muromachi (Ashikaga) Period (1392-1568)	The Hundred Years' War (1334-1434)
1400				Gutenberg's Press (1438) Columbus discovered America (1492)
1500			Momoyama Period (1568-1615)	Martin Luther launched reform of the Church (1517)
1600		Ch'ing Dynasty (1644-1911)	Tokugawa Period (1615-1867)	The Thirty Years' War (1618-48)
1700				American Independence (1766) French Revolution (1789-1793)
1800	Taehan Empire Proclaimed (1897)		Modern Period (1868-)	American Civil War (1861-65)
1900	Annexation by Japan (1910) Establishment of the Republic of Korea (1948)	Establishment of the Republic of China (1912)		World War I (1914-18) World War II (1939-45)

PART ONE
Introduction

Historical And Political Development

Korea, the East Asian country once known both as the "Land of Morning Calm" and the "Hermit Kingdom," has one of the oldest civilizations in the world, one dating back in history more than 5,000 years. Although this nation was little known to the West until the Korean War, Korea has been well known and highly valued for centuries by China, Russia, and Japan, the three nations surrounding the peninsula.

According to archaeological evidence and linguistic studies, as well as historical records, tribes inhabiting the Altaic Mountains started migrating eastward to Manchuria and Siberia thousands of years ago. Some of them, believed to be Tungusic in origin, came as far east as the coasts of the Korean peninsula. They liked what they saw and settled there, soon to become a homogeneous race, sharing distinctive physical characteristics, one language, and one culture.

The Korean people, as far back as history records and probably much farther, have inhabited a peninsula extending due south of Manchuria, curving gently east and then west, forming a tiger-like shape. They possess a culturally unique, homogeneous national identity, closely related to, yet independent of the cultures of their powerful neighbors, China, Japan, and Russia. A small country with a distinctive history and culture, influenced in part by others, but having its unique stamp, Korea has successfully maintained its national identity. Throughout history, Koreans have been victims of foreign attacks but the spirit of the Korean race and nation has never been extinguished.

The legendary past of the nation stretches back nearly 5,000 years. According to historical records, the Korean people once exercised control over Shantung and Shansi Provinces in China and almost the entire territory of Manchuria. In 2333 B.C., according to legend, Tan-gun united several tribes in the northern part of Korea and set up the first Korean nation under the ideology of Hong-ik In-gan or "Benefits to All Mankind." They named their nation "Chosŏn," which means the "Land of Morning Calm." Tan-gun taught his people about government, marriage, agriculture, cooking, housing and all aspects of civilized life. He ruled the nation of Chosŏn until 1122 B.C.

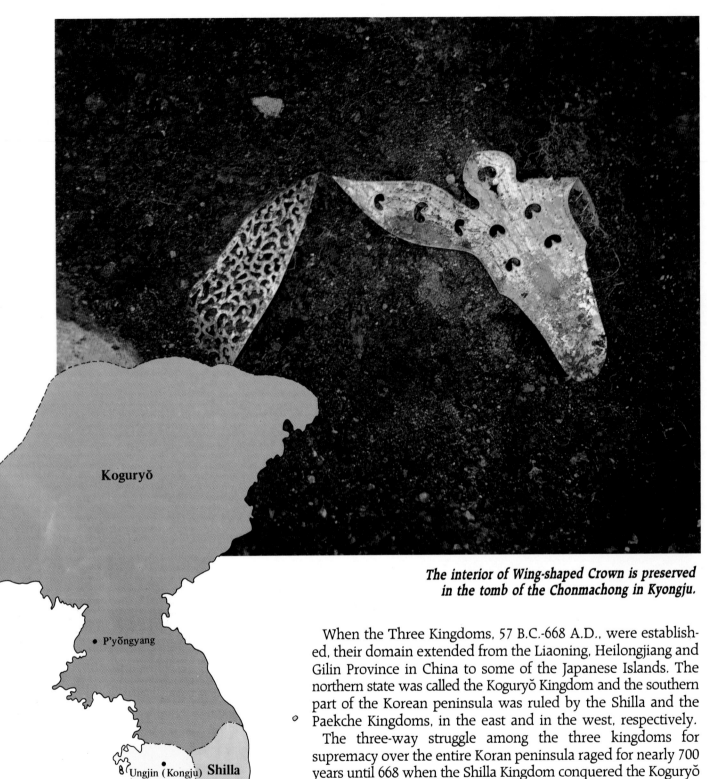

Koguryŏ

P'yŏngyang

Ungjin (Kongju) Shilla
Sabi (Puyŏ)
Kŭmsŏng
Kaya
Paekche

Chejudo Island

The interior of Wing-shaped Crown is preserved in the tomb of the Chonmachong in Kyongju.

When the Three Kingdoms, 57 B.C.-668 A.D., were established, their domain extended from the Liaoning, Heilongjiang and Gilin Province in China to some of the Japanese Islands. The northern state was called the Koguryŏ Kingdom and the southern part of the Korean peninsula was ruled by the Shilla and the Paekche Kingdoms, in the east and in the west, respectively.

The three-way struggle among the three kingdoms for supremacy over the entire Koran peninsula raged for nearly 700 years until 668 when the Shilla Kingdom conquered the Koguryŏ Kingdom, having conquered the Paekche Kingdom eight years before. When the Korean peninsula was thus unified, Shilla's territory extended up to the Taedong River, while most of the former Koguryŏ territory in Manchuria became Parhae, a new state founded by Koguryŏ refugees.

The Shilla kings presided over a cultural renaissance as brilliant as it was relatively brief. At this time, the Korean kings established a "younger brother" relationship with the emperors of China unlike any form of international linkage earlier known in the

Tombs in Tumulri Park in Kyongju.

Sanggyŏng

Parhae

Unified Shilla

Kŭmsŏng
(Kyŏngju)

Chejudo Island

Orient. Korean culture came to incorporate the cultures not only of China and of various tribes of northeast Asia, but also of many other tribes living west of the Chinese mainland. The archaeological remnants left behind by this ancient kingdom include remarkable jewelry, pottery, and Buddhist relics still to be seen around the ancient capital city, Kyŏngju.

Buddhist influence entered Korean culture mostly through China. The philosophy of Buddhism had presented itself as an entirely new world of thought to the Korean people, largely through Chinese characters. These borrowings were modified to suit local conditions and eventually were passed on to Japan. By the end of the Shilla period, Buddhist culture had become indelibly stamped on Korea, so much so that for a time it came to be identified almost wholly with Korean culture.

The long years of peace and prosperity after the unification of the Korean peninsula by the Shilla Kingdom, however, led to the decadence of the nobility and to the rise of powerful clan chieftains who weakened the power of the Shilla kings.

13

General Wang Kŏn was one of those military chieftains who helped to defeat the Shilla Kingdom and who succeeded in founding a new kingdom named Koryŏ, from which the present English word "Korea" is derived. The last king of Shilla offered his kingdom to General Wang Kŏn, signifying the peaceful transfer of government.

The Koryŏ Kingdom ruled the peninsula for 475 years, through a succession of 34 kings. Buddhism flourished as the state religion, and social and ethical principles of Confucian origin served as the moral standards. Innumerable temples were built throughout the country, and the arts found ready expression in Buddhist sculpture, painting, architecture and literature. The people of Koryŏ succeeded in developing a Buddhist world of their own, as evidenced by publication of the mammoth *Tripitaka Koreana,* historically significant as the first example of woodcut, block-type printing.

The publication of the *Tripitaka Koreana* was begun in 1011 by command of the eighth Koryŏ king, Hyŏnjong. It was compiled from more than 5,000 volumes of Buddhist scripture imported from China. More than 16 years were required to engrave woodblocks necessary to complete the project, which eventually comprised more than 6,000 volumes. Later, in 1232, movable, metal printing type was invented and used for the first time in the world in Koryŏ, over 200 years before Gutenberg first used movable cast lead printing type in Germany in 1450.

The Wooden blocks used to print the Tripitaka Koreana in Haeinsa Temple (above), Metal type invented in Korea during the 12th century (below).

Making a reproduction of the Koryo celadon pieces

The Koryŏ civilization flourished for many centuries, during which time the first civil service examination system was inaugurated, schools for education of the young were established, and taxation laws were instituted to stabilize national revenues.

During this era bronze coins were used, and the art of printing was highly developed. Koryŏ was renowned for its highly refined celadon ceramics, considered by many the most graceful ever made by man and still treasured in museums around the world.

Continual harassment of Koryŏ by northern invaders of central Asia, who had conquered China and who threatened both central Europe and Japan, was climaxed by the Mongol invasion of the kingdom in the 13th century when the Mongols crossed the Yalu River and marched on the capital city of Kaesŏng. The court moved to Kanghwado Island at the mouth of the Han River and resisted the invaders for over 40 years before it finally concluded a peace treaty under which the Koryŏ king accepted the overlordship of the Mongol Khan. The Mongols eventually withdrew after the failure of their invasion armada to subdue Japan, but their continuing influence at the Korean court resulted in political splits and eventually in a revolt in support of renewed nationlism. As a result, the Chosŏn Kingdom was established in 1392.

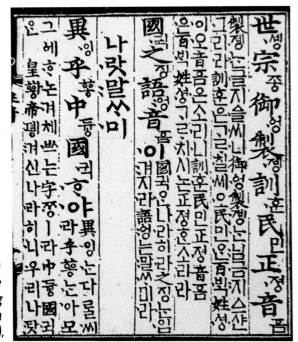

Hunmin-chongum or "script for the people," King Sejong is known for Han-gul (right).

General Yi Sŏng-gye, enthroned as the first king of the new kingdom in 1392, moved the capital city from Kaesŏng to the site of the present day Seoul. The early period of the kingdom brought major reforms in political and social structures. Buddhism, which had wielded great power during the previous kingdom, gave way to Confucianism, which the new kingdom espoused as the state cult.

Remarkable cultural strides were made during the first 70 years of the Chosŏn Kingdom. The man most responsible for the brilliant age of culture was King Sejong, the most enlightened ruler the kingdom had yet had. His encouragement and personal interest led to many scientific and technological inventions and cultural innovations.

To enable the Korean people to write their own language, King Sejong first developed *Han-gul*, the Korean alphabet of 28 letters, which was later reduced to the present 24 letters. It was simple in form and of such phonetic adaptability and clarity that anyone could learn to read and write it in a very short time. He also made contributions to the study of astronomy by constructing sundials and astronomical observatories. With the aid of scholars many literary works were published in the native language he had fostered.

In the late 16th Century, the Chosŏn Kingdom suffered its first major foreign invasion, by Japan. Toyotomi Hideyoshi, the new shogun of Japan at that time, had requested that the Chosŏn government grant his troops free passage up the Korean peninsula to facilitate a planned invasion of Manchuria and China, but the request had been refused. The Japanese responded with an invasion in 1592. The Japanese forces took less than three weeks to capture Seoul after disembarking at Pusan.

With Korea's very existence thus at stake, there emerged a great national hero, Admiral Yi sun-shin, who invented the "turtle war-

16

The ironclad "turtle-boats" (center). Rain gauge, dating from King Sejong's reign (left). A fashion show of the Choson Kingdom court costumes (below).

ship" (Kŏbuksŏn), the first ironclad warship in the world's naval history. With a fleet of these turtle warships he attacked the huge flotilla of Japanese vessels and defeated the enemy in battle after battle. The Japanese were finally driven back to their own shores.

During the next 300 years the Chosŏn Kingdom shut itself off almost completely from the rest of the world, largely because the invasion by the Japanese and the subsequent aggression by the Manchus showed how troublesome it was to live in open contact with warlike neighbors. This was a period of the "Korean dark ages," a period during which Korea came to be known as the Hermit Kingdom.

Despite remarkable achievements such as the invention of movable printing type, an efficient phonetic Korean alphabet to replace the Chinese ideographs, and the success of the ironclad warships, by the late 19th century Korea found herself in no position to resist, or even properly comprehend, the encroachments of Western technology, trade, and imperialism.

The Chosŏn Kingdom basked in complacent isolationism until 1866 when Western influence was physically felt. The state persecution of Catholics, including the execution of nine French Jesuits, led the French government to dispatch a punitive fleet to Korea, but its forces were driven back by Korean soldiers. Then, in 1871, an American flotilla under Admiral Rodgers was sent to the country in hopes of repeating Commodore Perry's exploits in Japan. But it was Japan, the latecomer on the scene, which succeeded in opening Korea in 1876. This was soon followed in 1882 by a treaty with the United States and other major powers contending in the area. Korea thus became the scene of bitter rivalry for domination among Russians, Japanese, and Chinese because of the strategic location of the peninsula, as well as its potential for exploitation. Japan emerged victorious over the others by defeating China in 1894 and then Russia in 1904-05.

Women demonstrating for Korean Independence from Japan on March 1, 1919 (above), Korea's liberation on August 15, 1945 (up).

Japan annexed Korea on August 29, 1910, in the 4243rd year after the legendary founding of Korea by Tan-gun, thus putting an end to the 500-year-old Chosŏn Kingdom. Now Koreans found themselves second-class citizens in their own country. Then began a 36-year "dark age," during which the Japanese made every effort to erase any trace of Korean national identity. Koreans, however, were not entirely without hope for the restoration of their independence. In March, 1919, Koreans carried out a nationwide peaceful protest demonstration against Japanese rule, hoping for support from the Versailles Peace Conference, which had proclaimed national self-determination as a principle of international law. This provoked further brutal persecution by the Japanese, but this attracted virtually no notice abroad. However, the occasioin served symbolically to focus the Koreans' new sense of nationalism and yearning for independence. The independence movement was advanced repeatedly by students or religious groups until Japanese rule was ended in 1945 with the defeat of Japan at the end of World War II. Prior to that, the Japanese colonial authorities had stepped up their attempts to "assimilate" the Korean people by forbidding the use of the national language, banning many books and periodicals written in Korea and forcing the substitution of Japanese names for all personal Korean names. Numerous young Koreans had been conscripted not only into the Japanese army but also to work at Japanese mines and factories during World War II.

No sooner had the Korean people heard the bells of liberation rung in 1945 than they found their fatherland divided into two parts at the 38th parallel. The northern half of the peninsula fell into the hands of Russia, and Americans held the south. Provisions contained in the Cairo Declaration and later resolutions of the United Nations in September, 1947, insured general elections in Korea under United Nations supervision. In accordance with the resolutions, the United Nations Commission for Korea

was dispatched to Seoul in January, 1948, to supervise the elections under which a unified Korean government would be formed. However, North Korea, which had rejected the United Nations resolutions, obstructed the entry of the United Nations Commission into North Korea, and the general elections were held in the only area to which the commission had access, that south of the 38th parallel.

On August 15, 1948, three years after Korea was liberated, the government of the Republic of Korea (ROK) was officially proclaimed. The United Nations approved the Republic of Korea as the legitimate government in the South.

The Korean War, a most tragic period of fratricide for the Korean nation, broke out on June 25, 1950, less than two years after the establishment of the rival governments. As the American General Douglas MacArthur described it, "North Korea struck like a cobra." Armed by their Soviet mentors, the People's Army of the North crossed the 38th parallel in a surprise attack and launched a full-scale invasion. Forty-miles of heavy artillery opened fire. Brigades of tanks roared southward. The Republic of Korea's Army, lacking both tanks and effective anti-tank weapons, was driven back. The government fled, and the invaders occupied the capital. Of the South's 65,000 defenders, nearly half had been killed or wounded. The free world was outraged. In response to a United Nations resolution, a 16-nation fighting force was sent in under the command of General Douglas MacArthur. The capital was quickly re-taken. Soon the invaders were driven north, beyond the 38th parallel, and MacArthur forced the war into the invaders' own territory.

However Red China entered the fighting on the side of the North, and the war reached a stalemate, ending with a negotiated truce. One result was the present 249.5 kilometer-long Military Demarcation Line cutting across the waist of the Korean peninsula.

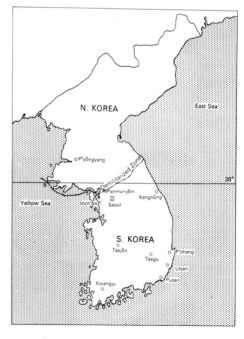

North Korean invasion of Seoul, June 1950, destroyed Myongdong in the Seoul (above left), Millions of North Koreans fled southward over destroyed bridges ahead of hordes of Chinese troops who entered the war in October 1950 (above right), Line on a map to mark a 193-kilometer Demilitarized Zone.

In the Republic of Korea, recovery from wartime devastation was slow until the 1960 explusion of the aged and authoritarian president, Syngman Rhee. After a year of political confusion, during which many violent demonstrations occurred and two governments attempted to restore order, an army junta seized power in a peaceful coup. The junta instituted rigorous discipline, made long overdue reforms, and eventually restored democratic civilian government in 1963.

The pattern of turbulent life brought about by the domination of foreign rulers continued to be evident, as Korea continued to suffer from poverty and instability. But the painful wounds of war and territorial division brought a fierce craving for peace and unity. While the nation's poverty and civil unrest were often almost unbearable to its people, their determination to achieve affluence and stability only became firmer. This national awareness led in the 1960's to the beginning of Korea's modernization.

In December, 1963, the Third Republic was inaugurated under the leadership of President Park Chung Hee. President Park, who was re-elected in 1967 and 1971, led the nation back to the course of revitalizing the ideology of "Benefits to All Mankind" and thus created one of the world's most remarkable national economic developments. For the first time in modern history, the human and natural resources of the nation were effectively organized. The economy began to grow at an annual rate of 9.2 percent, per capita. The gross national product (GNP) zoomed from $87 million in 1962 to $1,503 million in 1980 and exports rose by 32.8 percent a year, from $56.7 million in 1962 to $17.50 billion in 1980.

In the diplomatic area, relations were normalized with Japan and there was an active expansion of diplomatic relations throughout the world. On the Korean peninsula, the first contact after a quarter-century of national division was made between the South and the North in 1971. The Red Cross societies of the two parts of Korea began to meet in September, 1971, to discuss the question of locating and exchanging information about relatives dispersed in the South and the North. Political contacts were also started in May, 1972, culminating in the historic South-North Joint Communiques of July 4, 1972, in which South and North Korea agreed to work for peaceful reunification.

But the rapidly changing domestic and international situation was seen as embodying grave implications for Korea. Therefore the Park administration decided that to compete more effectively with North Korea and to cope with other challenges to the nation, all national strength should be consolidated into one cohesive force. Constitutional amendments were thus proposed in October, 1972, and approved overwhelmingly in a subsequent national referendum. With the promulgation of the revised Constitution in December, a new political order, referred to as the Yushin (Revitalizing Reforms) System was established and the Fourth Republic was inaugurated.

In the ensuing years, Korea successfully weathered the oil crisis

The South-North Red Cross Conference in Panmunjom in 1988 (above).

People gathered to participate in a family search campaign held by the network in 1983 (bottom).

and continued to grow. The Saemaŭl Undong or New Community Movement brought increasing prosperity to rural and urban areas and provided experience in democratic problem solving. Diplomatic relations continued to expand. Only the South-North dialogue hesitated and then came to a standstill.

Tragically, on October 26, 1979, President Park was struck down by an assassin's bullet. Prime Minister Choi Kyu-hah became acting President under the terms of the Constitution, and shortly thereafter he was elected President by the National Conference for Unification, an electoral college set up as part of the Yushin System.

During the next several months, Korea went through a difficult period characterized by political, social, and economic instability. Out of this seemingly chaotic situation, there emerged a consensus that there must be a new Constitution. A more sophisticated citizenry was entering a new decade with vastly different problems. It was also agreed that a number of negative side effects resulting from the country's rapid development needed immediate reform if Korea was to regain lost momentum and revive economic creativity.

However, feuding political groups were unable to agree on what basic directions the nation should take in shaping its political future, and domestic unrest persisted. This culminated in the Kwangju Turmoil in May, 1980, which was the most tragic national event since the Korean War.

During this period of turbulent transition, General Chun Doo Hwan emerged as the dominant leader of the nation, directing the reform government, restoring order and setting new priorities for the government. On August 16, 1980, President Choi resigned, citing the need to make the transition period as short as possible. General Chun resigned from the Army on August 22 and was elected president by the National Conference for Unification on August 27.

Immediate social and economic reforms were set in motion, and in October, the president offered a new Constitution, later approved by popular vote, guaranteeing political and civil rights and limiting the presidency to a single seven-year term. Thus began the Fifth Republic.

Following the establishment of the Fifth Republic, events moved quickly. Political parties, which had been abolished by the previous Constitution, began to organize again in December 1980. All political activities were resumed in January, 1981, and martial law was removed after a long 15 months. A presidential election was held in February, 1981 and National Assembly elections a month later. On March 3, 1981, President Chun took office, promising to build a "Great Korea" in a new era. On April 11, the opening session of the National Assembly, consisting of 276 members from eight political parties, was convened and the groundwork for the Fifth Republic was in order.

The accomplishments of the Fifth Republic were many and significant, including social reforms, the first-ever surplus in the balance of payments and a peaceful change of administrations,

21

which was no small feat, considering Korea's past record of tumultuous political upheavals at the end of every presidency. But the period was also plagued by many political problems that tended to overshadow the accomplishments, particularly near the end. These questions included the issue of the legitimacy of the government and the pressure for constitutional change toward direct election of the president. The Sixth Republic was born out of the solution to these pressing issues which had grown to crisis proportions.

The Sixth Republic began with the inauguration of President Roh Tae Woo and the simultaneous enforcement of the revised constitution. These events had been preceded by the June 29, 1987 Declaration of political reforms by Roh which accepted all the opposition demands, thus defusing the political crisis, and which proclaimed the first direct election of the president in 16 years. Thus, unlike the Fifth Republic, the Sixth Republic began on a positive note with the most serious political issues put to rest.

President Roh began his term of office promising that there would be an end to authoritarianism, with a new Bo-Tong-Saram or "ordinary man" empowered, and that the June 29 Declaration would continue to be faithfully implemented. Many steps have been taken to change not only the appearance but the substance of government. These steps range from the use of a round table at meetings to the careful review of all existing laws with the aim of repealing or revising any undemocratic ones. A number of people detained on political charges have been released and their civil rights restored. Institutional and non-institutional forms of interference in press activities and labor-management affairs have been discontinued. In short, all the na-

tion's institutions are being made democratic at a rapid pace.

As a result of the nation's hard work and dedication, the decade of the 80's has been one of the most significant in the annals of their country. By overcoming trials and tribulations such as few other nations have gone through, Korea now proudly joins the prosperous members of the international community, who are capable of helping the less fortunate. Not only have Korean citizens awakened themselves from long lethargy and stagnation to knock on the doors of a new historical era, they have begun to tap the national potential hidden in the five thousand years of the nation's recorded history.

During the past decade, progress in all fields has been rapid. Korea's industrial base is growing, and the nation is increasingly recognized as a source of high skills and quality production. As a result, new industrial complexes sparkle on the skyline of its cities. Korea now supplies a world market with everything from quality craftsmanship to high technology.

Through a difficult history that would have had it otherwise, South Korea has moved forward. In just a few decades, it has become a showplace of the Far East. As a host to the International Olympics in 1988, it showed that it has fully joined the world family of progressive nations. Despite the years of successive invasions, including the latest terrible one in the twentieth century, South Korea remains a beautiful country. The nation now faces the world with fresh confidence, pride, and optimism, armed with the philosophy of Benefits to All Mankind that has kept its people one nation and one people for so long and with a common language and culture, a clear sense of national identity, and a stubborn determination to shape its own destiny.

23

PART TWO
Educational Heritage

A. Classical Enlightenment

According to the *History of Three Kingdoms*, written in 1274 by the Buddhist priest Iryŏn, the Tan-gun established the "Chosŏn Kingdom" under the philosophy of "Hong-ik In-gan" or "Benefits to All Mankind." "Hong-ik In-gan" is a concept which is aimed at instilling in both people and government a resolve to do good in the interest of all mankind. Under the influence of this ideal arises the teaching that all human beings should be treated as brothers, with a respect for harmony and peace. A central idea is that the betterment of all private lives in each state leads to the betterment of all of human society, so the Korean state works to instill the ideal of love and peace in its people, with the ultimate goal of helping improve human society as a whole. Regardless of which country one belongs to, or how strange each person may look to another, all human beings on this globe are brothers and sisters. This philosophy of "Benefits to All Mankind" should be understood for its emphasis on peace and love for one's fellow human beings.

The idea that people in a society can achieve harmony transcending differences of personality and opinions, reflects the belief that human beings by nature are basically the same and are born equal. It is by no means a narrow individualism, but a broad philosophy that advocates sharing both joy and pain. This ideal is evident in the Korean tradition of going immediately to the aid of neighbors in any distress, of joining them on happy occasions without quite being invited to do so. It is also rooted in Korea's tradition of considering cooperation as a supreme virtue.

This ancient ideology of respecting one's fellow man naturally has led to the creation of a form of society based on humanism. There is evidence from ancient Korean history that the various kingdoms always considered the people as the essence of the nation. The ultimate goal of Korean politics was to assure the people of righteousness and justice following the Mandate of Heaven. The belief that only politics devoted to the public weal is worthy of the mandate of heaven produced the famed, ancient adage, "The minds of the people are the minds of heaven." The tendency in the Western democracies is to think that concepts such as equality and democracy were born in the west, but this ancient Korean philosophy of Benefits to All Mankind led very early to a democratic tradition.

This ideology of Benefits to All Mankind also became the foundation of Korea's ancient educational system. Throughout the ages this guiding principle has been used to deepen and to cultivate the spirit of harmony in the youth of the country and to assure their cooperation. The Hwarangdo or "Flower-of-Youth Corps" education during the Shilla Kingdom (57 B.C.-A.D. 935) showed this principle of providing the youth with training for developing character. Even in such an early civilization the aims, contents, methods, and evaluation of education were based on the principle of Benefits to All Mankind. Members of the Hwarangdo found their inspiration not only in tough physical training, but also in th cultivation of a taste for literature and the arts. In order to broaden their minds and to develop their character, the Hwarangdo made a practice of visiting places of scenic beauty, and they wrote poems and music and recited poetry when they visited such places.

Hwarangdo or the "Flower Youth Corps."

In the building of harmonious relationships, the Hwarang Knights also formed a powerful solidarity. Their prototype of a manly man was a knight who would fearlessly give up his life for other peoples, but who would also show compassion for life in all its forms. The ideal man was a fearless warrior at once determined to protect the cause and honor of the community, but one who was also romantic and appreciative of the great natural beauty surrounding him.

Another interesting feature of the hwarang Knights Schools is that virtues of filial piety, loyalty, trustworthiness, justice and restraint against unnecessary taking of life were stressed. The objectives were postulated by the famous priest, Wŏn-gwang, who brought together in his teaching all of the religious, philosophical, and social ideals in favor during that particular time. Above all, these virtues were necessary to promote Benefits to All Mankind. To implement these ideals, a new curriculum for teaching the Hwarangdo Knights was necessary. Thus, the Hwarangdo School inculcating a spirit of harmony and unity became the foundation for the unification of the Three Kingdoms whereby once again Tan-gun's Chosŏn people were brought under one government.

Thus the aims of Korean national education today have its roots in and its character shaped by the philosophy of Benefits to All Mankind. While the Constitution paraphrases the principle of Benefits to All Mankind in a general context, the Charter of National Education amplifies on this idea in terms of what is to be achieved by education.

The goals of education are defined by the Education Law (Chapter 1, Article 1) in this way: "Education shall aim at, under the great ideal of Hong-ik In-gan (Benefits to All Mankind), assisting all people in perfecting individual personality, developing the ability for an independent life, and acquiring good citizenship needed to serve for the development of a democratic nation and for the realization of human co-prosperity." This Constitutional directive is important in that it serves as a guide for all educational activities and represents the ideal traits of the Korean people which education should strive to cultivate. In this context, it is a spiritual guide for the people, one that offers a new set of ethical norms and a value system. The goals of education, as described in the Constitution, reflect the same philosophy which served as the original spiritual basis for this nation.

Improving ourselves in learning and the arts and inheriting the tradition of mutual assistance rooted in love and respect and faithfulness, promote a spirit of fair and warm cooperation.

Since education is designed first and foremost to develop a healthy nation, it is quite logical that a people's national characteristics and historical background should be reflected in the system of education. The guidelines that support a sense of national identity call for educational reforms that take into account national cultural characteristics and make education relevant to the indigenous setting. Additionally, efforts are made to ensure an effective transmission of the cultural heritage to succeeding generations and to create on this basis a culture contributing to national development.

With regard to ideological education, this idea of Benefits to All Mankind delineates the stance to be taken by the Korean people regarding Communism. As indicated earlier, in its political aspect, the philosophy of Benefits to All Mankind teaches that respect toward our fellow man has to lead to a society based on humanism. This ideology emphasizes human rights and regards politics as a means to an end: guaranteeing the people their basic rights. As declared by the Constitution, democracy is the ideological base of the nation. The political mission for education is to enhance the student's awareness of democracy as an ideal of human life and to strengthen the determination to counteract the aggressive and subversive schemes of Communism. The development of this attitude constitutes an important goal to be achieved by education in Korea. Furthermore, the territorial division poses a unique situation which calls upon education to foster patriotism and national pride awareness.

Hong-ik In-gan, the philosophy of Benefits to All Mankind has become the guiding spirit of the national system of education. Thus the nation has been stepping up efforts to develop a curriculum at all stages that stresses the revival of traditional ethical norms such as filial piety, respect for the aged, altruistic ideals, and mutual compromise and harmony. Educational efforts are focused on creating a climate conducive to the practice of these ethical norms in the family, schools, and society. This idea of Benefits to All Mankind also serves the individual Korean as a theoretical and practical aid toward understanding his own philosophy of life. It has promoted the enhancement of humanitarian ideals and human rights, and helps prepare Koreans for life in a global context and for participation in a continuing search for universal principles and propositions.

B. The Roots

The oldest available historical references to formal education in Korea date back to 372 A.D. when a state operated institution known as Taehak was established by King Sosurim of the Koguryŏ Kingdom. This institution was designed to prepare the children of the upper class for future government service. Classics, history, and literature were the mainstays of the curriculum. In addition, private schools called *kyŏngdang* were set up across the country to educate ordinary young people by teaching them both basic learning and military arts.

During the Three Kingdoms period, one of the most significant cultural developments was the introduction of Buddhism and Confucianism. Koguryŏ was the first to adopt Buddhsim as a royal creed, in 372 A.D., followed by Paekche in 328 A.D., and Shilla in 528 A.D.

Buddhism not only brought a civilizing influence to the wild tribes, but reformed the spiritual life of the early Koreans. Furthermore, Buddhism and Confucianism gave to the people of the Three Kingdoms a new vision in the world of art and education.

As a part of the overall growth of its culture, one of the most impressive developments in the Shilla Kingdom was the Hwarangdo, a unique system of training young men. Handsome and intelligent young men were selected for this school, which was similar to a fraternity of knighthood. The Hwarangdo (Flower of Youth Corps) students received an education that fostered both academic and military skills. In fact, nearly equal emphasis was placed on the study of classics, history, philosophy, and religion on the one hand, and military training on the other. Men of virtue and intellect were often selected from this group to serve the government as statesmen and military leaders.

The guiding principles of the Hwarang were loyalty, filial duty, trustworthiness, valor, and devotion to justice. The objectives were postulated by the famous priest, Wŏn-gwang, who synthesized indigenous Korean beliefs and Buddhist-Confucian virtues in the philosophy he developed to guide the education of the youth.

A spirit of chivalry and patriotism evolved from such education. In time of war Hwarang members fought valiantly on the battlefield.

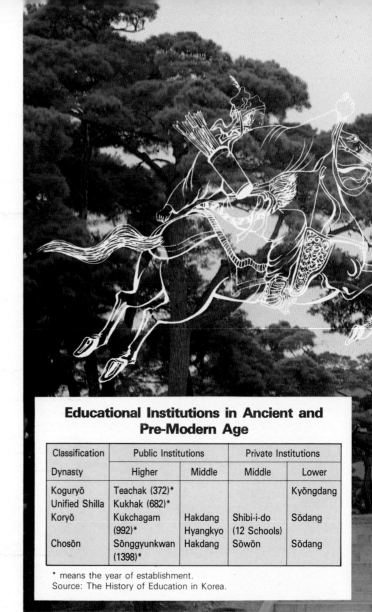

Educational Institutions in Ancient and Pre-Modern Age

Classification	Public Institutions		Private Institutions	
Dynasty	Higher	Middle	Middle	Lower
Koguryŏ	Teachak (372)*			Kyŏngdang
Unified Shilla	Kukhak (682)*			
Koryŏ	Kukchagam (992)*	Hakdang Hyangkyo	Shibi-i-do (12 Schools)	Sŏdang
Chosŏn	Sŏnggyunkwan (1398)*	Hakdang	Sŏwŏn	Sŏdang

* means the year of establishment.
Source: The History of Education in Korea.

General Kim Yushin, who played a key role in Shilla's unification of the Three Kingdoms, was a graduate of the youth corps.

Some of the most interesting features of the Hwarangdo Schools were their five commandments, which stressed the virtues of filial piety, loyalty to the king and keeping faith with friends (derived from Confucian teaching), prohibited the unecessary taking of life, and taught devotion to justice (the latter two principles taken from Buddhsim). The Hwarangdo teachers developed concepts that would harmonize beliefs taken from Buddhism, Confucianism, Taoism and native religions; they had used these to create a new curriculum for teaching the Hwarang.

The next educational development of the post-unification Shilla was the establishment of the Kukhak or the State School in the second year of King Shinmun (A.D. 682). A number of Paksa (Professors), Chogyo (Assistant Professors) and Taesa (12th grade officials of the state) were

Tomb of Kim Yushin in Kyongju.

nominated as teachers for the new school. This Kukhak, the institute for the training of public officials, had a nine-year course, deveoted primarily to teaching Confucianism and *Hsiaoching* (a dialogue on filial duty) but each year's instruction introduced different sets of additional classics. In one year the *Notes on the Rites and the Changes* were taught, in another were offered the *Tsochuan Annals* and *Poems* and in the third the *Writings of Old* and a selection of classic literature were taught. The students' ages ranged from 15 to 30.

The educational trend during the Koryŏ Kingdom (918 A.D.-1392 A.D.) was strongly influenced by Confucianism which was the dominant philosophy of the period. During the Koryŏ era the state educational institutes developed further, and the public civil service examination system was firmly established. In the early days of the Koryŏ Kingdom, there were three state-operated schools for training government officials.

The major state institute, Kukchagam, was founded in 992 A.D., The school had three major departments, each accommodating about 300 students. Students were admitted to different departments on the official rank of their parents. Students who finished more than three years of study at the school were eligible for the public civil service examination. The greater part of the curriculum of the school was devoted to the study of the Confucian classics, which consist of the Book of Changes, calligraphy, the *Poems, Notes on the Rites*, and the *History*.

The pattern of the educational institutes in the Koryŏ Kingdom mostly remained intact through the next dynasty.

The Chosŏn Kingdom, lasting from the close of the 14th century until the early 20th century, marked the beginning of the modern age.

In 1392, King T'aejo opened Sŏnggyun-gwan (the National Confucian Academy), an institution of higher learning. This institution was establish-

29

ed for the purpose of training the nation's future leaders. The first class was made up of 150 students who had successfully passed the first examination for government service, and the first faculty of 26 professors was appointed by the King. Admission to Sŏnggyun-gwan was restricted to boys from the ruling *yangban* class. Every student was required to reside in the dormitory on the campus, and his schooling and boarding expenses were fully paid for by the government. As *sŏng* means "maturity," *gyun* means "har-

mony" and *gwan* means "institution," the name of this educational institution explains the objectives of this school. It was meant to serve as an institution for building a harmonious society of perfected human beings. The curriculum for this institution consisted of manners, music, archery, horse riding, the classics (literature), and mathematics. Today, the legacy of Sŏnggyun-gwan, which dates back 588 years, is kept alive at Sŏnggyun-gwan University, a major modern institution of higher learning in Seoul.

During the Chosŏn period, primary education was provided to children from various social classes at the numerous *sŏdang* (private village schools), which taught them elementray Confucian classics and ethics. More advanced education was available at *hyangyŏ* (county schools) and other similar institutions.

With the massive introduction of Western influences in the latter period of the Chosŏn Kingdom, education became fertile ground for innovation. Intellectuals began to look critically at the kingdom's education because it was based on Chu Hsi's neo-Confucian philosophy which had lost much of its relevancy to changing Korean society. It was often held responsible for the perpetuation of a rigid hierarchial social structure, bolstered by the exclusionary civil service recruitment system. Such reflections led to the advent of Sirhak, a school of pragmatism, which argued that education, as well as government, must reflect egalitarian principles.

In the old days, village schoolhouses were a favorite subject of paintings (above), Songgyun-gwan or the "National Confucian Academy" (below).

C. Modern Education

The flow of Western influences into Korea in the last few decades of the Chosŏn Kingdom served to foster nationalism, which in turn triggered movements for modernization in every aspect of life. Accordingly, the need to revamp the century-old educational system became acute. Particularly, egalitarian thinking directed the innovative efforts of the time toward public education for women as well as men. Changes triggered by the rise of Sirhak and Sŏhak (Western Learning) led to the eventual abolition of the state civil service examination. This marked the first step toward democratic education. Until then, the government schools had admitted only those belonging to the upper class. In 1883, the first modern private school, called Wŏnsan Haksa (the Wŏnsan Academy), was founded at Wŏnsan, a port city on the east coast in central Korea, with enthusiastic support from local residents.

Shortly afterward, in 1885, American Protestant missionaries began to play an active role in promoting modern education and the Western ideas of democracy. A missionary group from the Methodist Church led by Henry G. Appenzeller of the United States opened the first missionary high school, Paechai Haktang, in 1885. This school with its new educational philosophy and modern curriculum, was truly the pacesetter of modern education in Korea. The Ewha Haktang, opened in 1886 also by American missionaries, became the first girls' school in Korea. Another boys' high school, Kyungshin, was established by a Presbyterian group in 1887. Five other missionary high schools were founded in major cities thereafter, all exerting impressive influence on Korean education.

The passion for education during this period burned still more brightly in the public at large. That "knowledge is power" was a conviction shared by Koreans from various walks of life, especially by the whole of the intellectual class. In 1985, the government began to found normal schools, foreign-language schools and elementary and middle schools, thereby accelerating the development of modern education. Numerous private schools thus came to be established, serving the growing interest in the education of the younger generation. As for higher education, Younhui College (Chosŏn Christian College) was founded in Seoul in 1905 and Sungsil College was established in P'yongyang in 1906, both sponsored by missionary foundations.

The turn of the century was thus a period of rapid changes in Korean education. Schools on all levels put great emphasis on the inculcation of nationalism and patriotism with a view to securing national survival and development in the

The Ewha haktang in 1886.

The Kyungshin high school in 1886.

face of the threat of encroachment from foreign powers, especially neighboring Japan. Thus high priorities in the curricula were given to national history and the national language. Many Korean patriots directly committed themselves to educational endeavors, with the intention thus of laying the foundation for an indepndent and thriving Korea. By 1910, when Korea was annexed by Japan as its colony, more than 5,000 private schools had been founded across the country.

Missionary schools established and managed with the Christian spirit to teach the sciences and humanities by Western methods had a profound impact on education of the period, especially by demonstrating the concept of brotherhood and equality for all. In fact, for the first time in Korean history, Christian missionaries opened up education for everyone, upper or lower class, rich or poor, and even women. This helped to spark a tremendous social, as well as educational, revolution. By stressing the spirit of national independence and the importance of human rights, Christian missionaries' educational endeavors significantly contributed to the growth of a democratic spirit in a land with a long history of absolute monarchy.

But in 1910 the Japanese annexation of Korea snuffed out the flame of educational innovation before a sufficiently large and solid basis for popular education could be laid. Schools during the colonial period were increasingly forced to primarily serve egocentric Japanese interests by converting Koreans into "loyal subjects" of the Japanese empire. Despite some increase in the number of schools, only a small fraction of the expanding Korean population was able to benefit from education, even on an elementary level, as the result of the colonial policy of limiting educational opportunities for the natives.

As Korea fell to Japanese colonial rule, progressive Korean leaders endeavored to initiate and promote national independence movements. Efforts were first focused on enlightening the people and fostering a sense of nationalism and patriotism. A considerable number of wealthy patriots thus contributed land and property for the establishment of more schools, especially on secondary and higher levels. These private schools played an important role in educating the children of ordinary families as well as those of the middle and upper classes, inspiring them with a spirit of self-respect and independence.

In that way, the missionary and private schools served as a spiritual beacon for the oppressed Korean people. However, schools soon came under mounting pressures of Japanese authorities intent on using education as a means of "Japanizing" Koreans. The aims and contents of education in those days were thus made to fall increasingly in line with the imperialist goals of the Japanese government. Korean teachers and students were ordered to make regular visits to the Shinto shrines, and a number of American missionary schools were shut down for refusing to comply.

After Japan declared war on the United States and Britain in December 1941, the Korean educational system was further adjusted to meet

Schools were forced to serve egocentric Japanese interests by converting Koreans into "Loyal subjects" of the Japanese empire.

Japan's war needs. The middle school course was shortened from five years to four and the combined length of college preparatory courses and college courses was also shortened, from five years to three. Schools with names readily identifiable as of foreign missionary origin, as well as those with names reflecting the Korean national heritage, were given new Japanese names. English language lessons were cut back or even terminated and Korean teachers and students were ordered to speak only in Japanese at school and even at home. The Japanese authorities also pressured Koreans into Japanizing their names. To meet the manpower shortage at the height of the war, the Japanese began conscripting Korean students into the Japanese military services, falsely calling them "volunteers". Schools were virtually closed in the last months of the war as students were mobilized to help the war efforts by serving in large labor units.

The liberation of the country in August 1945 at the end of World War II pointed to a need in the South to quickly shift Korean education away from the past, Japanese-imposed totalitarian modes of teaching to democratic ones, even while North Korea fell under Communist control. Educational renewal in the immediate post-liberation years, however, was not smooth sailing. The repatriation of Japanese nationals left schools acutely short of qualified teachers, necessitating the employment of many inexperienced instructors. Democratic ideals also often clashed with the traditional largely Confucian values which were too deeply rooted to be replac-

ed overnight. Schools also faced increasing financial difficulties.

A new stage for educational development was set in 1948 when the government of the Republic of Korea was established. The Education Law promulgated in October 1949 set forth lofty ideals of Korean education, based on the concept that all nations must contribute to the common prosperity of mankind through the development of democracy and by nurturing the integrity of individuals, equipping them with the ability to lead independent lives and to become good citizens with altruistic ideals. This law clearly emphasises the ancient Hong-ik In-gan or philosophy of 'Benefits to All Mankind."

However, resurgent education in Korea was all too soon devastated by the Korean War that broke out in 1950. More than 70 percent of the elementary school classrooms were either totally or partially destroyed during the three-year conflict. School activities were carried on in tents and makeshift barracks while the war was still being fought.

Following the armistice, rehabilitation of the educational system was undertaken at a fever pitch with the active assistance of such international agencies as the United Nations Korean Reconstruction Agency (U.N.K.R.A.) and the United States aid mission. Given this help and impetus, postwar education was restored to the prewar level in a matter of a few years and its growth quickly accelerated, especially with six-year compulsory elementary education introduced in 1954.

Expansion of Elementary School Education 1945-1989

Year Classification	1945	1960	1970	1980	1989
Schools	2,834	4,496	5,961	6,487	6,396
Index	100	158	210	229	226
Teachers	19,729	61,605	101,095	119,064	134,898
Index	100	312	512	603	684
Students	1,366,024	3,622,685	5,749,301	5,658,002	4,894,261
Index	100	265	420	414	358

Expansion of Middle School Education 1945-1989

Year Classification	1945	1960	1970	1980	1989
Schools	166	1,053	1,608	2,121	2,450
Index	100	634	968	1,277	1,476
Teachers	1,186	13,053	31,207	54,858	81,699
Index	100	1,100	2,631	4,625	6,889
Students	80,828	528,593	1,318,808	2,471,997	2,371,215
Index	100	654	1,631	3,508	2,934

Expansion of High School Education 1951-1989

Year Classification	1951	1960	1970	1980	1989
Schools	307	640	889	1,353	1,672
Index	100	208	289	435	545
Teachers	1,720	9,627	19,854	50,948	87,277
Index	100	559	1,154	2,962	5,074
Students	40,271	273,434	590,382	1,696,792	2,326,062
Index	100	678	1,466	4,213	5,776

Expansion of Higher Education 1945-1989

Year Classification	1945	1960	1970	1980	1989
Schools	19	85	168	236	536
Index	100	450	890	1,240	2,821
Faculty Members	1,490	3,808	10,435	20,900	39,950
Index	100	260	700	1,400	2,681
Enrollments	7,819	101,041	201,436	601,994	1,434,259
Index	100	1,290	2,586	7,700	18,343

The most striking development in education since liberation was its quantitative growth. In 1945, there were only 2,834 primary schools, with a total enrollment of a little less than 1.4 million in what is now the Republic of Korea. As of April, 1988, the number of primary schools had reached 6,463, with a total enrollment of 4.8 million students. The number of students is equivalent to 98.4 percent of the school-age children in the country.

The explosion in the number of schools was even more noticeable at the secondary education level. There were 165 secondary schools with about 83,514 students in South Korea in 1945. The Republic of Korea in 1988 had 2,429 middle schools and 1,653 high schools with a combined enrollment of over 3.9 million students.

A rapid quantitative growth is also seen in higher education. There were only 19 institutions of higher education with about 7,800 students throughout the country in 1945. Today, the Republic of Korea boasts 115 four-year colleges and universities with a total enrollment of a little over one million. In addition, nearly 300,000 students attend 119 junior colleges, while over 97,000 are pursuing advanced studies at 278 graduate schools.

The middle school curriculum is composed of 12 basic or required subjects, elective subjects and extracurricular activities.

Education System

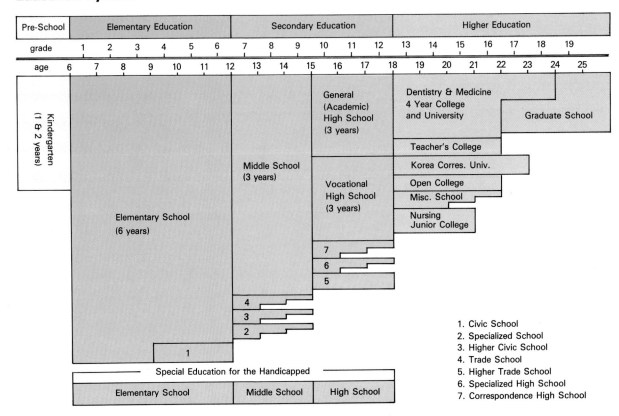

1. Civic School
2. Specialized School
3. Higher Civic School
4. Trade School
5. Higher Trade School
6. Specialized High School
7. Correspondence High School

General Conditions of Schools, 1989

Classificiation	Number of Schools	Number of Classes or Departments	Number of Students	Number of Teachers
Grand Total	19,483	229,334	11,528,676	363,558
Kindergarten	8,246	13,922	410,824	14,886
Elementary School	6,396	116,170	4,894,261	134,898
Middle School	2,450	45,301	2,371,215	81,699
General High School	1,084	26,964	1,490,846	54,333
Vocational High School	588	15,708	835,216	32,944
Special School	100	1,624	19,137	2,485
Civic School	1	3	198	4
Civic High School	16	37	675	93
Trade School	1	1	24	2
Trade High School	28	479	24,181	751
Miscellaneous School (Middle school course)	7	82	4,840	135
Miscellaneous School (High school course)	30	800	43,006	1,378
Junior College	117	1,161	291,041	6,999
Teacher's College	11	346	17,182	679
College & University	104	3,854	1,020,771	31,675
Graduate School	278	2,774	81,171	—
Miscellaneous, School (Undergraduate courses)	26	108	24,094	597

*The number of professors in Graduate School is included in each college and univ.

The total number of students on all levels thus rose from 4,716,000 in 1960 to 11,531,000 by mid-1989. In 1985, compulsory three-year middle school education was introduced on a phased basis, first covering remote inland areas and islands. In 1989, about 223,000 students were benefiting from this arrangement, which is scheduled to be extended to towns and smaller cities over the next several years, with the goal of eventually providing all Korean children with free nine-year education.

Korea has made unprecedentedly rapid economic growth through the successful implementation of a series of five-year economic development plans. Underlying this dynamic growth is the rapid development of the nation's educational system.

In response to the challeges of industriatization, vocational and technological education were given special emphasis in the early 1960's and steps were taken to more closely link education to economic development. Such efforts were spurred by the enactment of the Industrial Education Promotion Law of 1963, which provides financial

39

Primary School Curriculum

(Unit: teaching hours)

Classification		1st year	2nd year	3rd year	4th year	5th year	6th year
Subjects	Moral Education	Education for Freshmen (70)		68(2)	68(2)	68(2)	68(2)
	Korean Language	330(1)	374(11)	238(7)	204(6)	68(2)	68(2)
	Social Studies			102(3)	102(3)	136(4)	136(4)
	Arithmetic	108(6)	204(6)	136(4)	136(4)	170(5)	170(5)
	Science			102(3)	136(4)	136(4)	136(4)
	Physical Education	180(6)	238(7)	102(3)	102(3)	102(3)	102(3)
	Music			68(2)	68(2)	68(2)	68(2)
	Fine Arts			68(2)	68(2)	68(2)	68(2)
	Crafts			—	68(2)	68(2)	68(2)
Extracurriular Activities		*30(1)	*34(1)	68(2)	68(2)	68(2)	68(2)
Grand Total		790(24)	850(25)	925(28)	1,020(32)	1,088(32)	1,088(32)

- The hours shown on this table represent the minimum school hours alloted for 34 weeks per year.
- One teaching hour in this table represents 40 minutes.
- Extracurricular Activities in the 1st & 2nd year are the principal's optional subjects.
- Figures in the parentheses are hours taught per week.

Middle School Curriculum

(Unit: teaching hours)

Classification		1st Year (7th Grade)	2nd Year (8th Grade)	3rd Year (9th Grade)
	Moral Education	68(2)	68(2)	68(2)
	Korean language	136(4)	170(5)	170(5)
	Korean History	—	68(2)	68(2)
	Social Studies	102(3)	68-102(2-3)	68-102(2-3
	Mathematics	136(4)	102-136(3-4)	68-102(2-3)
	Science	136(4)	102-136(3-4)	136-170(4-5)
	Pysical Education	102(3)	102(3)	102(3)
	Music	68(2)	68(2)	34-68(1-2)
	Fine Arts	68(2)	68(2)	34-681(1-2)
	Clasical Chinese	34(1)	34-68(1-2)	34-68(1-2)
	English	136(4)	102-170(3-5)	102-170(3-5)
	Vocational Skills (Boys) Home Economics (Girls)	Sel 1 102(3)	Se 1 136-204(4-6)	—
	Agriculture, Technical, Commerce, Fisheries, Housekeeping	—	—	Se 1 136-204(4-6)
	Elective	0-68(0-2)	0-68(0-2)	0-68(0-2)
Extracurricular Activities		68-(2-)	68-(2-)	68-(2-)
Grand Total		1156-1224 (34-36)	1156-1224 (34-36)	1156-1224 (34-36)

- The hours shown on this table represent the minimum school hours alloted for 34 weeks per year.
- Figures in the parentheses are hours taught per week.
- Elective is principal's optional subjects.
- One teaching hour in this table represents 45 minutes.
- Se: Select

Training for students of the vocational high schools.

General (Academic) High School Curriculum

(Unit: teaching hours)

Classification	Subjects	General Curriculum: Required Subject Units (10th Grade)	Students Select One of Three Majors: Humanities Major (11th-12th Grade)	Science Major (11th-12th Grade)	Vocational Major (11th-12th Grade)
Moral Education	Moral Education	6			
Korean Language	Korean Language	10			
	Literature		8	8	] 4
	Composition		6	4	
	Grammar		4		
Korea History	Korea History	6			
Social Studies	Political Economy	6			
	Geography	4			
	World Hostory		4	4	] 4
	Social Studies & Culture		4		
	World Geography		4		
Mathematics	Mathematics (1)	8	10		6
	(2)			18	
Science	Science (1-2)	10	8		
	Physics			8	] 4
	Chemistry			8	
	Biology			6] Se	
	Earth Science			6] 1	
Physical Education	Physical Education	6	8	8	4
Military Training	Military Training	12			
Music	Music	4			] 2
Fine Arts	Fine Arts	4			
Classical Chinese	Classical Chinese		8	4	4
Foreign Language	English (1.2)	8	12	12	8
	German		] Se 1	] Se 1	]
	French				
	Spanish				6
	Chinese		10	10	
	Japanese				
Industrial Arts & Home Economics	Industrial Arts (Boys)		] Se 1	] Se 1	] 4
	Home Economics (Girls)		8	8	
	Agriculture		] Se 1	] Se 1	
	Technology				
	Commerce				
	Fisheries		8	8	
	Housekeeping				
Elective			2	2	2
Extracurricular Activities		12			
Grand Total		204-216			

- (1) means required subjects.
- (2) means the elective subjects by course and program.
- 1 unit means a period of 50 minutes per week during one term (17 weeks). One week equals 5 1/2 days.
- Technical curriculum in Vocational Major is selected from 50 to 100 units. • Se: Select

incentives for teachers and students involved in industry-related learning.

Efforts have been made to update curricula at all levels and to reform higher education in particular with specific reference to the emerging needs of newly industrializing society. These efforts are all aimed at better relating classrooms to work places—but not to the detriment of the general goals of education. Innovations in education are constantly sought in line with long-term plans.

Especially remarkable is the high proportion of Koreans attending institutions of higher learning. At present, college students account for 29% of the entire college-age population. Compulsory and free elementary education, initiated in the mid-1950's, produced a labor force needed for the economic development of the 1960's. The expansion of higher education, especially in the 1970's, has supplied highly trained manpower for the continued growth and sophistication of the nation's economy.

It is rare indeed for any nation to attain such a phenomenal growth in education in such a

Students of College & University by Course, 1989

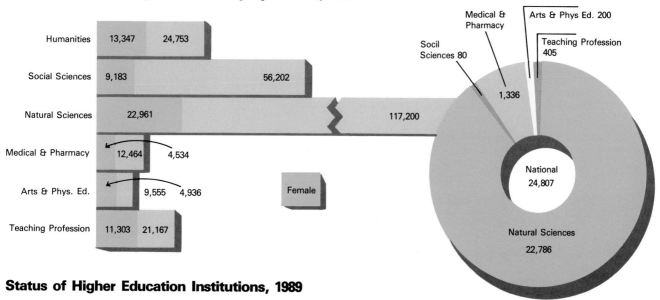

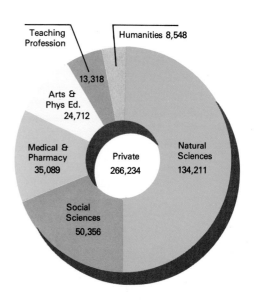

Status of Higher Education Institutions, 1989

| Classification | Number of Schools | | | | | | | Departments |
| | Total | By Time | | | By Sex | | | |
		Day	Eve.	Day & Eve.	Men	Women	Coedu.	
Grand Total	536	244	141	151	5	49	482	8,243
National	104	64	19	21	2	4	98	2,301
Public	3	1	1	1	—	—	3	48
Private	429	179	121	129	3	45	381	5,894
Junior College	117	56	—	61	3	24	90	1,161
National	16	16	—	—	2	4	10	123
Private	101	40	—	61	1	20	80	1,038
Teacher's College	11	4	—	7	—	—	11	346
National	11	4	—	7	—	—	11	346
College & Univ.	104	63	1	40	1	10	93	3,854
National	22	21	—	1	—	—	22	1,111
Public	1	—	—	1	—	—	1	25
Private'	81	42	1	38	1	10	70	2,718
Graduate School	278	108	140	30	1	15	262	2,774
National	55	23	19	13	—	—	55	721
Public	2	1	1	—	—	—	2	23
Private	221	84	120	17	1	15	205	2,030
Miscellaneous School	26	13	—	13	—	—	26	108
Private	26	13	—	13	—	—	26	108

Students of Junior College, 1989

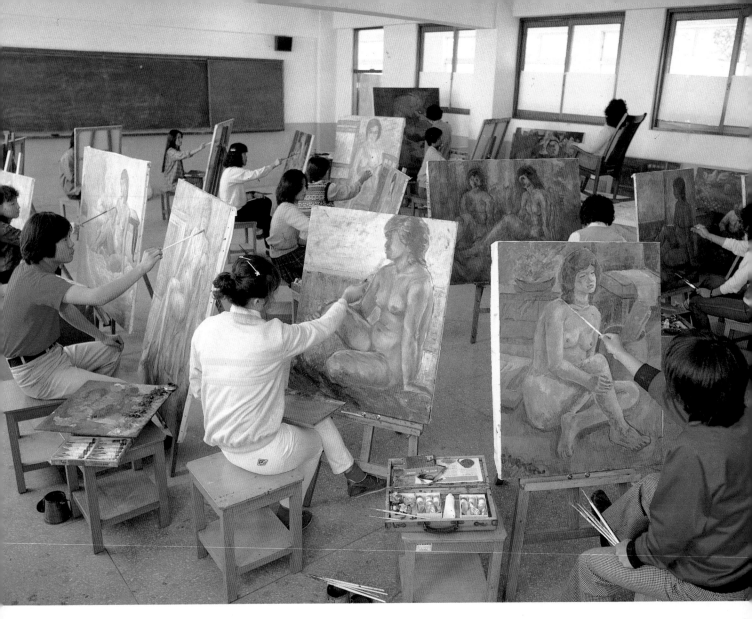

A student who has completed 140 credit units is awarded a bachelor's degree.

Youths Exchanged Under
Bi-lateral Programs 1965-1988

	Year Classification	Total	'65-82	'83	'84	'85	'86	'87	'88
	Grand Total	1,726	682	131	99	133	177	252	252
Dispatched	America	69	—	—	6	20	17	14	12
	Japan	529	70	17	19	50	60	152	161
	Malaysia	133	74	10	10	10	9	10	10
	Saudi Arabia	88	36	34	—	8	—	10	—
	Others	256	210	46	—	—	—	—	—
	Sub Total	1,075	390	107	35	88	86	186	183
Invitation	America	89	—	—	17	23	22	14	13
	Japan	230	55	13	29	12	37	42	42
	Malaysia	117	53	11	10	10	9	10	14
	Saudi Arabia	70	139	—	8	—	23	—	—
	Others	45	45	—	—	—	—	—	—
	Sub Total	651	292	24	64	45	91	66	69

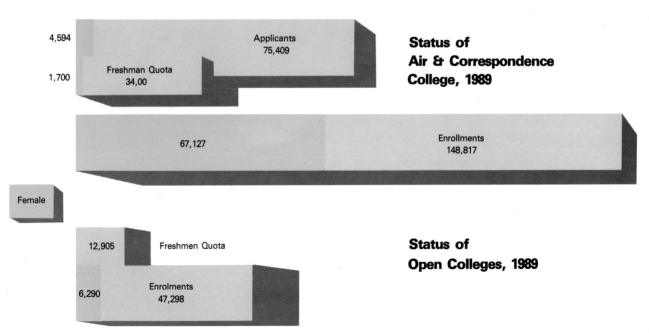

4,594

Applicants
75,409

1,700

Freshman Quota
34,00

**Status of
Air & Correspondence
College, 1989**

67,127

Enrollments
148,817

Female

12,905

Freshmen Quota

6,290

Enrolments
47,298

**Status of
Open Colleges, 1989**

short span of time. Such a rapid expansion of education has resulted from the government's forward-looking educational policy, social traditions that value learning and the public's zeal for education.

Despite its progress, Korean education has drawn criticisms that its quality is still not high enough and that it tends to lag behind the times. In particular, the rapid population growth that has continued until recently has seriously handicapped efforts to provide better education, especially at elementary and secondary levels. In order to cope with this and other related problems, the potential of non-formal education is being tapped. Most notable in this direction is the establishment of broadcast and correspondence courses at the college and high school levels.

The unfortunate political situation of the Republic of Korea, deriving chiefly from the division of the land into hostile halves and its consequent deadly confrontation with the Communist north, suggests yet another role to be performed by education—that is, to exhibit the innate superiority of a free society to Communist totalitarianism. Having put decades of authoritarian rule behind it, the Republic is currently in the process of evolving a truly democratic education philosophy and system. This is a task warranting serious attention of all those who are interested in promoting the cause of freedom and democracy through education.

The Status of Graduate School, 1987

Classification	Number of Schools			Number of Programs					Number of Students				
	Total	General Graduate Sch.	Pro. Graduate Sch.	Total	MA Courses			Doctor Courses	Total	MA Courses			Doctor Courses
					Sub-Total	General Total	Pro. G. Sch			Sub-Total	General G. Sch.	Pro. G. Sch	
Total	278	95	183	4,013	2,774	2,026	748	1,239	81,171	67,840	34,540	33,300	13,331
Humanities				613	400	369	31	213	8,962	81,171	34,540	33,300	13,331
Social Sciences				951	689	419	270	262	22,934	20,493	6,808	13,685	2,441
Natural Sciences				1,656	1,023	897	126	633	23,859	18,670	14,119	4,551	5,189
Arts & Physical Ed.				215	195	182	13	20	4,207	3,963	3,020	943	244
Medical Sciences and Pharmacy				153	94	79	15	59	7,549	4,811	4,233	578	2,738
Teaching Profession				425	373	80	293	52	13,660	13,135	1,459	11,676	525

The Status of Nation-Wide Libraries, 1989

Classifi-cation	Libraries	Staffs	Seats	Collection of Books	Clients	Volumes in Circulation	Budget
Total	977 (6,306)	7,292 (1,271)	410,011 (454,778)	39,675,020 (22,136,168)	98,737,901 (24,111,749)	39,648,868 (21,392,252)	82,168,202 (15,093,184)
Central National Library	1	239	4,089	1,437,991	1,226,364	1,797,909	5,585,575
National Assembly Library	1	256	526	622,864	66,367	190,733	2,360,716
Public Library	197	2,917	103,741	6,111,451	24,516,703	14,520,382	33,621,31
College & Univ. Library	287	2,680	228,275	25,008,360	67,525,319	19,846,281	26,731,990
High School Library	160 (1,532)	163 (568)	53,091 (174,807)	1,274,265 (5,797,532)	3,043,936 (8,466,084)	854,635 (4,375,767)	313,271 (1,696,574)
Elementary School Library	51 (2,929)	11 (253)	4,910 (145,444)	181,144 (10,009,514)	249,137 (10,743,140)	234,687 (12,543,729)	88,568 (12,439,549)
Special Library	250	1,016	10,678	4,901,680	1,950,459	2,056,708	13,450,343

* The figures in (   ) indicate the data by item with respect to the number of reading rooms.

PART THREE
Models for Economic Development

A. Background

To gain an insight into a nation's economy, it is important to understand its cultural background —its education, customs, traditions and beliefs that have affected its national character, its economic and social structures and its people's way of thinking. For a national economy is strongly colored by conscious and unconscious influences of its cultural and historical background. In other words, economic policies and practices of a nation are, in general, deeply rooted in its tradition and culture.

When one examines different cultures, one of the most indispensable tools of study is the recognition of the national spirit. As presented earlier, Korea's national spirit is based on the ideal of *Hong-ik In-gan*, or the philosophy of "Benefits to All Mankind." This national spirit has played a fundamental role in shaping the people's way of thinking and their way of life. In a way the concept of Benefits to All Mankind is the foundation of this society and is at the root of the national character. By examining some of the basic principles in this philosophy, one can better understand the real characteristics of the Korean economy, its organization, policies, and management style.

The "Benefits to All Mankind" ideal requires one to practice the virtues of perseverance and concentration. For most of its long history, Korea has been an economically impoverished country. As late as 1960, Korea was still in the grip of many of the difficulties facing underdeveloped countries today. Adding to its extreme poverty, the nation's population was growing by three percent annual-

ly, and unemployment and underemployment were pervasive. While domestic savings were negligible, Korea had no significant natural resources and exports were virtually nil. It depended on imports for both raw materials and a wide range of essential manufactured goods. Over and above these problems, the country was still lacking in progressive leadership critically needed to get the war-shattered economy off the ground for sustained growth. Throughout the 1950s, the government failed to provide sufficient stability and clear direction in the affairs of state. Under these conditions, it was nearly impossible to mobilize the creative energies of the Korean people. However, through the virtues of perseverance and concentration, the people of Korea managed to rebuild the country from the ashes of the Korean War of 1950-53. In the early 1960's, more effective government leadership emerged and set "liberation from poverty" as a top national goal. The nation has since carried out a series of six successful five-year development plans, thereby completely transforming its economy over the span of only a generation or so.

The phenomenal growth of the Korean economy over the past three decades or so has been one of the great modern success stories of national development. Between 1960 and 1988, Korea's gross national product (GNP) soared from $2.3 billion to $169.2 billion in current prices, representing an average increase of more than 8 percent annually in real terms. Meanwhile, per capita GNP rose from $87 to $4,040 in current prices over the same period. Korea's growth was

G.N.P.

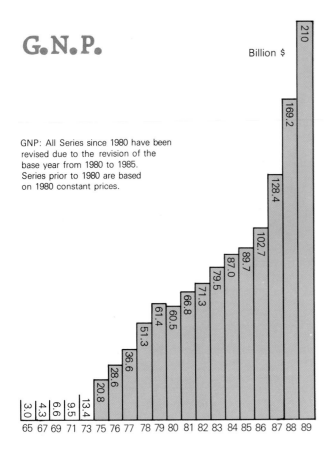

Billion $

GNP: All Series since 1980 have been revised due to the revision of the base year from 1980 to 1985. Series prior to 1980 are based on 1980 constant prices.

210
169.2
128.4
102.7
89.7
87.0
79.5
71.3
66.8
60.5
61.4
51.3
36.6
28.6
20.8
13.4
9.5
6.6
4.3
3.0

65 67 69 71 73 75 76 77 78 79 80 81 82 83 84 85 86 87 88 89

Per Capita GNP

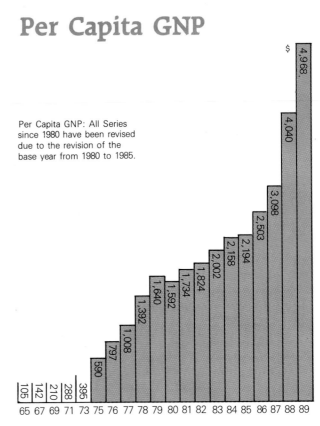

$

Per Capita GNP: All Series since 1980 have been revised due to the revision of the base year from 1980 to 1985.

4,968
4,040
3,098
2,503
2,194
2,158
2,002
1,824
1,734
1,592
1,640
1,392
1,008
797
590
395
288
210
142
105

65 67 69 71 73 75 76 77 78 79 80 81 82 83 84 85 86 87 88 89

fueled by the explosion of its exports, which rocketed from a mere $50 million to over $59 billion during this period.

The creed of the simple way of life has been at the heart of the Benefits to All Mankind teaching. This idea has been emphasized in both family education and formal schooling, and it has therefore been absorbed by Korean society generally. Korean business encourages economizing and saving, then reinvesting those savings. With the invested monies the business upgrades the plant and equipment and thus improves productivity and product quality. In truth, the Korean people have been taught the value of, and have cherished, simple living for millenniums. Thus in a Buddhist temple one can easily identify who is the chief monk because he is the one who wears the oldest, most worn-out, most patched clothes.

Although loyalty may be considered by some to be an archaic remnant from the philosophy of Benefits to All Mankind, one could hardly be considered sincere to himself, without such a notion guiding one's life. Although there is an element of collectivism in it, the ideal of loyalty has as its central theme the obligation of individuals to one

another. For an individual life to be sound and for meaningful human and social relationships to be possible, there must be harmony within a collective entity. In ancient times, Korea was known as a land of loyalty. Virtues then considered to be of social value included decorum and truthfulness, compassion for the young, and respect for the aged. To help improve the nation's modern-day economic development, the ancient principle of loyalty is now being stressed. Certainly the notion of loyalty fits into modern day standards of honor and ethics. The guiding principle of mutual obligation that underlies this tradition of loyalty leads also to patriotism and the unusual passion that Koreans have for their country. Thus, loyalty has been one of the most important elements in Korea's recent economic and industrial revolution.

Throughout the ages, the Benefits to All Mankind concept has held in high regard human relationships based on a spirit of harmony. Koreans have seen harmony as the essence of life and thought. Its characteristic is to view human or social relationships, not in terms of conflict and struggle, but in terms of consensus and cooperation. It is an attitude of life, a mentality that in-

EXPORTS

Export: Based on customs clearance.

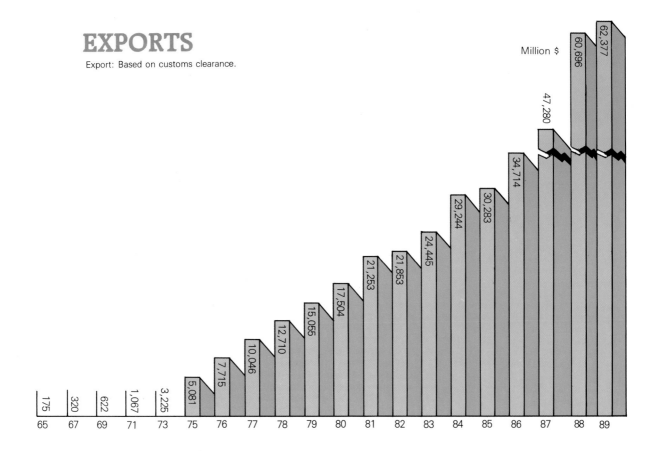

Million $

65	67	69	71	73	75	76	77	78	79	80	81	82	83	84	85	86	87	88	89
175	320	622	1,067	3,225	5,081	7,715	10,046	12,710	15,055	17,504	21,253	21,853	24,445	29,244	30,283	34,714	47,280	60,696	62,377

sists that although conflicts and confrontations often divide people and organizations, there is always bound to be a common ground that makes possible complementary relationships for greater social and economic development. The ideal of harmony emphasizes the need for tolerance to arrive at a "golden mean" and the use of reason to avoid confrontation, contradiction, struggle, and bickering. Throughout history, the Korean people have preferred harmony to conflict, and peace to violence. The devastation wrought by the many wars of invasion that mark their history is often said to be a result of this trait. Its roots are to be found in the people's deeply ingrained mild temperament and their dedication to the harmonious development of their country.

Eventually, this tradition formed the backbone of the Korean economy, as it was applied to the employer-employee relationship in business and industry.

Another ideal emphasized by the Benefits to All Mankind philosophy is creativity. Korea invented the world's first movable metal type, built armored turtle ships when the rest of the world was sailing in wooden vessels, constructed a rain

51

gauge, and invented a scientific and easy-to-use system of writing called *Hangul*, the Korean alphabet. In the field of political institutions, one is reminded of the *Hwabaek* system of the Shilla Kingdoms, devised in A.D. 502, which made unanimity of opinion on political subjects possible through consensus building. *Uichang* and *Hwangok* were two economic-welfare policies of the Koryŏ and Chosŏn Kingdoms by which grains were collected and stockpiled in peacetime for distribution in time of war or distress. Some of Korea's greatest cultural accomplishments were attained while it was engaged in a struggle for survival. One instance was the carving of the 80,000 woodblocks for printing *The Tripitaka Koreana.* These are some of the shining cultural legacies on which was built the country's technological and industrial revolution.

As mentioned earlier, one of the most important virtues based on the Benefits to All Mankind philosophy is concern for others. Those who have experienced life both in Korea and the United States often conclude that American companies care only about output and meeting the profit projection, whereas Korean companies are more concerned about their employees. In Korea, companies most often treat their employees as whole persons rather than as so many productive units. The creed of caring about people, together with other intrinsic elements of the Benefits to All Mankind philosophy, seems to result in both high output and a healthy profit as well. This concern for the employee has been instrumental in attaining high productivity and high standards of quality through Korea's industrial revolution.

One of the most important secrets of the Korean economic success is that most often there is a cheerful willingness on the part of employees to accept continuing changes in technology. In the West, having learned a certain skill or technology, an employee often tends to believe that he is finished learning in that area, but the Korean thinking is influenced by the Benefits to All Mankind ideal, that once one is finished with a certain process or function he is just beginning to learn only part of the many aspects of that whole area. The Benefits to All Mankind concept teaches that one of the most serious failings is ignorance. The whole of Korean society encourages young people to go to school and continue their education afterward. Most executives are enrolled in evening graduate studies classes.

In the Western countries, if one learns or acquires a new skill then he acquires a new position. In a sense, Western training is promotion-focused, while Korean training is performance-focused. In the West, as illustrated by the Peter Principle, if the man who pushes a broom does an excellent job, then he gets new training and will be promoted to a higher job.

In Korea the man working as an electrician will automatically attend various training sessions but he will stay an electrician until he retires. Koreans carry a considerabe spirit of competition from school to workplace. Even on the job or on a manufacturing shop floor, work groups compete with one another just as group members compete among themselves individually. All promotions are open to contest on a seniority basis.

Another interesting characteristic of Korean business, industrial, and academic organizations is that relatively few executives are employed. One saying in the United States is that often there are "too many chiefs and not enough Indians" in a business or institution. In Korea, supervisory positions are rotated on a seniority basis. Most promotions and wage increases are also based on seniority. In a typical United States univeristy, executive administrators include a university president and five or more vice-presidents. Some big universities have a chancellor under the president and within the president's office and the vice presidents' offices as well there are usually several special assistants. However, in a Korean university there is only one president and one vice-president. Also, the offices of president, vice-president, dean, and chariman are rotated every four years. Occupants of these positions are paid salaries based on the professor's rank and seniority. There is no special administrative pay scale.

Perhaps the spirit of self-reliance is the most priceless teaching of the Benefits to All Mankind philosophy. In the Korean mind "self-reliant" means that one is the master of his own house. In times of national hardship ahd tragedy the spirit of self-reliance has always asserted itself to generate an atmosphere conducive to cooperation and solidarity. It has often galvanized the Korean people to produce unity needed to overcome national emergency and ensure national survival. The Korean people have always resolutely met the challenges presented by numerous foreign invasions. When Japan invaded Korea in 1592, the Korean people, with the spirit of self-reliance,

quickly organized militias to fight a guerrilla war against the invaders. Even Buddhist monks rose from their monasteries to bear arms for the salvation of the nation. Indeed, it was a time for all Koreans, beyond the differences in sects or classes, to stand up and offer their lives for the defense of the homeland. Even while the Mongols under Genghis Khan were trampling China, Asia, and many parts of Europe under their feet, the Koryŏ Kingdom put up a fierce resistance against Mongol occupation. It is a fact of history that even in the severest moments of foreign domination, the Korean spirit of self-reliance never died out. Both at home and abroad, Korean patriots rallied forces to fight for national emancipation. The most notable modern example is the Samil (March First) Independence Movement of 1919, nationwide peaceful demonstrations protesting the 1910 Japanese annexation of Korea. Subsequently, as the harsh Japanese colonial authorities sought to exterminate the Korean language and ethos, the traditional spirit of self-reliance again rose to tenaciously preserve Korean culture until the day of final liberation.

B. Saemaul Undong or The Community Movement

In order to vigorously mobilize the energies of all Koreans for development, the Saemaŭl Undong, the New Community Movement, was inaugurated in 1971 and played a key role in building the foundation of the 1970s industrial revolution. Like many other developing countries, Korea, until the 1960s, was predominantly agricultural, with over two thirds of its population living on farms. The Saemaŭl Undong, like the 4-H Club program in the United States, was a national reconstruction and development campaign. The primary aim was to inspire the nation's farmers with the ideal of Benefits to all Mankind and to encourage them to provide the manpower necessary to greater rural development and modernization with a view to facilitating the industrial revolution. It was in part a national morale-boosting movement to cultivate in the people's minds a spontaneous urge for speedier national development in keeping with the spirit of Benefits to All Mankind. Self-reliance, perseverance, concentration, loyalty, harmony, creativity, cooperation. concern for others, willingness to work, and preference for the simple way of life were the lessons to be learned. These attitudes begin with one's sense of pride, independence and belonging. The self-help spirit springs from one's recognition of his own worth and responsibility combined with a determination to solve his problems through his own efforts, with confidence in his own ability. In this way, he develops a life of self-reliance and independence.

Since the Saemaŭl Undong aims at bringing prosperity to villagers through self-help projects, it naturally helps to cultivate their community consciousness and eventually to build the people's sense of national identity. In a more general sense, it encourages a spirit of national self-reliance—an attitude looking to do away with dependence on economic assistance from foreign countries.

The Saemaŭl Undong reflects the Korean people's yearning to create a society in which each

56

*A power cart on its way to work on an arrow-straight
farm road recently constructed by the cooperative
efforts of the villagers.*

member can count on community cooperation in
meeting his basic human needs. So that such
a society may be created, all villagers are urged
to participate in various community projects, such
as the improvement of village roads and the construction of bridges, irrigation ponds, village halls
and so forth. When villagers see what they have
achieved, through mutual contributions and
teamwork, their morale is strengthened as they
are convinced that there is nothing they cannot
do if they cooperate and work in unity toward
common goals.

The Saemaŭl Undong places a special emphasis
on action. It tries to teach the people that com-
pletion of the simplest task is important and that
its basic objective is to revitalize the ideology of
the Benefits to All Mankind. This concept is
nothing new in Korea and is not difficult to
understand because this has been the Koreans'
guiding principle throughout the nation's history.

The Saemaŭl Undong is aimed at enhancing
community wealth through the people's self-help
efforts. The government assists villagers,
however, when they are unable to handle difficult

problems. Government support is composed of
three categories: financial, administrative, and
technical aid. Priority support is provided to exemplary villages that are moving ahead with enthusiastic community-wide participation in their
projects. This is done in order to spur villages lag-
ging behind into action.

The role of the government is aimed primarily
at promoting a spirit of diligence, self-help and
cooperation among the rural populace, the
Saemaŭl Undong being a movement stressing
local initiative, participation and self-
management. Though the government offers administrative, technical and philosophical guidance
as the catalyst, the Saemaŭl Undong must be carried out basically through voluntary participation,
self-help efforts and village-wide cooperation.
Government support is provided as needed only to such an extent as can be properly utilized
by residents. It is meant to help stimulate local
initiative, not to coddle the village residents. The
extent of government support provided is deter-

mined by examining such factors as the technical and economic characteristics of proposed projects, and their feasibility in terms of local conditions, the villagers' self-government ability, the degree of the residents' participation, as well as the expected ripple effects of the projects.

In providing support, the government's goal is to see to it that under no circumstance should the impression be created that the government is implementing projects by proxy. It is also government policy to see to it that once a project is launched, guidance and support continue to be provided until the project is fully completed. In particular, due attention is paid to granting support at the proper time.

The basic objectives of all Korean rural development movements have been to increase the income of farmers and to improve their living standards and well-being. Financial and technical support have been necessary for such purposes. Another priority, however, is the promotion of local economic independence necessary for the development of a viable rural sector. As a first step, farmers first have had to develop a spirit of self-help and a positive outlook on the future before government assistance could be effectively utilized, and so that the tendency to depend continuously upon official help could eventually be eliminated.

One basic feature of the Saemaŭl Undong is its strong emphasis on education of farmers in development possibilities. The Saemaŭl Undong thus first emphasized projects aimed at improving farmers' immediate living environment, followed by projects to enhance the economic infrastructure, then by projects designed to more directly increase their income.

At the initial stage, the government gave incentives to farmers to improve their own living environment by installing or building more durable roofs, improved kitchens and sanitary facilities. These projects were undertaken by individual farmers working as teams, and the materials required were provided by the government, partly as grants and partly as loans. All farmers really needed was to provide labor with a desire to help themselves.

As the self-help spirit of individual farmers was cultivated, the government encouraged villagers to take up larger-scale projects aimed at creating the infrastructure needed for increased agricultural production—projects which would require the cooperation of all villagers, such as the con-

Today, farmers use modern machinery and techniques such as tractors and vinyl sleeves producing high-priced fresh vegetables all year round.

struction of small bridges and small-scale irrigation facilities, the installation of running-water systems, village beautification, and the establishment of credit unions. These projects did not immediately increase income, but they nevertheless significantly benefited the villagers by improving the quality of rural life and demonstrating the value of some sacrifice and spontaneous cooperation from everyone.

Having successfully completed these initial projects, the villagers were encouraged to take up income-generating projects such as group farming, off-season vegetable cultivation in plastic greenhouses, pig farming, and the establishment of Saemaŭl factories and cooperative marketing facilities. Here again the government provided much of the necessary materials and some of the funds, together with technical advice, but villagers also had to put up their share of the funds and provide the labor and management. As such income-generating activities required a much higher degree of cooperation and active participation by all the villagers, they were introduced only after the village had passed the second stage, which was intended to foster a spirit of cooperation.

Villagers regularly meet in their respective town halls and discuss problems of mutual interest and learn from others' experiences.

This step-by-step approach is considered one of the major reasons for the success of the Saemaŭl Undong. Many government-sponsored rural development projects failed in Southeast Asian countries because the villagers were asked to do too much too fast.

There were three types of projects: individual household projects for which farmers receive no financial support but are given continuous technical guidance; village projects for which the government provides materials and cash; and inter-village projects from which the entire community benefits through government support.

Basic guidelines for the preparation of projects were issued by the Saemaŭl Undong Central Consultative Council which was chaired by the Minister of Home Affairs. A village project based on the guidelines and selected by the Village Development Committee (comprised of 15 elected villagers chaired by a Saemaŭl leader) had to be approved by the general assembly of the village. The various village projects were coordinated by the township chief in consultation with the township Saemaŭl Committee, which he chaired. The coordinated projects were reported to the county chief who examined and approved them in consultation with the County Saemaŭl Council of which he was chairman.

Only those projects with problems which could not be resolved at the county level were referred to the provincial governor. The provincial governor works out the problem through consultation with the Provincial Saemaŭl Consultative Council which he chaired.

In this manner, all the projects were finally summated and coordinated at the Central Saemaŭl Consultative Council, which was chaired by the Minister of Home Affairs and was composed of the vice ministers of 17 ministries and the heads of seven concerned semigovernmental agencies. The Saemaŭl Planning Division of the Ministry of Home Affairs functioned also as the secretariat of the Central Committee.

Saemaŭl projects were first selected by a consensus of villagers at the village assembly and implemented with their total participation. The projects had to contribute to the common benefit of all villagers, not to any particular participant's interest alone. They were evaluated with full consideration of the specific conditions of the village and the village's potential. Each project had to be designed to directly or indirectly increase the participants' income.

One of the most important purposes of the

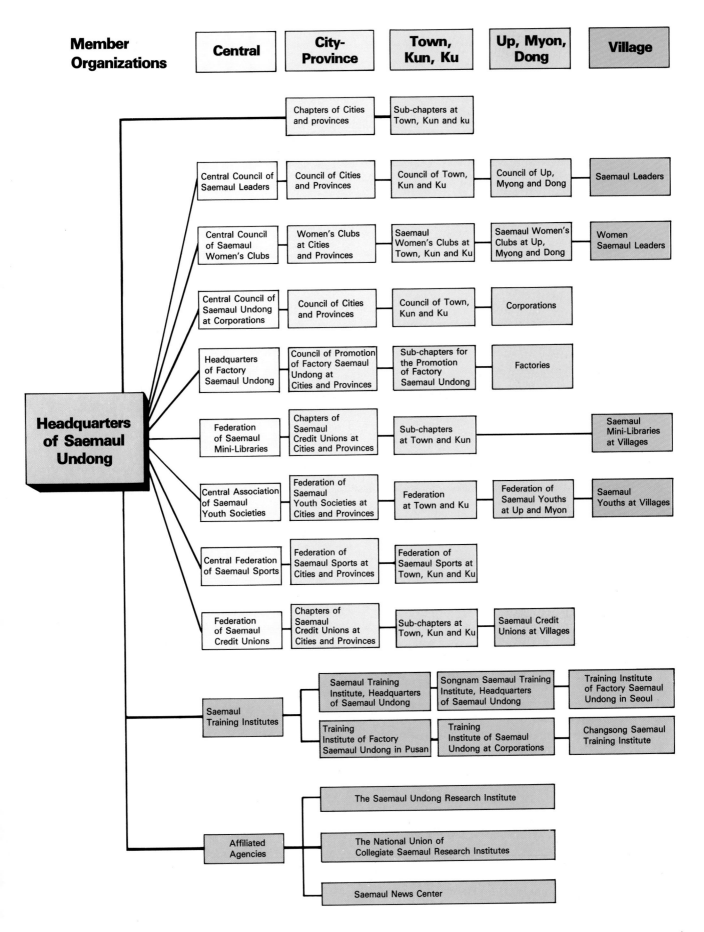

Member Organizations	Central	City-Province	Town, Kun, Ku	Up, Myon, Dong	Village
Headquarters of Saemaul Undong		Chapters of Cities and provinces	Sub-chapters at Town, Kun and ku		
	Central Council of Saemaul Leaders	Council of Cities and Provinces	Council of Town, Kun and Ku	Council of Up, Myong and Dong	Saemaul Leaders
	Central Council of Saemaul Women's Clubs	Women's Clubs at Cities and Provinces	Saemaul Women's Clubs at Town, Kun and Ku	Saemaul Women's Clubs at Up, Myong and Dong	Women Saemaul Leaders
	Central Council of Saemaul Undong at Corporations	Council of Cities and Provinces	Council of Town, Kun and Ku	Corporations	
	Headquarters of Factory Saemaul Undong	Council of Promotion of Factory Saemaul Undong at Cities and Provinces	Sub-chapters for the Promotion of Factory Saemaul Undong	Factories	
	Federation of Saemaul Mini-Libraries	Chapters of Saemaul Credit Unions at Cities and Provinces	Sub-chapters at Town and Kun		Saemaul Mini-Libraries at Villages
	Central Association of Saemaul Youth Societies	Federation of Saemaul Youth Societies at Cities and Provinces	Federation at Town and Ku	Federation of Saemaul Youths at Up and Myon	Saemaul Youths at Villages
	Central Federation of Saemaul Sports	Federation of Saemaul Sports at Cities and Provinces	Federation of Saemaul Sports at Town, Kun and Ku		
	Federation of Saemaul Credit Unions	Chapters of Saemaul Credit Unions at Cities and Provinces	Sub-chapters at Town, Kun and Ku	Saemaul Credit Unions at Villages	

Saemaul Training Institutes
- Saemaul Training Institute, Headquarters of Saemaul Undong
- Songnam Saemaul Training Institute, Headquarters of Saemaul Undong
- Training Institute of Factory Saemaul Undong in Seoul
- Training Institute of Factory Saemaul Undong in Pusan
- Training Institute of Saemaul Undong at Corporations
- Changsong Saemaul Training Institute

Affiliated Agencies
- The Saemaul Undong Research Institute
- The National Union of Collegiate Saemaul Research Institutes
- Saemaul News Center

Mutual learning through group discussions and presentation of successful cases of Saemaul leaders training activities.

Saemaŭl Undong program was public enlightenment. Therefore, education and training were given the greatest emphasis. Although the Saemaŭl Undong itself was a mass training process, the formal training of the Saemaŭl and other community leaders in rural development expertise was also much emphasized.

Formal training programs for village Saemaŭl leaders were started in 1972. As the movement progressed, it became obvious that the social elite as a whole should be armed with the Saemaŭl spirit. Therefore, starting in 1974, urban Saemaŭl leaders, prominent citizens in various fields and high-ranking government officials were included in the training. The new trend was intensified in 1975 to include the entire spectrum of social leaders (from businesses, universities, religious circles, the labor movement, the news media, etc.).

Development of rural community rural leadership was one of the most important factors in the effective implementation of the Saemaŭl Undong. The intention was to cultivate leadership from among the villagers themselves, not to be brought in from the outside.

The 1972 Saemaŭl proclamation has set forth several criteria in selecting a village Saemaŭl leader. The candidate had to be thoroughly imbued with the Saemaŭl spirit and was required to set an example by practicing it. He had to be a man of ability and action, not necessarily a person of a good family background or with a good education. He had to be trusted and respected by the villagers and it was essential that he had a power of persuasion. Since the Saemaŭl Undong was aimed in part at shaking off unproductive old conventions, a Saemaŭl leader had to be able to convince people to discard antiquated customs and counterproductive practices. He had also to possess a pioneering spirit and creativity, and be capable of innovative thinking. He had to have a strong sense of mission and be ready to sacrifice his personal interests for the sake of the community. Finally, he was to be democratic in exercising his leadership and to be ready to

*Training of social elite and
high-ranking government officials.*

Major Components
of the Curriculum

	Village *Saemaŭl* Leaders' Course	Social Leaders' Course
Curriculum	(6 days)	(6 days)
Philosophy of *Saemaŭl Undong*	19%	22%
National Security and Economy	13%	13%
Saemaŭl Project Planning Implementation	13%	—
Case Studies	13%	14%
Field Tours and Others	14%	24%
Group Discussion	28%	27%
Total	63hrs (100%)	63hrs (100%)

Source: Ministry of Home Affairs

accept the ideas of others.

Two leaders, a male and a female, were elected by the villagers from among themselves. Education and age were not limiting factors. The Saemaŭl leaders were to be responsible for planning and implementing Saemaŭl projects for the village. Their service was voluntary. Though they received no salary, leaders enjoyed administrative and moral support from all levels of the government and other concerned agencies. When selected, they were sent to the Saemaŭl training institutes for one to two weeks of training. When they returned home, the villagers were ready to give their full support to the leaders in their administration of Saemaŭl projects.

As rural people started to participate in the Saemaŭl Undong more actively, it became obvious that high-ranking government officials who were making public policy for the movement and whose job was to monitor, guide and support the movement must also be armed with the Saemaŭl spirit. Furthermore, it became increasingly clear that those who used to be considered to be not directly involved in rural development (business

executives, religious leaders, university students and professors, bankers, journalists, labor leaders, police chiefs, military leaders, etc.) could profit from Saemaul training. All the ministers and vice ministers of the government have been trained under this program, including a large number of members of the National Assembly. They have received training together with village Saemaŭl leaders at the same institutions. Their Saemaŭl training has made the social elite reevaluate their roles in light of the Saemaul spirit, bringing them closer to the village leaders and fostering a spirit of solidarity with the rural population.

The training methods developed at the sŏngnam Saemaŭl Leaders Training Institute have become a model for all Saemaŭl training institutions on various levels. The training centers' emphasis is not on teaching, but rather on self-motivated learning through case analysis, group discussions, study tours, field work, and other practical activities. These courses last for one to two weeks, and the participants are undisturbed by outside intrusions. All trainees and instructors stay in a dormitory during the training period.

The objectives of the training institutes are: to train grassroots leadership for the Saemaŭl Undong, to support Saemaŭl leaders as catalysts for the movement, and to contribute to the nationwide promotion of the Saemaŭl spirit of diligence, self-help, and cooperation.

Education at the Saemaŭl training institutes focuses on sharing experiences and trainees and staff members share room and board to promote personal exchanges of views and ideas. Cultivation of the Saemaŭl spirit is brought about through actual doing and mutual learning is fostered through group discussions and seminar-type presentation of successful Saemaŭl projects. There is also continuous follow-up and support for the graduates.

There are three main features of the training. First, the presentation and discussion of case studies and the experiences of successful village Saemaŭl leaders is considered a very effective and persuasive means of educating other Saemaŭl and civic leaders. Especially instructive for members of the social elite, who make policies for others to implement, is the account of a poverty-stricken village woman with no formal education who has

Formal training of village Saemaul leaders (right above), the village Saemaul women leaders participate in farm-technical training to learn (right below).

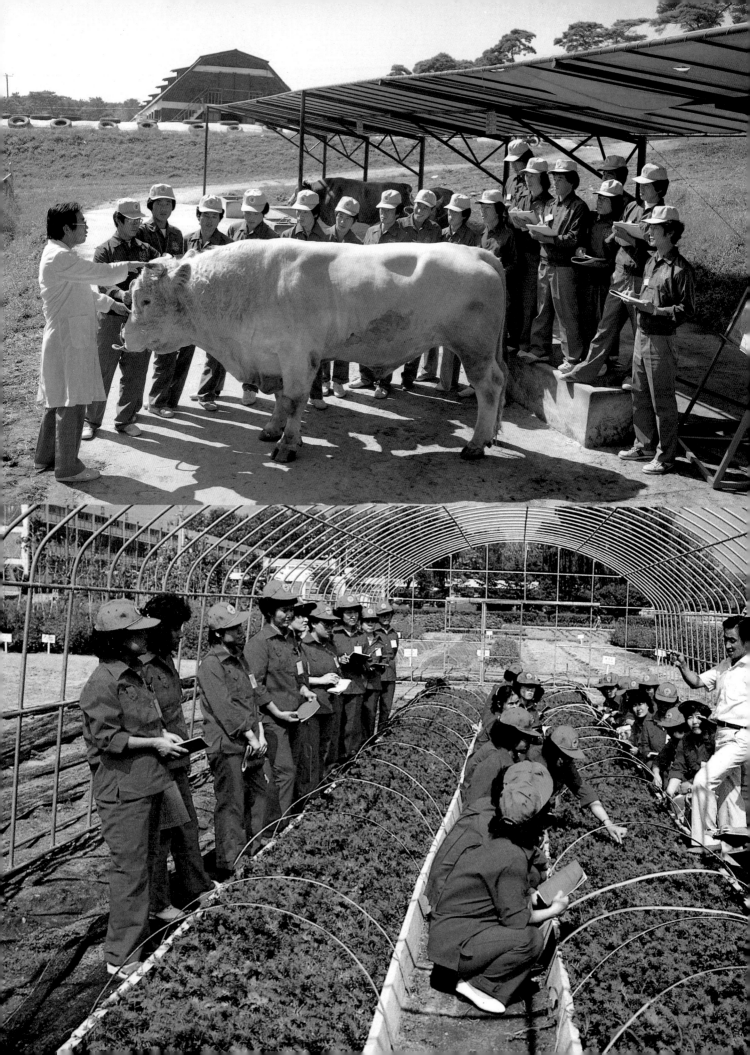

managed by dint of hard work and frugality to extricate herself from the grip of poverty and is now helping other villagers to find ways to improve their economic lot. This makes a long-lasting impression on a participant in the seminar and causes him to feel that perhaps the village woman is contributing much more to society than he is. After listening to such stories, the prominent personage reexamines his mode of life and begins to sincerely respect the village Saemaŭl leaders. He becomes eager to offer as much support to the Saemaŭl Undong as possible.

The training emphasizes "doing" as a means of learning. Every trainee lives under the same conditions, eats the same food, makes his own bed, and cleans his living quarters. Every trainee participates in a two-kilometer morning jog and uses the stairs instead of the elevator. No one expects or receives special treatment. Everyone is treated equally. A simple diet is served, consisting mainly of coarse grains, and with no alcohol, coffee, or tea.

Through such a regimen, the trainees learn that "doing" is much more difficult than "talking" and that the farmers' rough hands become a symbol of victory over adversity.

Another phase of the training involves self-evaluation through group discussion. This makes the trainee evaluate his past mode of life. The evaluation first focuses on analyzing what he has done in the past and then on charting what he should do in the future as an individual, as the head of a family, as the head of an office, and as a leader in society. The trainee is taught to concentrate on thinking about what he should do himself, rather than what others should do.

The greatest achievement of the Saemaŭl Undong so far is that there has been a substantial change in the people's outlook. This achievement is significant, because the primary goal of the Saemaŭl Undong has been, from the outset, to transform the people's attitudes.

Through the Saemaŭl Undong, the confidence that "we, too, can make it if only we try hard" and that "we, too, can live well" has spread rapidly among farmers and the rest of the population. The Saemaŭl Undong has thus contributed greatly to implanting a firm sence of confidence and a proper manner of life among the people.

Social elite received the training together with village Saemaul leaders under the same conditions.

When Saemaul leaders finish training, their companies are ready to give them full
support in carrying out various Saemaul projects under their leadership.

The Saemaŭl Undong's most outstanding result has been a dramatic rise in the rural standard of living. Briefly, a revolutionary change has taken place in the clothes, food, and dwellings of the rural populace. Housing facilities have been drastically renovated in villages, improved means of production have been developed, and transportation and communication networks have been significantly expanded. Today, even in the remote areas or isolated islands, the rural people are also enjoying cultural amenities.

To achieve these successful results, efforts were made to see to it that rural residents first improved their basic living environment through joint community projects, and then venture into production and income-increasing undertakings on the strength of spiritual enlightenment.

The Saemaŭl Undong is in part aimed at correcting regional and industrial imbalances caused by the rapid economic development and the "export-first" policies of the 1960s. In fact, the movement has helped bring about more balanced industrial growth through the intensive development of rural areas and productivity increases in various industrial sectors.

The Saemaŭl Undong has developed industries by speedily tapping rural economic potential through channeling many underutilized rural resources into these development projects. Because of the maximum possible use of local resources, relatively small amounts of additional inputs have been required from the national budget.

In particular, the rational allocation of local resources into rural development has had a spillover effect even in the industrial sector, contributing significantly to overall increases in productivity.

In addition, the recognition of the importance of savings and the frugal way of living promoted in the Saemaŭl Undong program have accelerated the accumulation of domestic capital badly needed for national development.

The Saemaŭl Undong has now developed into an international model for development, capable of profiting all the world's peoples by sharing its ideals and experiences. It has drawn keen interest and attention from numerous foreigners because it has succeeded in stimulating rural residents' positive interest and voluntary participation in self-help projects. Much interest has been focused on finding out the reasons for the success of the Saemaŭl so that other countries may apply

The Saemaul Undong has not only modernized farming but has given the farmers a completely new life style as well.

SAEMAUL UNDONG

Focal Points	Orientation of Saemaul Projects
1971—1973 Creation of a Base	
*A Saemaul concept is kindled and proliferated *A people's autonomous attitudinal posture is enhanced.	*A project to make up Saemaul villages is begun. *A base is created for the improvement of living environment and enhancement of productivity. *Targets for the developmental phase of villagers are established and relevent projects are propelled forward.
1974—1976 Self-Reliant Socio-Economic Development	
*Efforts were concentrated on the socio-economic development. *An increasing number of people from various quarters of Korean society came to participate in the Saemaul Undong.	*Income-boosting projects for villages were worked out. *Urban and factory Saemaul Undong and the movement at corporations began to evolve. *An increasing number of leading figures in Korean society came to participate in the Saemaul Undong.
1977—1980 Creation of Self-Reliant Posture	
*A base for socio-economic development was intensified as a means to further cultivate national resources. *A matured spiritual posture of the people was pursued paralled with the attainment of a high rate of economic growth.	*A base was expanded to bring about an increased welfare state of farming and fishing villagers. *Urban Saemaul Undong was intensified. *Efforts were made to establish righteous social ethics.
1981—People's Welfare State to Take Roots	
*The Saemaul Undong was diverted into a civilian-led movement. *People's potentials were pooled and the movement was so guided to create a culturally advanced motherland.	*The network for an efficient performance of the Saemaul Undong under civil stewardship was established. *A sense of people's unity was formed. *People came to have a reasonable and democratic way of thinking.

Saemaul training for Koreans as well as for foreigners is conducted both in the field and in indoor sessions.

the same principles and methds to their own national development.

In particular, many developing countries in Asia, Latin America, and Africa, finding the Saemaŭl Undong the best model for their own rural development, have introduced its principles directly into their development programs. Foreign colleges and other academic circles are also closely studying the Saemaŭl program.

A total of 29,000 foreigners from 125 countries had visited Korea to study or observe the Saemaŭl Undong as of the end of 1985. On sixteen occasions 690 of these foreigners underwent the regular Saemaŭl training course together with the Korean Saemaŭl leaders.

The basic philosophy of the Saemaŭl Undong should be useful to the efforts of the Sixth Republic to build on the experience and achievement of the past decades. The foremost goal of the Sixth Republic—namely to usher in a "great era of ordinary people" by creating an advanced democratic nation devoted to welfare for all—is is complete accord with the ideals of the Saemaŭl Undong.

73

C. Korea's Industrial Revolution

The nation's economy began to change appreciably in the early 1960s, when Korea launched its first five-year plan. At this time, the government had to decide between two alternative approaches to economic development: an inward-looking strategy based on import substitution or an outward-oriented strategy emphasizing exports and participation in the world economy. Korea chose the latter strategy to break out of constraints posed by its poor natural resource endowment and small domestic market. Given Korea's long history of isolation, this decision was considered unrealistic by many, but it turned out to be well suited to realizing the potential of the Korean economy.

The essence of the outward-looking development strategy was to promote exports of labor-intensive light manufactured goods in which Korea had a comparative advantage. In implementing this strategy, the government counted heavily on the market mechanism. For example, to create domestic savings the government at one point allowed commercial banks to raise their interest rates to as much as 26 percent per year. After 1965, when the government took this step, savings deposits in Korean banks nearly doubled annually for three consecutive years. To encourage the inflow of foreign investment, the government enacted a comprehensive Foreign Capital Inducement Act, whereby generous tax breaks were offered to foreign investors.

As part of its strategy to promote exports, in 1965 the government devalued the Korean won by almost 100 percent, and replaced the previous multiple exchange rate system with a unified exchange rate. In addition, it provided short-term export financing, allowed tariff rebates on materials imported for export production, and simplified customs procedures. These policy changes eliminated the previously existing policy bias against exports, enabling Korean exporters to do business much more efficiently.

Progress in the new development strategy also enabled the government to readjudst its previous

policy of tight import controls which had been adopted in view of severe hard currency shortages. For example, realizing that it was uneconomical for Korea to insist on self-sufficiency in all major grains, the government allowed large-scale imports of many grains for human and animal consumption for the first time. In addition, it shifted from a "positve list" of import controls—which allowed only specified products to be brought in from abroad—to a "negative list" system, which permitted the imports of all products except for those specifically prohibited. This system emphasized the need to prove that specific "infant" domestic industries required import protection and thus marked the first step toward eventual import liberalization.

The government's outward-looking strategy did not receive universal acceptance in Korea at first. Many conservative economists felt that it could even endanger national independence through an excessive reliance on foreign capital and markets. Indeed, foreign funds financed 83 per-

cent of total Korean investment in 1962, even though they were mostly "soft loans" from foreign governments and international financial organizations like the World Bank. Not until late in the decade did Korea boost its exports enough to attain a credible debt servicing capacity and make it possible to borrow development funds from foreign commercial sources. Korea's efficient use of foreign credits for productive purposes resulted in rapid economic growth even in the face of dire shortages of domestic capital and laid the foundations for subsequent self-financed economic development. During the 1950's, Korea depended first on grants-in-aid and later on concessionary public loans—both mainly from the United States—to finance essential imports and implement industrial projects. This external assistance was crucial to rehabilitating the war-devastated economy but in the long run, it would have been counterproductive for the country to become addicted to such aid.

The results of the outward-looking policy were

astonishing. Between 1961 and 1971, Korea's exports rose more than 36 percent per year in real terms, and real GNP grew by an annual average of 8.7 percent. This growth was accompanied by persistent inflation, with wholesale prices rising at an average yearly rate of 12 percent during the period. But this inflation was not steep enough to blunt growth momentum and was certainly milder compared to what was to follow in the next decade.

Of course, this performance was not entirely ascribable to the government's policy orientation; there were at least three other factors working to Korea's advantage. First of all, Korea was fortunate to be endowed with a well-educated and highly-motivated population. For centuries, the Korean people have placed a high value on education. By the early 1960s, the literacy rate in Korea was already close to 80 percent, and today literacy is almost universal in the age group below fifty. This heritage of respect for learning has made South Korea one of the most literate countries in

the whole world, contributing to labor efficiency throughout the past decades of growth.

In addition, the outward-looking strategy would not have succeeded without Korea's dynamic entrepreneurs who had the energy and daring to exploit new opportunities. In this respect, Korea benefited from its large pool of highly trained managerial and professional manpower. In addition, many Korean college graduates had obtained advanced degrees in developed countries. The military was also a source of managerial talent and experience, and many retired officers made successful transitions to managerial careers in private business. Finally, the international economic environment of the 1960s was conducive to Korea's development. Throughout the decade, the volume of world trade was expanding by nearly 8 percent annually, the barriers of trade protectionism were relatively low, and world economic growth had yet to be hampered by serious shortages of oil or other major raw materials.

In the early 1970s, this positive environment deteriorated in a number of areas. In 1971, for example, the Nixon Administration reduced the U.S. troop level in Korea by about one-third, a decision which was seen as the possible beginning of an eventual withdrawal of all U.S. forces from the country. As a result, the government resolved to develop Korea's defense industry by diverting resources from peaceful industrial development so that the nation could stand alone if necessary.

Another highly significant international development in 1971 was the demise of the Bretton Woods monetary system. For a quarter century, the Bretton Woods system had ensured relative stability in exchange rates and international trade. Nevertheless, the system was widely considered to encourage protectionism because it dissuaded trading nations from adjusting their payment balances via exchange rate modifications. The advent of a flexible exchange rate system, however, failed to reverse the trend of protectionism. On the contrary, restrictions on trade increased. Many industrial countries were unwilling to make the necessary but temporarily painful structural adjustments and instead sought an easy way out by hiding behind taller protectionist walls. This only worsened fluctuations in exchange rates and payment balances.

The worldwide commodity shortage of 1972-73 and the quadrupling of oil prices in 1973-74 hit Korea hard also. In particular, the soaring oil prices led to an alarming deterioration in Korea's trade balance. Similarly, significant price rises for imported grains put further pressure on the nation's balance of payments, resparking the argument that Korea should achieve self-sufficiency in all major food grains.

To meet the challenges of these jolting developments, Korea took, among other things, the following actions: restructuring the composition of its merchandise exports in favor of more sophisticated, higher value-added products and diversifying its trading partners, both to boost export earnings, and increasing domestic agricultural production to hold down imports. As it carried out this shift in development strategy, the government intervened extensively in the functioning of the market mechanism.

To upgrade the composition of its exports, Korea turned to its budding heavy and chemical industries. Already a priority sector of the third-five year plan (1972-76), these industries receiv-

ed greater emphasis in view of the changes in Korea's external trade environment. In 1973, the government announced its Heavy and Chemical Industry Development Plan, which set an accelerated development schedule for technologically sophisticated industries. In order to help finance the more rapid development of the heavy and chemical industries, the government established a National Investment Fund to mobilize public employee pension funds and a substantial portion of private savings in regular banking institutions.

Korea's investments in new, more sophisticated industries produced significant results, leading soon to successful manufacturing operations in electronics, shipbuilding, petrochemicals and other fields. The ratio of ship exports to total Korean exports, for example, rose from 0.06 percent in 1973 to 16 percent in 1984. However, the Heavy and Chemical Industry Development Plan had a number of negative side effects on the overall economy. Because the projects in question often had long payback periods, the government set very low interest rates for loans from the National Investment Fund. These low rates, together with overly optimistic projections of world trade growth, led to excessive investment in several capital-intensive industries, such as power generation equipment, heavy machinery, and diesel engines, and caused many firms to accumulate excessive debt loads.

In addition, the huge demand for low-interest loans swelled the domestic money supply. At the same time, the low interest rate policy made it difficult for banks to offer interest rates high enough to attract savings, thus impeding the growth of a sound domestic capital base. Finally, producers of light manufactured goods found themselves losing competitiveness during the 1970s because the government's emphasis on creating new industries was throttling the availability of investment funds for their modernization.

Korea's efforts to diversify its markets were directed toward all regions, and they achieved considerable success especially in the Middle East and Europe. The Middle East's share of total merchandise exports rose from 1.8 percent in 1973 to 11.7 percent in 1976, and the European percen-

Korean exports include heavy construction plant and equipment.

1988 Exports and Imports

Unit: Million $

	Exports	Imports
Total	60,969	51,810
North America	24,294	14,291
Asia	22,915	23,959
Europe	9,657	7,022
Africa	1,211	452
Oceania	1,120	2,174
South America	404	1,107
Others	1,095	2,806

Note: 1) From 1986 excludes repaired vessels.
Source: Office of Customs Administration.

tage went up from 11.8 percent to 17.5 percent. However, Korea made little progress in the Latin American and African markets.

An important aspect of Korea's market diversification was the growth of its construction activities abroad. Particularly in the Middle East, Korea sold construction services, as well as goods, on a massive scale. Gross earnings from construction contracts in the region totaled almost $15 billion by the end of 1978, and some 122,000 Koreans were employed on Mideast projects by that time.

Despite the invaluable experience and opportunities these projects provided to Korean workers and firms, the immediate consequences of the Middle Eastern ventures were a mixed blessing to some extent. They drained a large number of skilled workers for the construction of heavy industry. As a result, the wage differential between skilled and unskilled workers widened during the decade. In addition, the sudden surge in remittances from the Middle East rapidly expanded the domestic consumer demand, providing an added stimulus to inflation.

In order to redress the income disparity between urban and rural workers, the government re-emphasized the self-help Saemaŭl Movement to improve productivity and living standards in rural areas, and it also adopted a strengthened price support program for food grains, especially rice. These programs were successful in raising crop yields and rural income and in reducing the disequilibrium in Korea's standard of living. Nevertheless, the grain price support measures were extremely costly to the government, leading to substantial budget deficits which also contributed to inflation. In addition, price support en-

couraged the production of excess grains at a time when consumption was shifting towards more non-grain foods. Therefore, the program contributed to an imbalance in the demand and supply of agricultural products.

Korea's policy shifts in this period did, however, produce impressive overall results: GNP growth between 1972 and 1978 averaged 10.8 percent annually, and from 1976 to 1978 annual growth reached 11.2 percent. Meanwhile, the share of heavy and chemical industry products in total exports rose from 21.3 percent in 1972 to 34.7 percent in 1978. Nevertheless, this progress came at the cost of high inflation. Wholesale price rises accelerated to nearly 18 percent each year from 1972 to 1979, compared to about 12 percent between 1962 and 1971. In addition, Korea's industrial structure was distorted by overinvestment in heavy industries and underinvestment in light industries, and government controls distorted prices and stifled domestic competition. At the same time, real wages were increasing faster than productivity, weakening Korean export competitiveness.

By 1979, the government realized the dangers posed by these contradictions. Accordingly, it began a broad stabilization program to mop up excess liquidity, realign credit priorities, eliminate price distortions, and promote competition. This program had positive effects on prices, but its results were soon negated by a series of external and internal shockers. The organization of Petroleum Exporting Countries (OPEC)'s second round of oil price hikes nearly doubled Korea's oil import bill in only twelve months, and the resulting worldwide recession limited Korea's exports.

Moreover, the violent death of President Park Chung Hee in October, 1979, accelerated the mounting political and social instability, which dampened investment and consumer spending and undermined the resistance of employers to demands for higher wages. Further economic damage was inflicted by a disastrous harvest in 1980. As a result of all this, Korea's economic performance in 1980 was the poorest in over 20 years. The economy contracted by 5.2 percent during 1980, wholesale prices soared more than 38 percent and the current account deficit shot up to $5.3 billion, the highest in Korea's history.

This critical economic situation obviously called for decisive policy responses, and in late 1980, a new government that came into being under the leadership of President Chun Doo Hwan began to act toward that end. The reforms that were begun during those days are still the centerpieces of Korea's economic policies. These reforms address three major needs: price stability, continued economic growth, and more equitable income distribution.

The importance of price stability is obvious, especially in the light of Korea's experience during the 1970s. If the nation is to allocate its resources efficiently, it must depend upon free-market forces to do the job, rather than on centralized bureaucratic decisions as in the past. However, such free-market allocation is effective only if inflation is low enough to avoid price distortions.

Korea's need for high growth is also obvious. During the 1980s Korea's work force has been expanding by about three percent per annum, sending about 400,000 new workers into the job market annually. In order to create as many jobs, Korea's GNP must grow by at least five to six percent annually. Furthermore, if Korea is to maintain its high defense expenditures even while meeting its debt service obligations, its economic growth must continue steadily.

As regards income distribution, Korea is committed to ensuring that all of its people share the benefits of the nation's growth. In addition, there is a widely perceived need in Korea to demonstrate that the nation's free-market approach to economic development is superior to the central planning followed by the Communist regime in the North. To achieve all these objectives, the Korean government has since 1980 tried to further invigorate the economy, especially by liberalizing its external economic policies to expose Korean businesses to more foreign competition, while cracking down on monopolies and ensuring fair trade.

In 1986, Korea achieved a trade surplus, as well as an overall balance of payments surplus, for the first time in its history. In spite of continuous expansion in production and exports over the previous 25 years, the country had until then remained in chronic trade deficits on top of a perpetual imbalance in its international balance of payments due largely to the heavy borrowings overseas to finance economic development. Korea registered a balance of payments surplus of $4.6 billion that year and $9.9 billion in 1987, as against an average annual deficit of $3.1 billion recorded in the 1980-1984 period.

Korea's export surplus vis-a-vis the U.S., amounting to $7.3 billion in 1986 and $9.8 billion in 1987, was largely responsible for turning the balance of payments into the black, in spite of its large, intractable trade deficit with Japan, which reached $5.6 billion in 1986. As a result, Korea began to face increasingly strong pressures,

Balance of Payment

In millions of dollars

Year	Current Balance	Trade Balance	Export	Import	Invisible Trade Balance	Unrequited Transfers (net)
1970	− 622	− 922	882	1,804	119	180
1975	− 1,886	− 1,671	5,003	6,674	− 442	226
1980	− 5,320	− 4,384	17,214	21,598	− 1,385	449
1985	− 887	− 19	26,441	26,460	− 1,446	577
1986	4,617	4,205	33,913	29,707	− 627	1,038
1987	9,853	7,659	46,243	38,584	977	1,217
1988	14,160	11,445	59,648	48,202	1,267	1,448

Source: The Bank of Korea

particularly from the U.S., to open its markets, especially for beef, cigarettes, and advertising services. It was also pressed to accept an intellectual property rights agreement.

This was only the beginning of Korea's integration into the economy of the increasingly interdependent global village. Korea has taken a series of steps in the direction of liberalizing imports of goods and financial and other services. It has been repaying its external debts on schedule; it has been the lenders that have refused Korea's offer to repay before maturity. Korea is now being considered for membership

Exports and Imports by U.S.A.

In millions of dollars

Year	Exports	Imports	Surplus
1984	10,478	6,875	3,603
1985	10,754	6,489	4,265
1986	13,879	6,545	7,334
1987	18,310	8,758	9,552
1988	21,404	12,756	8,648

in the OECD (Organization for Economic Cooperation and Development), an exclusive club of advanced nations including the U.S., Japan, and the European Community (EC) countries.

It did not take long for Korea's economy to benefit from these reforms in economic policy. In 1981, the economy bounced back from a recession the year before to record 6.6 percent growth, and wholesale inflation declined to barely half its rate in the previous year. In addition, the current account deficit shrank $0.7 billion, to $4.6 billion, helped by a $3.5 billion increase in merchandise exports, and unemployment fell. This progress continued throughout the first half of the decade. Real GNP growth from 1982 through 1989

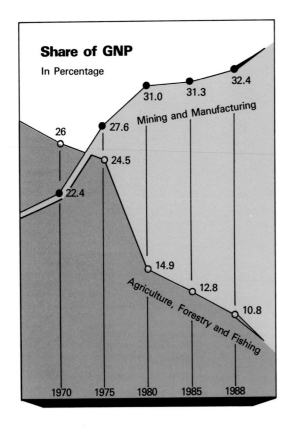

Share of GNP

In Percentage

32.4

31.0 31.3

Mining and Manufacturing

27.6

26

24.5

22.4

14.9

12.8

10.8

Agriculture, Forestry and Fishing

1970   1975   1980   1985   1988

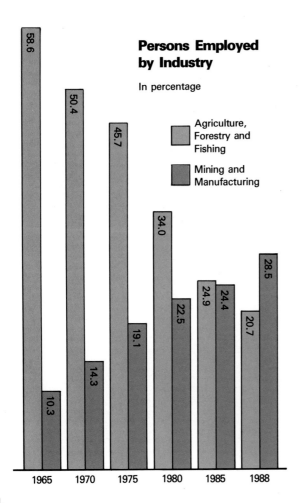

Persons Employed by Industry

In percentage

Agriculture, Forestry and Fishing

Mining and Manufacturing

58.6

50.4

45.7

34.0

24.9 24.4

28.5

22.5

20.7

19.1

10.3

14.3

1965   1970   1975   1980   1985   1988

averaged 7.7 percent per year, and inflation in both the wholesale and consumer sectors was well below 5 percent annually after 1982. Moreover, the current account deficit shrank steadily to about $900 million in 1989; Korea's trade deficit by that time was a mere $30 million. During this period, the Korean economy generated some 887,000 new jobs, although the rapid growth of the labor force thwarted any substantial improvement in the unemployment rate.

The expansion of Korea's economy was accompanied by dramatic changes in its structure. The mining and manufacturing sector grew much faster than the agricultural sector between 1972 and 1989. As a result, the share of agriculture in Korea's GNP sank from 37.0 percent in 1962 to 13.8 percent in 1989. Agriculture, forestry, and fisheries accounted for 63.1 percent of all jobs in 1963, but this percentage fell to 24.9 percent in 1989. Meanwhile, mining and manufacturing grew to make up 29.6 percent of GNP, up from 16.3 percent in 1963, and jobs in this sector swelled to 24.5 percent of Korean employment up from 8.7 percent in 1963.

The makeup of Korea's manufacturing sector itself was also transformed as industrialization continued to progress. During the 1960s and early 1970s, Korea based its growth on light industries making wigs, footwear, textiles, and other labor-intensive products. Reflecting this concentration on labor-intensive industries, the portion of total investment going to manufacturing increased only slowly, from 19.3 percent in 1954-60 to 19.8 percent in 1961-72. The share allocated to utilities and transportation facilities rose from 23.9 percent to 34.9 percent, however, giving entrepreneurs the advantage of a better infrastructure in producing and distributing their goods.

In the 1970s, the share of investment coming into the manufacturing industries again showed only a slight rise, despite the initiation of Korea's drive to develop heavy industries. Manufacturing-sector investment edged up to 20.7 percent of the total from 1973-76, but it fell to 19.1 percent from 1977-81. These relatively low figures reflect the large increase in overall investment, particularly in services, during the decade. The 1977-81 figure also shows the dampening effects of high inflation and the 1980 recession on business investment. Investment in agriculture, meanwhile,

Loans and Foreign Investment

In millions of dollars

Year	Arrivals		Approval basis	Loans Debt Service	
	Public Loans	Commercial Loans	Foreign Investment	Public Loans	Commercial Loans
1980	1,516	1,402	143	638	1,503
1981	1,690	1,247	153	774	1,765
1982	1,868	914	189	1,003	1,845
1983	1,493	973	269	1,076	1,761
1984	1,424	858	422	1,338	1,773
1985	1,024	964	532	1,343	1,689
1986	880	1,620	354	1,789	2,105
1987	1,109	1,558	1,060	3,261	3,103
1988	891	988	1,283	2,648	2,526

increased to 8.8 percent of the total from 1973-76 but it sank to 7.5 percent in 1977-81.

Throughout Korea's development, the nation's investment has exceeded its domestic savings. As a result, Korea has relied on foreign savings to make up the difference. Foreign savings equaled about 7 percent of GNP in the first half of the 1960s, rising to 9.3 percent in 1970. The rate has declined since then, and foreing savings induced in 1989 made up some 3.1 percent of the GNP that year.

In the early 1960s, Korea obtained much of its foreign savings from U.S. aid, but such aid was phased out during the decade in favor of loans. Trade credits made up a majority of Korea's capital inflow during the 1960s and 1970s, compensating for chronic trade deficits. The U.S. and Japan provided most of the public and private lending to Korea during this period. In more recent years, as Korea gained a favorable credit rating, the nation has turned increasingly to bank loans, bond issues, and other sources of capital. In 1985, such long-term funding exceeded short-term loans for the first time.

An inevitable consequence of Korea's need for foreign savings has been its accumulation of a large foreign debt. At the end of 1989, Korea owed $30 billion to creditors in other countries. Nevertheless, Korea's export earnings have allowed it to maintain a comfortable debt service ratio, which has hovered around 20 percent in recent years. The government also has managed the composition of the debt to protect Korea from instability in world financial markets, while raising the share of long-term obligations.

Foreign investment in Korea made up only a small fraction of capital inflow in the 1960s and 1970s. However, Korea's liberalization of foreign investment laws, and its evident economic performance have attracted a rising level of invest-

Foreign Investments by Country (Approval Basis)

In millions of dollars

Year	U.S.A.	Japan	Hong Kong	Germany	Netherland	Switzerland	U.K.	France
1980	70	42	0.5	8.5	1.8	2.1	2.3	—
1981	59	37	33.8	3.5	1.3	12.6	—	1.1
1982	101	40	27.1	3.9	5.1	3.2	1.7	—
1983	54	168	6.9	2.5	9.5	5.8	0.8	1.5
1984	193	164	4.2	3.6	—	18.3	4.1	22.1
1985	111	360	13.4	11.2	0.5	6.9	12.0	5.0
1986	125	137	12.8	5.7	4.3	31.5	15.4	0.2
1987	255	494	43.3	40.9	45.8	55.6	48.3	11.3
1988	284	696	13.8	74.0	48.9	24.4	21.7	47.3

The Sixth Five-Year Economic and Social Development Plan

			1987	1988	1989	1990	1991
National Income	Growth rate	Constant prices	12.0	10.0	8.0	7.5	7.5
	Gross National Product	Current prices $100 million	1,186	1,450	1,700	2,000	2,260
	Per Capita GNP	Current prices	2,826	3,600	4,270	4,840	5,500
Balance of Payment	Current Balance	$ 100 million	99	95	75	60	60
	Trade Balance	$ 100 million	77	72	60	50	60
	Exports	$ 100 million (custom clearance basis)	473	575	640	705	795
	Gross Foreign Liabilities	$ 100 million	356	310	270	245	230
	Foreign Assets	$ 100 million	132	180	210	235	265
	Net Foreign Liabilities	$ 100 million	224	130	60	10	−35
Industrial Structure	Economic Activity Participation rate	%	58.3	58.6	58.8	59.0	59.2
	Employment — Agri., For., & Fishing	%	21.9	20.5	19.1	17.9	16.7
	Employment — Mining & Manufacturing	%	28.1	28.6	29.3	29.9	30.5
	Employment — Others	%	50.0	50.9	51.6	52.2	52.8

ment during the 1980s. In 1989, foreign investment totaled $1.28 billion on an approval basis, compared to $419 million in 1984, $268 million in 1983, and an average of $108 million per year during the seventies.

Korea's medium- and long-term prospects are good, with the promise of continued improvements in exports, the gross national product, and living standards. Barring a severe deterioration in the world trading environment, projections for Korea's sixth five-year plan show an average growth rate of 7 percent per year from 1987 to 1991. By the end of the sixth plan period, Korea's per capita GNP is expected to stand at $3,650 in current prices. Commodity exports on a customs clearance basis are projected to expand by some 12 percent annually to $55 billion by that time, while imports will rise to almost $52 billion. Thus, by the early 1990s Korea should enjoy a moderate trade surplus, which in turn will bring the current account balance into the black. Freed of the economic drain caused by balance of payments deficits, Korea will be more able to expand its investment in other countries, bringing down the nation's net foreign indebtedness. Eventually, a positive balance of payments will enable Korea to reduce the gross size of its debt as well.

Korea's economic expansion should be accompanied by continued low inflation. Prices for most imported raw materials are expected to remain stable for much of the decade, and the government will continue to keep money supply growth and budget deficits in line. In addition, the increasing level of competition in the Korean market will likely restrain price increases throughout the economy.

The economic shift from primary to secondary industries has beeen another factor during the late 1980s. By 1991, only about 12 percent of GNP will be generated by the agriculture, forestry, and fishing sectors, while manufacturing industries will account for nearly 32 percent of GNP. The share of the service sector is expected to remain constant at its current 50 percent level.

The Korea Development Institute projections for the year 2000 carry on this optimism. Korea's GNP at the beginning of the next century should exceed $250 billion in 1984 prices, giving a per capita GNP of over $5,000. With projected exports of some $123 billion and imports of $119 billion, Korea will play a major part in the vitality of the world economy.

There are a number of solid reasons for these optimistic forecasts. First of all, Korea's share of world trade is still small, accounting for only about 1.5 percent of the 1984 total. The nation

1988 Production of
Iron and Steel Basic Industries

Pig-Iron	M/T	12,577,754
Ferro-alloys	M/T	173,108
Slab	M/T	11,663,791
Bloom	M/T	1,478,814
Billet	M/T	5,882,402
Steel bars	M/T	865,512
Concrete reinforcing bar	M/T	3,539,246

Iron and Steel Industries

Angles and shapes of steel	M/T	1,505,231
Medium heavy plate	M/T	2,373,870
Hot rolled sheet	M/T	515,567
Steel for casting	M/T	114,702
Steel pipe	M/T	2,173,208
Wire rods	M/T	1,234,445
Cost iron pipe	M/T	124,241
Tin plates	M/T	243,799
Galvanized sheets	M/T	810,553

Non-Ferrous Metal Industries

Electrolytic copper ingot	M/T	168,334
Unwrought aluminium ingot	M/T	16,101
Unwrought zinc ingot	M/T	225,987
Copper wire bar	M/T	232,864
Copper plates & stripe	M/T	92,907
Copper tubes & hollow bars	M/T	38,490
Aluminium plates	M/T	85,063
Aluminium sash bar	M/T	110,344

1988 Production of Fabricated Metal Products

Metal structural product on land	M/T	421,625
Gas storage tank	M/T	64,248
Container	Each	296,155
Stainless household products	M/T	42,494
Metal can	1,000 each	2,203,085
Screw products	M/T	200,634
Wire netting	M/T	61,534
Wire rope	M/T	138,978
Welding rods	M/T	113,303

1988 Production of Machinery

Plought & rotary tiler	HP	481,142
Lathe	Each	7,225
Milling machines	Each	2,802
Press machines	M/T	409,264
Looms	Each	10,386
Knitting machines	Each	5,197
Electronic caculators	Each	4,150,795
Room airconditioner	Each	676,309
Gas range	Each	3,137,117
Elevator	Each	4,885
Fork lift	Each	20,598

should thus be able to expand its sales abroad, particularly if it devotes energy to doing business in new markets and to developing new products. Although protectionism has frequently inhibited Korea's exports in the past, the increasing size and openness of the Korean market will reduce the basis for such actions in the years ahead. Korea's location in the heart of the Pacific Basin will also be an asset to its future growth. In close proximity to some of the most vibrant economies in the world, Korea is well-positioned to benefit from intra-regional trade. Here again, the nation's economic liberalization will help it make the most of its potential as a center for banking, retailing, and manufacturing in the Pacific.

On the supply side of the economy, there are also grounds for optimism. Korea's labor force is expected to grow at about 3 percent annually for some time to come, compared to about 1.5 percent yearly growth in the total population. This labor force growth will require Korea to generate many new jobs, but it will increase the ratio of labor force to population. Raising this ratio means that the average worker will have fewer dependents to support and hence will be able to save more. With higher domestic savings, Korean industries will be more able to finance their investment needs at lower interest rates. Meanwhile, the growing labor force will help keep the returns on investment high.

Productivity improvements will be another important factor in Korea's continued development. Each new generation of Koreans is better educated than the one before, and the nation's workers will thus be more able to take advantage of the

productivity inherent in new technologies. Furthermore, Korea will be able to raise overall output by shifting workers from the less efficient agricultural sector to high-productivity industries. Agriculture still accounts for about one third of all employment in Korea, so the potential gains in output from such a personnel transfer are great. Korea's growing technological capabilities will be yet another spur to its productivity improvements. Rising business expenditures on research and development, along with the increasing capabilities of the nation's research institutions, suggest that Korea will have a growing reserve of domestic technology for its entrepreneurs to draw upon.

Finally, one of the most important reasons for optimism about Korea's long-term economic prospects is the aspiration of the Korean people to improve their standard of living. These aspirations and the willingness to make sacrifices to realize them will continue to add dynamism to the Korean economy. Just as they have done when faced with difficult situations in the past, the Korean people will do whatever is necessary to overcome challenges in the future and to attain their dream of a better life.

As mentioned earlier, Korea's economic development over the past quarter century has resulted from a number of factors and conditions. One of these sources of growth has been the series of five-year plans instituted by the government. In the early years of the nation's growth, these plans set specific, numerical targets for the development of industries and infrastructure, and the government backed up the targets with its financial and organizational capabilities. More recently, the plans have become more general, setting forth the economic orientation of the government and the direction of policies during the plan period. The approach allows most investment choices, except for some involving large scale public work projects, to take place unimpeded in the private sector.

Korea's early plans concentrated strictly on

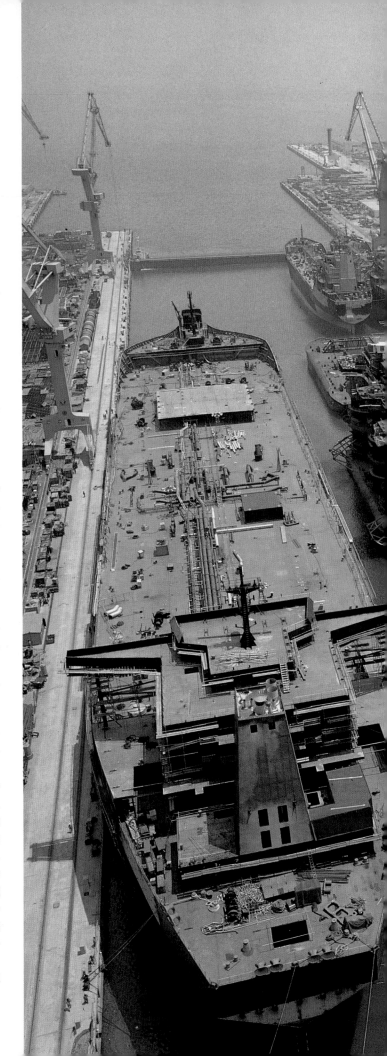

The shipyards of Korea's largest shipbuilder, the Hyundai Company.

building the economy, in keeping with the nation's desperate need for growth. In the 1970s, however, the plans began to include more social policy tasks, such as health care improvement, educational planning, and housing programs. In recognition of this trend, in 1982 the government adopted the term "Economic and Social Development Plan" to describe its fifth five-year plan. Thus, the importance of social welfare objectives in the overall plan has grown over the past decade, just as the emphasis given to specific economic targets has declined.

The planning process has continued with the Sixth Five-Year Economic and Social Development Plan, in effect from 1987 to 1991. The government has sought to design a plan that is truly representative of the desires and needs of the Korean people, by making the planning process more open and comprehensive than ever before. Concepts and methods employed in the sixth plan have been aired and refined in consultations with business people, scholars, and representatives of citizen's groups, as well as in public hearings. Moreover, the plan's stress on decentralizing government functions will make it more flexible and more responsive to changing conditions while in operation.

Under the Sixth Five-Year Plan, the government will direct its greatest attention to continuing and reinforcing the stable, long-term growth of the Korean economy. In all aspects of the nation's economy and society, the government will work to eliminate destabilizing factors while stressing more efficient use of the nation's physical, financial, and human resources.

At the same time, the government will encourage the reshaping of Korea's industrial structure to ensure that its economy will be ready for growth in new markets and under new conditions. These efforts for stability and restructuring will be accompanied by programs to increase the balance of development between regions and to improve the standard of living of the nation's people.

91

The sixth plan's emphasis on stability and efficiency in the Korean economy translates into four major policy categories. The first is to promote competition domestically by reducing government involvement and eliminating restrictive business practices. To this end, the plan calls for transforming the government's role from one of regulation to one of promotion.

The government will simplify its procedures of approval, registration, and permission, especially in relation to founding a new firm or expanding an existing one. It will also abolish or consolidate laws which support or promote specific industries, giving market forces and private management decisions the greatest importance in deciding business success or failure. The government may still intervene in cases where a business failure threatens the health or stability of the broader national economy, but such intervention will be strictly limited in scope and duration.

To end the inefficiency of restrictive business practices, the government will bring Korea's fair trade practices up to a level comparable to those in advanced economies. The government will set guidelines for the activities of trade associations to prevent them from collusive or market-restricting behavior. The sixth plan period will also see an increase in sanctions against collusive activity by groups of firms, as well as the formulation of criteria for approving exceptional cartels to overcome a recession or to rationalize an inefficient industry.

Other fair-trade actions under the sixth plan will include coordinating the related policies and enforcement activities of different ministries and formulating long-term education and training programs to help the government analyze and enforce its laws more effectively. Special attention will go to the small and medium industries, which have often suffered in the past from unequal relationships with their larger competitors and contracting partners. Government activities in this area will include strengthening regulations against abuses of economic power by larger firms, improving legal standards for subcontracting regulations, restricting takeovers of smaller firms by large ones, and ensuring greater access to distribution channels by small and medium industries.

The second category of policies designed to stabilize and increase the competitiveness of the Korean economy during the sixth plan period will be to broaden external access to its markets.

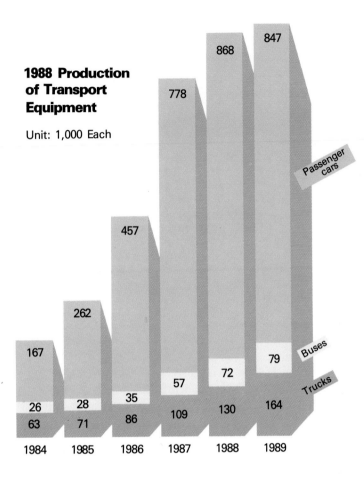

1988 Production of Transport Equipment

Unit: 1,000 Each

Passenger cars

Buses

Trucks

	1984	1985	1986	1987	1988	1989
Passenger cars	167	262	457	778	868	847
Buses	26	28	35	57	72	79
Trucks	63	71	86	109	130	164

An automated car assembly line of the Hyundai Company.

Korea's import liberalization ration will rise to over 95 percent in 1989, a level similar to those in advanced countries, and it will continue reducing tariffs during the period. To minimize any domestic disruption or opposition caused by these steps, the government will employ shock-absorbing techniques such as advance warning of liberalization of import restrictions, imposition of temporary adjustment tariffs, or surveillance applied to rapidly increasing import items.

Similar liberalization will take place in the investment sector. The number of Korean industries open to direct foreign investment will increase steadily during the plan period, and the government will continue to reduce the approval and paperwork requirements for foreign investors. Investment in Korea's capital markets will also be

1988 Production of Electric and Electronic Equipment

Motors	HP	5,366,938
Power transformers	1,000 KVA	17,016
B/W Television receivers	Each	4,389,292
Color television receivers	Each	10,431,207
Video cassette recorders	Each	8,683,000
Cassette recorders	Each	19,876,000
Telephones	Each	6,956,290
Video tapes	Each	214,947,000
Electric refrigerators (household)	Each	3,930,512
Washing machines (household)	Each	1,930,012
Micro wave ovens	Each	10,311,000
Air humidifer or dehumidifers (household)	Each	2,199,293
Transistors	Each	6,380,148,000
Integrated circuits	Each	3,116,430,000
Wire & cable of communication	M/T	51,408
Power wire & cable insulation	M/T	104,561

Korea ranked among the world's top ten producers of electronic goods.

opened up, with foreign investors being able to buy stocks and bonds directly before the end of the decade.

A third and broader step to stabilize and streamline the economy will be to increase the efficiency of the government's role in the market-based economy that Korea is developing. The government will restructure itself by consolidating similar or duplicated functions and by privatizing them wherever possible. On top of this restructuring the government will strengthen its cost control, holding the growth of its budget to no more than the GNP increase rate. Through fiscal moderation, the government will be able to use public finance as a stabilizing influence on the business cycle.

For greater efficiency in carrying out tasks that

it cannot privatize or eliminate, the government will upgrade the coordination of policies between ministries. It will also increase the level of specialized education available to officials, helping them to plan and execute policies more effectively. To promote broader public support and understanding of the nation's economic strategies, the government will make administrative procedures more convenient for individual citizens and concerned private sector groups, and it will work to make government statistics both more reliable and more widely disseminated.

The government's fourth method of promoting a stable and efficient national economy is to make the best possible use of natural, financial, and human resources. To avoid destabilization from fluctuating raw material prices, the government will encourage better demand management and the stockpiling of affected commodities. It will also stress the need to absorb overseas price increases as much as possible, rather than translating them into accelerated domestic inflation.

In the financial sector, the sixth plan calls for raising the domestic savings ratio from 28.4 percent in 1985 to 33 percent in 1991. To accomplish this task, Korea will diversify savings instruments, promote greater public access to and use of the banking system, encourage firms to retain a higher level of their income, and restrain government spending. The plan also includes guidelines for achieving and maintaining a balance of payments surplus, by encouraging the domestic production of parts and machinery now imported, by encouraging exports by small and medium-sized firms, and by supporting productivity improvements by industry.

To make the best use of this higher level of domestic resources, the government will enhance incentives for productive investment in such fields as manufacturing, technology development, training, and small and medium industries. Meanwhile, it will intensify its efforts to stamp out real estate speculation.

Naturally, among the most important aspects of financial resource management is the condition of the institutions which distribute these resources. Therefore, the government is focusing on improving the efficiency of the financial sector. Under the sixth plan, the government will cut back its involvement in the allocation of loans and in executive staffing decisions, making financial institutions responsible for their own management. It will also liberalize interest rates gradually, and continue the phasing out of policy preference loans to favored sectors. To bolster the competitiveness of domestic banks, the government will work with them to find ways of reducing their bad debt burden. It will also encourage more sophisticated financial techniques and more diversified banking functions in order to raise bank profits.

Other steps toward more efficient financial resource management will refine the government's monetary and fiscal controls, with emphasis on the use of indirect instruments of monetary policy such as discount rates and reserve requirements. The plan also calls for a greater appreciation of the importance of social development financing, such as housing loans and those to middle and lower income families, as well as for a more balanced use of funds by region.

To make better use of Korea's human resources, particularly in an era of rising competition from lower-wage countries, the sixth plan calls for heightened training of workers and scientific researchers. The plan calls for an increase in the number of researchers in science and technology from 32,000 in 1983 to 72,000 in 1991. In addition, university enrollment quotas will be increased for students of science and technology, and an exchange program will be introduced to advance the quality of research by scientists in universities, industry, and government.

On the worker level, the government will improve the current vocational training system, integrating it to cover manpower demand projections, training, and employment services. On-the-site training will be promoted to help industries meet their own manpower needs, and public training courses will be upgraded to supply more high-level workers. Meanwhile, the government will encourage the formation of professional training institutes in the private sector.

The international conditions in which Korea's economy must operate have changed dramatically during the past decade. Developments such as the debt crisis in the developing world, the rise of protectionism in advanced nations, the growing industrial capabilities of a number of less developed nations, and the increasing specialization of national economic strategies have meant that Korea can no longer operate under the same set of economic assumptions that fueled its growth in the past.

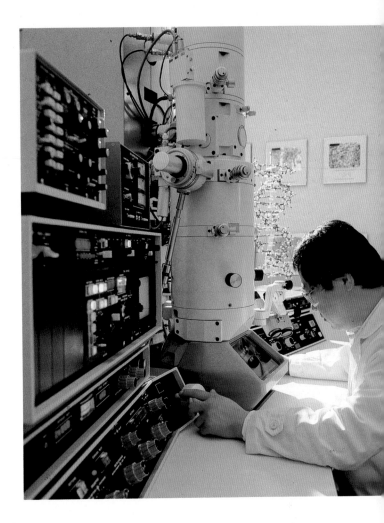

Genetic engineering and automobiles are just a few of the high-tech fields Korean companies are moving into.

Therefore, the sixth plan aims at transforming Korea's industrial structure into one more suited to the demands and changes of the world economic environment. To achieve this goal, the plan calls first of all for greater efficiency in the structure and operation of Korean firms. Therefore, the government will develop an institutional apparatus to help consolidate industries which suffer severe structural problems. Such consolidation will be based on the premise that the affected industries should solve their problems through their own decision-making and self-help ability. In addition, the government will encourage the heavy and chemical industries to make greater use of their strength in attracting investment and in technology transfer, helping them to reach their potential for productivity and exports.

The sixth plan also calls for changes in government policies toward business management. The government will encourage corporations to increase their separation of ownership and management through greater use of equity financing and professional managers. Similarly, the government will strengthen incentives for conglomerates to specialize in their main lines of businesses and to avoid excessive dependence upon debt.

A major part of the sixth plan's program for structural revision will be promoting technological innovation. The plan calls for enlarged government support for basic scientific research and for greater use of the research capabilities of universities. In addition, the venture capital industry will be expanded during the plan period, and the government will introduce a technology credit guarantee system to aid in the commercialization

97

of new technology. Through these and similar steps, the ratio of investments in science and technology to GNP should rise to 2.5 percent by 1991. At that time, Korea's firms are projected to plow back 23 percent of their turnover into research and development.

The importance of small and medium industries will rise as part of the transformation of Korea's economy. During the plan period, the government will strive to implement support for small and medium firms with solid competitive poten-tial, through providing such firms with greater access to financing and other non-specific support. In the agricultural sector, Korea will move away from its past emphasis on increasing rice production. Instead, it will focus on expanding the scale of farm businesses, the level of mechanization, and the efficiency of distribution channels. To promote the confidence and well-being of farm families, sixth plan programs will help stabilize the prices of agricultural and fisheries products and will augment sources of non-farm income.

What useful lessons can one draw from Korea's economic policies and experiences over the past 20 years? One of the most important lessons one can draw from Korea's experience has to do with the merits of an outward-looking development strategy. Without such a strategy, Korea's economic progress to date world have been impossible. Some critics have argued that Korea's heavy dependence on trade has made its economy highly vulnerable to unfavorable external developments, and have supported their argument by pointing to the painful adjustments Korea has had to make to two rounds of oil shocks and to the current wave of protectionism. Certainly, an outward-looking strategy is vulnerable to external shocks, but it is still a better option than an inward-looking orientation. In general, an open economy adapts better to external shocks than a closed economy, simply because entrepreneurs in an open economy are more capable of exploiting new opportunities arising from changes in the external environment

The Pohang Iron and Steel Company.

Future Prospects

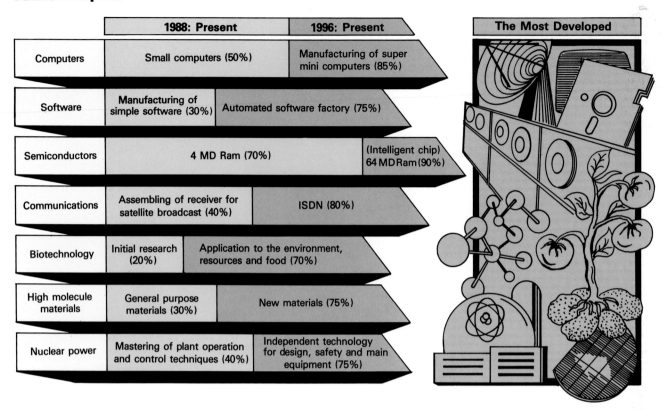

	1988: Present	1996: Present	The Most Developed
Computers	Small computers (50%)	Manufacturing of super mini computers (85%)	
Software	Manufacturing of simple software (30%)	Automated software factory (75%)	
Semiconductors	4 MD Ram (70%)	(Intelligent chip) 64 MD Ram (90%)	
Communications	Assembling of receiver for satellite broadcast (40%)	ISDN (80%)	
Biotechnology	Initial research (20%)	Application to the environment, resources and food (70%)	
High molecule materials	General purpose materials (30%)	New materials (75%)	
Nuclear power	Mastering of plant operation and control techniques (40%)	Independent technology for design, safety and main equipment (75%)	

than are businessmen or bureaucrats in a closed economy.

A second lesson is the importance of the market mechanism in promoting long-term growth. In the 1960s, Korea successfully established a high growth economy by following the basic principle of the market, that scarce resources should be allocated on the basis of price signals through the initiative of entrepreneurs operating in a competitive environment.

During the 1970s, the allocation of resources was not as efficient as in the 1960s, because the government interfered in the working of the market mechanism in its effort to promote certain strategic industries. A case in point is the use of low interest rates to encourage certain high-priority industries. Such support invited misinvestment, resulted in chronic inflation, and prevented the normal growth of the capital market whose efficient operation is so essential to the long-term growth of any economy.

A related lesson concerns the importance of price stability for growth. Korea's experience with macro-economic management over the past 20 years indicates that there is no trade-off between price stability and gowth. As a matter of fact, Korea's experience shows that growth is not sustainable in an inflationary environment. Moreover, if the present government had not curbed inflation in the early 1980s, the country would probably not have enjoyed the growth it showed during the first half of the decade.

The fourth lesson has to do with inflow of foreign capital. Korea's experience in this regard indicates that at least in the early phase of development, when foreign confidence in the economy is weak, the greatest barrier to the international movement of capital is the uncertainty of investors or lenders. A government can reduce this uncertainty significantly by providing guarantees for repayment or repatriation or profits. In a later stage of development, when foreign confidence in the economy has grown, a country should be more liberal in regard to direct investment and joint venture requirements. After all, direct investment is an effective vehicle for the transfer of technology. Direct investment is also helpful in avoiding serious mistakes in investment decisions because foreign investors are often better informed about marketing conditions abroad.

The fifth lesson relates to the capacity to absorb new technology and manpower training. Korea's remarkable ability to absorb new technology from abroad has stemmed directly from the high level of education in the country, and

Major Indicators' for the Korean Economy in the Year 2,000

		1980	1990	2000
Total Population	1,000 persons	38,124	42,793	46,830
Gross National Product	$ 100 million	605	2,230	7,570
Per Capita GNP	dollars	1,592	5,220	16,150
Current Balance	$ 100 millions	−53.2	20.0	75.0
Exports	$ 100 millions	175	640	1,800
Net Foreign Liabilities	$ 100 millions	196	0	−500
Population per Physician	persons	1,492	952	833
Housing Supply Ratio	percentage	71.2	69.8	88.2
Telephone Subscribers	per 100 persons	7.2	30.9	49.6
Pipe Water Supply Ratio	percentage	54.6	78	90
Water Service per Person/Daily	liters	256	340	440
Passenger Car Supply	per 1,000 persons/each	4.9	43.9	146.3
Paved Roads Ratio	percentage	33.2	82.4	100
Length of Express highway	kilometers	1,225	1,550	2,931
Length of Subways	kilometers	22.1	240.4	689.2
Electric Power Consumption	per persons/year KWH	858.6	2,097.7	3,343.3
Petroleum Consumption	per person/year Bbl	4.78	7.73	10.18

in the future, the government will devote still more resources to education and to training skilled workers and technologists.

For a nation that depends almost exclusively on educated and trained manpower for continued progress, the emphasis on education and training is not only good economics but also good social policy. Government investment in education and technical manpower training, coupled with a policy providing for continued expansion of employment opportunities, serves as the most effective structural basis for an equitable distribution of income.

The sixth lesson relates to the effects of protectionism on growth in developing countries. Too many industrial countries ignore the cost of adjustment they impose on the developing world through sudden protectionist moves. Protectionism often shortens the life of investment capital in the developing countries or forces these countries to leap to stages of industrial development beyond their capacity. As a result, it adds to the high cost of industrialization in the developing world. If protectionist measures are unavoidable they should be limited in duration and should be regressive in order to provide time for adjustment on the part of developing countries. The developing countries themselves would do

well to minimize protectionist resistance against their exports by promoting exports based on intra-industry specialization.

The seventh lesson has to do with an exchange rate regime and the monetary system. The rise in worldwide protectionism and resource nationalism in recent years has been aggravated to a great degree by the highly unstable international monetary climate since the breakdown of the Bretton Woods system. Sudden shifts in the exchange rates of developing countries, due to forces beyond their control, have compelled them to bear heavy adjustment burdens.

The final point goes beyond economics. The critical precondition for economic development is social and political stability. Korea's rapid growth in the 1960s would not have been possible without the social stability provided by the government at that time. As indicated earlier, uncertainty in the nation's social and political environment was in part responsible for the severe problems encountered by the Korean economy in 1980. In light of these experiences, the importance to economic growth of stable and efficient government should not be overlooked.

PART FOUR
Social Changes

A. The New Ideological Movement

One of the goals set by the New Ideological Movement in the 1960s was to create a nation not only materially affluent, but spiritually healthy, a society which is ruled by the spirit of Benefits to All Mankind. While the pursuit of the advantages of modern civilization and the comfortable life it offers remain the goals of Koreans, they have not overlooked the importance of creating a society in which compassion rules. They desire a highly modernized society without the usual ills that are displayed by other advanced nations.

The causes of problems that normally accompany modernization or industrialization should be thoroughly examined well in advance of their arrival. Examining the problems of other advanced countries, one finds at their roots the problem of dehumanization. A highly industrialized society is a society that is extremely mechanized, specialized, organized, and rationalized. Ironically, however, the more complex a society has become, the more unhappy and fettered has become the citizen's lot. In the shadow of a highly mechanized civilization, man has turned into a slave of machines and materialism, with his individuality and personality lost in the organization. With mass society taking over, fraternity and compassion disappearing, man finds himself feeling increasing alienation and loneliness. The cases of shoe manufacturing can serve as an instance. A shoemaker who handles all the work attendant on making a pair of shoes may be moved by a feeling of accomplishment. But this is not true of the factory employee who is reduced to making the same part day after day in a tedious factory routine. He is a victim of drudgery, powerless before the machine and lonely within himself.

Modern man, under such circumstances, is apt to lose control of himself and to become the victim of an obsession for consumer goods, his value system turned upside down by the onslaught of his society's consumption orientation. He is then swept away by the force of fads and fashion. Reeling under a daily bombardment of advertisement, everyone is literally pushed into buying new and ever newer products. One finds oneself a prisoner of fashion, aping other people's lives and other nation's standards of living. The more materialistic a society becomes, the more prominent is this phenomenon.

It is natural for people enjoying an increasingly better life, but struggling under the pressure of an industrial society, to seek the comfort of modern civilization and the amenities it offers. Under no circumstances, however, should material wealth be allowed to become a standard by which to judge human or social values. The idea that money answers all problems, and the sacrificing of compassion and faith in pursuit of material rewards not only destroys a nation's spiritual life, it threatens its social equilibrium and harmony by negating individual social discipline. If such a materialistic tendency is compounded by individual or collective egotism, people eventually forfeit their sense of belonging to a viable social unit.

The plethora of organized activities in an industrialized society may give the semblance of frequent human contact and exchange. But with most of them likely to be associations based on narrow professional interests, modern society in fact turns into more of a theater for barren competition. With a variety of different *weltanschauungen* and other value systems competing for attention among different generations, races, classes, and professional groupings, solidarity in its broad sense within society has become almost impossible to achieve. In urban day-to-day life, family units have become smaller and smaller with friendship circles ever narrowing. Loneliness and nihilism cannot but be increased by their developments.

How does one explain the fact that the suicide rate is usually the highest and the number of psychiatric patients largest in the most civilized and advanced of countries? The question only underlines the barrenness of a materialistic and individualistic society. As one imagines the picture of aged couples, abandoned by their children, forlornly strolling in parks, or unwanted children, neglected by their divorced parents, he senses the causes of social tension and instability, with the attendant phenomena of juvenile delinquency, rebellion of youth, increased criminality, confusion, drug abuse and psychological instability. Youngsters turn to decadence, desperately trying to fill a spiritual vacuum. Some of these ills may seem inevitable, but the problems are insistent: How can we cope with them? The answer may depend to a large degree on the strength of the individual or social values a country has, or on the texture of its spiritual culture. Take the case of a poor family suddenly becoming rich, yet finding itself unhappy. In this case, it is not so much the wealth itself as the family's failure to cope with it that is the cause of unhappiness. With every one making his choice as to the meaning of happiness, defining it becomes even harder.

For all that, there is something universal about man, making it not impossible to find a common standard. Every one wants convenience in life, as well as survival and safety. Indeed, it is to free the people from the yoke of poverty and provide them with greater material affluence that economic growth is sought. But a materially affluent life alone hardly guarantees happiness, for things in themselves can never produce it.

Man develops a liking for things that he sees, hears about, or feels. We react the same way to family and neighbors. It is said of man that he is a social animal, which means he cannot live apart from others. Either in human relationships or in doing something good for others, he craves respect and fulfillment. By sharing poverty with neighbors, or by seeking common development rather than individual wealth, one may find deeper satisfaction and happiness. Others, out of

their love for community or for their nation, gladly offer their lives to protect it. A society's soundness is measured not in terms of the number of high-rise apartments or the efficiency of its traffic system, but by the amount of its compassion and humanity.

In many advanced industrialized countries, a growing number of people are beginning to talk about the recovery of humanism. They are talking about stronger value systems and deeper spiritual beliefs, warmer human relationships and more communication within families and communities.

In the advanced industrialized society Koreans seek to achieve for themselves, the nation's traditional concepts of social harmony and cooperation should be strongly established and even more brightly manifested. Some Westerners are beginning to show interest in their ancient ways and wisdom, some even getting immersed in the study of Korean religions and philosophy.

Korea has not yet entered the stage of having to worry about the innumerable ills that afflict other advanced countries. However, from time to time, beautiful native customs and ways are being eclipsed by the progress of urbanization; or fads and fashions are overwhelming the traditions of the society. The more common such trends become, the stronger should be Koreans' assumption of the spirit of Benefits to All Mankind as an identity. It should be Korea's ultimate aim to blend Western modernism with Korean traditional culture and values so that, out of such a marriage, a new society free of the familiar ills of industrialization can arise.

The higher the economic growth and the more sophisticated our civilization becomes, the larger, rather than smaller, should be man's place in it. Unless human dignity is given its rightful recognition, a materially rich civilization is only a dead one. So it was in the Renaissance movement in the West, which began with an attempt to recover mankind from medieval darkness. That was how the study of ancient man and his thought began.

As Korea prepares to greet the opening of an advanced industrialized society, it should attempt to give greater effort to reviving the wisdom and spiritual traditions of the past, for what is sought is not just the facade of an advanced civilization but a truly livable society in which material affluence will go hand in hand with humanism. It should be a society dedicated to mutual development based on compassion and cooperation, not

105

one rent by conflict and struggle; not a society rejoicing in decadence, but one ruled by respect for honesty, sincerity, and industry. Instead of being overly competitive, tense and lonely, our life in such a society should be relatively stable and happy.

By making the expression of sympathy almost a virtue, the Korean people throughout the ages have cherished the tradition of helping the less fortunate under the spirit of Benefits to All Mankind. To see how this tradition still lives, one need only watch the reaction of the general public to each natural calamity or man-made disaster. Almost instinctively, they rush forward with aid ready to help with rehabilitation. Never unmoved by their countrymen's sympathy, the victims rise from the rubble to make a fresh start.

As another example of Korea's strong spiritual tradition, one may cite the strong family relationships and respect for the aged in the nation. Foreigners who come to Korea for the first time marvel at these attitudes. Here, no children would dare send their aged parents to an old people's home. The number of old people's homes in a nation is certainly not considered by Koreans to be a good indication of a socially just system. The sight of neighborhood people helping the aged is commonplace in Korea. When such a beautiful custom permeates society, the proper atmosphere for maintaining warm human relationships is created even in the midst of an industrialized society. A relationship based on trust, whether it involves teacher and student, old and young, or employers and employees, should be the guide for all associations.

The New Ideological Movement implemented in Korea in the 1960s is an excellent guide for the creation of a society of genuine compassion. New villages are not simply villages or administrative units but entities of cooperative life where national traditions are harmonized with modern civilization. Inside factories, offices, schools, or on the farm, the spirit of Benefits to All Mankind movement should create a balance. In a country undergoing Korea's scale and speed of change, this spirit assumes a special significance.

As in every other country in the world, Korea's urban life, in Seoul as well as in other cities, is becoming increasingly characterized by the citi-

zen's indifference to neighbors. If the urbanites succeed in leading a healthier life, yet still manage to combine spiritual values with the amenities of modern civilization, Korea's cities can make the positive contribution of becoming windows through which foreign cultures are successfully absorbed and distilled.

As a result of the New Village and the New Spirit movement, life in the cities is becoming a little more healthy and compassionate. Discarding the old habits of waste, distrust, and discord, and ushering in a pattern of thrift, diligence and

harmony, more and more people are becoming a little more sensitive to their neighbors' needs. Surely, the society they are on the way to building will not be just a collection of fragmented individuals; its marks will be sincerity, truthfulness, and fraternity. By preserving compassion and morality, it should be one in which man will be able to control the things he invents, rather than letting them control him.

Given the present tempo of growth and a definite vision for the future, by the 1990s Korea will have built an affluent society whose citizens will not envy the life of other countries. Per capita income of Koreans will have reached the level of those in advanced industrial countries. Their income from exports will rank among the highest in the world.

When that time comes, Korean's citizens will be able to choose the work they like, demand compensation justly reflecting their labor, and fashion for themselves a future bright with hope. Whether in the city or on the farm, people will be freed from lacking the basic necessities of life and will enjoy the benefits of modern civilization.

The children of Korea, with the opportunities for advanced education wide open, will then pursue their studies without worry about jobs or tuition. They will then show the world their talents as a people with a long tradition and history.

Korea's lands will have turned verdant, becoming "the field of ocean green," as once proudly described by the nation's forefathers. The face of the country will be criss-crossed by expressways; nearly every part of Korea will be within a day's driving distance of any other. Seoul and other large urban centers, and the countryside, laced with industrial plants and farms, forests and resorts, historical sites and shrines, will be a beautifully balanced picture. New cities will rise alongside factories, lands retired from agriculture

108

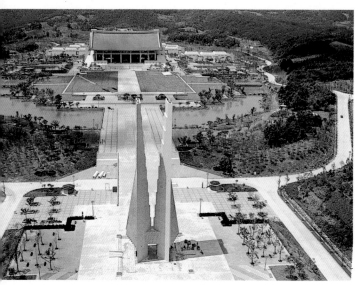

will form the suburbs, and the countryside will be dotted with pretty farm houses. Differences in income or cultural standards will be unknown. Korea's ancient culture will flower. Together with rehabilitated historical sites, the well-preserved environment will present a fresh image of a vibrant Korea. To meet the requirements of a modern age, healthy mass entertainment will satisfy everyone's emotional needs. Beyond all this, Korea, while becoming materially affluent, will not have lost its tradition of compassion. It will have turned into a brighter country, with its ancient spiritual culture flowering.

Perhaps this Korean ideological movement offers a modest contribution to the cause of world peace and international understanding. The spirit

109

of peace as manifested in the philosophy of Benefits to All Mankind and the non-violent pacifism of the 1919 March First Independence Movement, appealing as it did to the principle of human justice and self-determination of peoples, are expressions of Korea's confidence that harmonious relations among nations are attainable. This spiritual movement is the basis of the attitude and the ethics necessary to bring about a unified Korea, and it can serve to create the ethics necessary for all nations to live peacefully together as a world family. It is often forgotten that, although the world is torn apart by conflict and strife, it is fated to live in interdependence. Developments in communications and transportation have sharply reduced the size of the world, making it essential for nations to cooperate and carry on peaceful exchanges with each other. All forms of conflict, whether they involve racial differences, ideology, or natural resources, have to be resolved through dialogue in a peaceful manner.

The achievement of peace and cooperation among nations, perhaps partly based on Korea's spiritual movement of Benefits to All Mankind, would be a positive contribution to the shaping of a world culture. Although the international community today is said to form one cultural sphere, it cannot be denied that Western values have played a dominant role.

For a genuine world culture to flourish, however, it must reflect within itself aspects of all other cultures and traditions. A world culture can claim to represent a true cosmopolitanism when it achieves harmony in diversity. When a world culture is shaped by the participation of people around the world, it will then have helped to create the peace and prosperity which have remained humanity's dream for a long time. a genuine peace among nations would then be supported by common ethics and morality that arise from a single culture. With some nations still believing in the principle of the survival of the fittest, these hopes and ideals will hardly be

realized soon. Some nations do not hesitate to flout international law or human decency. Even though a part of today's international political reality is affected by these blind pursuits of egotism, they are but a temporary aberration when seen from the perspective of the long history of human civilization. Law, ethics, morality, equality, faith, and credibility, are still the elementary ingredients which sustain peaceful relations among nations. Both a permanent peace and continuing prosperity in the internationl community are possible through the rule of law over naked force and strife, through harmony and cooperation taking precedence over conflict.

It has been the mission of the Korean people to overcome the greatest tragedies of the twentieth century, poverty and war, and to achieve prosperity and peace. The fulfillment of this mission has been possible only through the spiritual movement based on the ideology of Benefits to All Mankind. Perhaps Korea can serve as a model for the world.

111

B. Population

In 1989, South Korea had a population of 42,380,000, a density of 427 persons per square kilometer. The population of North Korea was estimated at 21,964,000 in 1989. The population of the Republic of Korea increased rapidly after World War II. Between 1960 and 1982, both the birth rate and mortality rate dropped significantly. The birth rate was 42 and the mortality rate 13 per thousand in 1960, while the birth rate was 23 and the mortality rate 6.5 per thousand in 1982.

The annual population increase in South Korea was 2.7 percent during 1960-66, but dropped to an average of 1.9 percent during 1966-70, 1.5 percent during 1975-80, and 1.25 percent during 1980-85. This drop reflects the changing attitudes towards family planning and the impact of national family planning campaigns over the decades.

Before World War II, Koreans migrated to two major regions, Manchuria and Japan. It is estimated that about 600,000 Koreans remain in Japan. The most important migration in recent times is the north-to-south movement of people after 1945 and during the Korean War (1950-53). It is estimated that about 2,000,000 people have migrated from North Korea to South Korea since 1945. There are no significant racial minorities in Korea.

Despite rapid urbanization after World War II, Korea still has a large rural population, comprising 42.7 percent of the total in the 1980 census. As most of the rural population engages in agriculture, it is highly concentrated in the lowlands of the west and south coasts, along the major river valleys.

Agglomerated villages are common in the rural areas with a few exceptions in the mountainous areas and in areas of reclaimed land on the west coast. Such villages may have developed as a means of protection and to accommodate large extended families. Villages where most of the residents share the same family name are not uncommon, and the names of many villages indicate a certain clan, for example, Kimgach'on (Kim's Village) and Yigach'on (Yi's Village). In agglomerated villages, farming activities such as

Percentage of Each Age Group in 1988

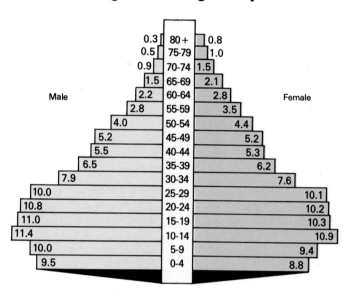

Trend of Population

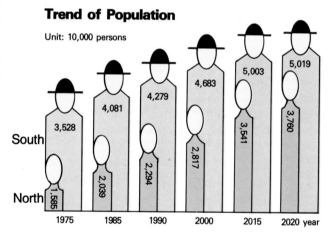

Expenditure per Household by the Family Size

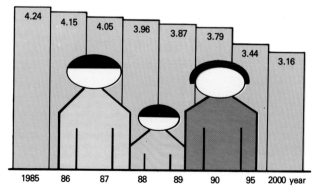

113

transplanting rice from seedbeds and harvesting and threshing rice are often accomplished through the cooperative efforts of the villagers. However, farm mechanization has resulted in changes in many agricultural activities, and recent farm labor shortages are being met partly by agricultural machines.

Rural villages are usually located in the foothills and face southward, for such a location provides protection from the severe cold winter monsoons, and allows maximum use of the lowlands for cultivation. The location of settlements and houses has also been influenced deeply by folklore tradition, according to which the ideal site for a house or village has a hill behind it and faces a stream. Consequently, topographic maps usually show villages along the boundaries between hills or mountains and plains or river valleys.

Rate of Employed Persons by Industry

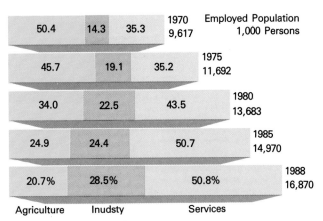

Agriculture	Industy	Services		
50.4	14.3	35.3	1970	Employed Population
			9,617	1,000 Persons
45.7	19.1	35.2	1975	
			11,692	
34.0	22.5	43.5	1980	
			13,683	
24.9	24.4	50.7	1985	
			14,970	
20.7%	28.5%	50.8%	1988	
			16,870	

The Saemaŭl Undong (New Community Movement) and the introduction of farm machinery have resulted in a gradual changing of the rural landscape. Farm villages are gradually being developed into well-organized communities with a systematic arrangement of houses which increasingly are constructed of cement and tile. In fact, most straw-thatched houses disappeared during the 1970s. The use of wood fires for heating in the rural areas is decreasing rapidly with the increasing use of coal. However, the most significant change in the rural areas has been a rapid decrease in population and subsequently a remarkable migration of rural population to the urban areas. The total urban population rose from seven million to over 21 million, or from 28 percent to 57 percent, during the period 1960-80. It has been a period of rapid industrialization and of rapid growth in Korea's GNP.

114

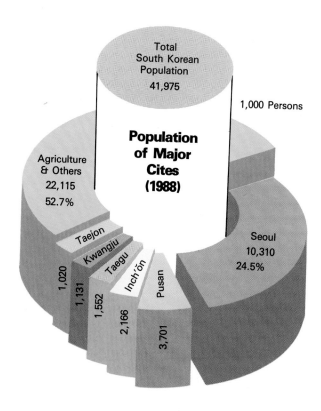

Population of Major Cites (1988)

Total South Korean Population 41,975

1,000 Persons

Agriculture & Others 22,115 52.7%

Taejon 1,020

Kwangju 1,131

Taegu 1,552

Inch'ŏn 2,166

Pusan 3,701

Seoul 10,310 24.5%

The concentration of population has been especially great in Seoul, the capital of the Republic of Korea, and in Pusan, the largest port and industrial center. The population of Seoul has increased from 2.5 million in 1960 to about 10 million in 1989, multiplying about four times during two and a half decades. Urban landscapes have changed greatly, especially since the late 1960s. Before 1960, there were no buildings of more than 30 stories in Seoul's business districts and the Yŏuido area. Now there is a 63-story building in Yŏuido, as well as in Seoul.

Public services, such as water lines, communications, and gas lines are being expanded, but supply seems always one step behind demand.

The number of cities has increased. There were only 12 major cities in 1945. Today there are 57 cities, one special city, the capital Seoul, and four metropolitan areas—Pusan, Taegu, Inch'ŏn and Kwangju.

C. The Christian Movement

In the first part of the 17th century, the Korean envoys returning from Peking brought home a book entitled *Introduction to Catholic Religion*, and it attracted their countrymen's special attention. In 1783, Yi Sŭng-hun went to Peking to study Catholicism and passed the catechism examination and was baptized with the Christian name of Peter. In the following year, he returned home, carrying some religious articles and the Bible, and began to spread the new teaching among learned people. He bapitized several other Koreans. However, the new faith suffered successive persecutions in 1785, 1801, 1839 and 1866. Despite these intermittent persecutions, the Foreign Mission Society of Paris sent missionaries to Korea continuously. Finally the Catholics obtained freedom of worship as a result of treaties of friendship with some of the Western nations in 1882. In 1889 the Catholics held a grand ceremony for the consecration of the Seoul Cathedral.

The protestant missionary who left his first footprint on Korea was German minister Charles Gutzlaff, who arrived in 1832. He was followed by R. J. Thomas, a Scotsman who came to Korea on September 13, 1865. He came back again the following year aboard an American merchant marine ship. The boat sailed up the Taedonggang River, and Thomas distributed Bibles and preached to the people gathered along the riverbanks. This vessel was fired upon by Korean troops and citizens near P'yongyang and its crew members were killed. Thomas was seized and taken before the magistrate of P'yŏngyang for questioning. He was found guilty of treason and beheaded. The story is that just before the axe fell, the English "man of Christ" gave his Bible to a wrestler who was watching the execution and prayed for the man's soul. Subsequently, the wrestler became a Christian.

Yongnak Presbyterian Church founded in 1945, is the oldest and largest Presbyterian Church located in Seoul.

In 1882, Korea signed its first treaty of friendship with the United States. This opened Korea's doors to representatives of Christian faiths. The first two American missionary pioneers, Henry G. Appenzeller (Methodist) and Horace G. Underwood (Presbyterian), arrived at the same time at Inch'ŏn, on Easter Sunday of 1885.

Since Christianity developed from Judaism, an ethnic religion, and at the same time, taught universal truths and was based upon the concept of brotherhood, without distinctions based on wealth, sex, or age, ideas compatible with the philosophy of Benefits to All Mankind, it was readily accepted by the Korean people, who believed that they were themselves heaven-descended. Meantime, the archaic philosophies of Confucianism and Buddhism had somewhat lost their spiritual significance and their hold on the people. Both suffered the common fate of all religions espoused by a people exposed to undue temptations and surfeited by material possessions. A materialistic outlook had begun to replace a spiritual one.

Koreans could understand not only the moral lessons of the Bible, but also its historical background. A small nation in the Near East and a small nation in the Far East were surrounded alike by hostile neighbors and experienced many miseries of a similar kind. The Exodus which Moses led out of Egypt was the story which expressed Korea's cherished hope of being an independent nation liberated from foreign forces. The tragedy of Jerusalem and the fate of Palestine under the Roman Empire were identified with Korea's own story under the domination of Japan.

The wonderful development of the Korean Christian Church was influenced by several other factors, too. First of all, the philosophy of the Christian religion was very much like principles in the philosophy of Benefits to All Mankind, which had been very familar to Koreans for centuries. Another was the strong Korean desire for Westernization and modernization. The Christian teachings opened the way to understanding modern thought and, especially, modern ideas of democracy. In 1885, an American Protestant missionary group began founding modern schools in Korea. For the first time in Korean history, thanks to these Christian missionaries, education was opened up for everyone. Only a relative handful of upperclass boys were students in the traditional schools in Korea until this time. This marked a tremendous social revolution as well as the beginning of a new era for Korean education. Thus, Christians introduced Korea to a modern system of education which included everybody, upper or lower class, rich or poor, even women. They introduced the sciences and humanities, bringing to the nation the modern ideas which awakened the Korean educators to the need to modernize their system of education. By stressing the spirit of national independence and the dignity of human rights, Christian teaching of these moden ideas laid the foundation for the growth of the democratic spirit for the first time in Korea.

Later on, when 33 patriots signed the Declaration of Independence against the Japanese occupation on March 1, 1919, 16 were Protestants. Indeed, Korea's independence movement was developed around Korean churches and mission schools.

One other way in which Christian missionaries exerted a strong influence was through the social welfare programs and organizations they started. They established nursery schools, homes for orphans, and homes for the poor. The churches also helped improve social conditions by launching anti-vice campaigns. They built hospitals and churches on military bases and in prisons as well.

The momentum begun long ago still continues to be evident in the development of Korea's churches. In general Korean Christian churches have been great contributors to Korean culture, education, and social development.

In 1900, the number of Korean Christian churches had reached about 3,000, with about 2,000 ministers and about 300,000 members. The Great Holy Spirit Movement began in early 1900 in the Korean churches. At this time, Korea was slowly coming under Japanese political control and occupation, and on February 23, 1904, Japan forced the Korean government to sign the Korean-Japanese Protocol. The first Korean-Japanese Agreement was concluded on August 22, 1904 and the second was signed in 1905. Under the terms of these agreements, all Korean foreign

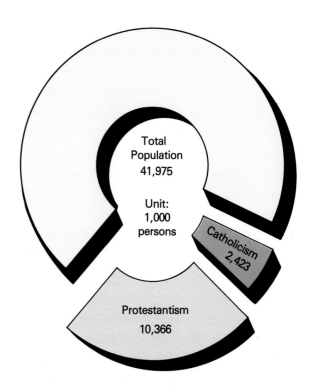

Protestantism in Korea

In Persons

Denomination	Churches	Reverend	Missionary	Christian
The Presbyterian Church	18,496	15,692	16,331	5,948,197
The Methodist Church	3,896	3,320	2,605	1,202,178
The Evangelical Church	1,970	1,564	1,463	758,933
The Baptist Convention	1,524	1,087	814	583,560
The Pentecostal Church	1,045	776	971	404,930
The Church of Christ	306	208	163	93,848
The Seven-Day Adventists	699	213	151	105,399
The Salvation Army	211	412	28	100,239
The Church of Nazarene	190	162	50	45,810
The Anglican Church	78	98	11	47,505
Others	1,906	1,101	1,124	1,046,276
Total	30,321	24,623	23,711	10,366,875

diplomacy was placed under the control of the Japanese government. Thus, the Christian churches became not only the sources of the impetus toward Korea's modernization, but also the main source of their hope to win Korea's freedom from Japan. Korean Christians felt much the same way as ancient Israel had in its Egyptian slavery. Meanwhile, they discovered for the first time the works of the Holy Spirit in their Christian studies. They realized that personal faith as well as the construction of churches was based on fellowship with the Holy Spirit. Therefore, this Great Holy Spirit Movement, which began in 1900, strengthened the foundation of the Korean Christian religion and from these roots revival meetings began to take place throughout the country.

Korean churches were growing even during the 36 years of the Japanese occupation. But from the 1970s on, Korean churches witnessed their most significant growth in quality as well as quantity. At the present time, that is, in June 1988, according to the Government census, there are 32,688 churches with 54,940 ministers and 12,649,403 members in Korea. This number represents about 30% of the national population. These churches are sending 498 Korean missionaries to over 50 nations throughout the world. Also, there are 68 Christian periodicals and newspapers, 14 Christian universities and colleges, and 25 seminaries in Korea.

Yonsei University (Choson Christian College) founded in Seoul in 1905 (below).

Korea now has five of the largest churches in the world as measured by size and membership. For example, the largest church is the Full Gospel Central Church in Seoul which was started by the Reverend Yonggi Cho in 1958, with five members meeting in a small tent. In 1970 the church had a membership of 8,200; in 1975, it had 22,000 members, in 1980, 147,000, and by mid-1988, 330,000. Every Sunday, from 6:00 A.M. until 9:00 P.M., the minister is holding worship services—seven in all. The main chapel seats 10,000, but people sit in the hallways and on steps. Television is used to broadcast to the education building, the mission center, and temporary church buildings in order for the many members of this church to hear and see Reverend Cho as he delivers his sermons.

For each service on Sunday, people must line up beforehand with it requiring 30 minutes for them to go in and out for each service. The congregations are organized like the military, from 12-member squads to 12-squad platoons to 12-platoon companies and finally to 12-company divisions. The church activities are very well organized and managed.

Reverend Cho's sermons focus on real life stories rather than difficult theological interpretations. His sermons are based on the Third Letter of John, Verse 2, "I pray that you may enjoy good health, and that all may go well with you, as I know it goes well with your soul." According to Reverend Cho's interpretation, the salvation is not only meant spiritually but is also meant for blessing our present physical life. He says the meaning of the words, "All may go well with you," refers to having a successful life in this world. "Good health" means physical health. Therefore, the three blessings, according to Reverend Cho's interpretation, are not only spiritual blessing by the Holy Spirit but also blessings of good health to assume successful living. Thus he says in his preaching to his congregation, "You are not poor, nor weak and neither are you a useless person. But you are a wealthy and healthy person that God bought by His only Son's blood."

Reverend Cho emphasizes the principles that Christians should have more positive, active and creative attitudes toward life, that with constant striving one will achieve success, and that God's blessings include those needed for everyday living, too. These three blessings have become a source of great hope and strength to the millions of this minister's followers. Reverend Cho's message is especially appealing to the poor and to unskilled workers, because he offers them dreams of a better life.

This minister says that observing laws and rituals, and attaining understanding of theoligical points, will not bring a Christian salvation and those three blessings. But by exercising faith in Jesus Christ and his grace, he teaches, one can expect these blessings. Therefore, he tells the members of his church, if one believes in and trusts God and prays hard with all his heart and with tears, then he can expect these blessings. He uses for illustration such a passage as that addressed to King Hezekiah in II Kings Chapter 20:5-6, "I have heard your prayer, I have seen your tears, surely I will heal you... And I will add to your days fifteen years." Reverend Cho preaches this as a literally true promise word by word, and one applicable to every Christian.

There are special features in this Full Gospel Church's teachings, which are quite unique and different in philosophy from other, more traditional Christian Churches of Korea. All Korean Protestant Churches teach the importance of being "born again" in order to be a Christian, but this Full Gospel Church emphasizes the ideas that through being born again by the cross of Jesus Christ and His grace one should be enabled to build his self-esteem and to feel good about himself. Further, Reverend Cho teaches that Jesus Christ's cross is not only the symbol of suffering, but it is also a symbol of our hopes, dreams, and strengths. When one is born again, Cho teaches, he should change from a negative to a positive person, from a sickly person to healthy one, from one filled with despair to one filled with hope, from being a desperate sinner to being a respectable person, and from feeling poor and cursed to feeling oneself rich in God's blessings. Therefore, he maintains that church members should not think of themselves always as sinners but as having become Children of God.

Secondly, the Full Gospel Central Church gives its members a sense of belonging to the collective life of a communal society, filling their need for security in these troubled times. In an unsettled society that is becoming more and more individualistic, man feels more anxiety and becomes alienated.

Youido Assembly of God founded in 1958, has the largest membership, 540,000 people, of any other church in the world. It sponsors 241 missionaries in 16 countries throughout the world.

Semoonan Presbyterian Church founded in 1887.

However, this church welcomes everybody and gives its members a sense of belonging, and its proclamation of its holy mission provides a sense of peaceful refuge. The church says, "Here we have a truly communal society for everyone." Thus the worship services are full of enthusiasm rather than strict ceremony. Their worshipers feel a warm welcome as if they are going to a festival. The preacher and the members of the church feel a warm relationship. They feel that the Day of Pentecost has fully come and that they are all fill-ed with the Holy Spirit. Whenever the preacher says, "Pray by the name of Jesus Christ," all the audience will respond with "Halleluia" or "Amen." Also, whenever the preacher emphasizes certain texts, the audience always responds with "Halleluia" or "Amen." Sometimes during prayer the preacher speaks with other tongues and all the audience feels the prayer has reached God. They all achieve the mystic feeling that they are finally face to face with God and are experiencing an exalted state.

Joong-ang Penecostal Church founded in 1907.

This church also presents a nationalistic faith. This nationalistic faith has no reference to the salvation of the nation from the Japanese occupation nor to the hope of unification with the North. This faith also differs from commitment to the fight for social justice or for basic human rights or political freedom. The faith is nationalistic in its teaching that Korea is the new chosen nation for a Christian Kingdom. According to the Reverend Cho, as seen in Genesis 10:21-31, Noah had three sons, Ham, Shem, and Japheth. Ham was punished but Shem and Japheth were blessed by God. Among Shem's descendants there were two sons, Peleg and Joktan. Peleg became an ancestor of Israel and Joktan became an ancestor of Asia. From among Peleg's descendants Jesus Christ was born, but Israel crucified him and never has built a Christian Kingdom. Now only Joktan's descendants have the chance to build Christiandom. In Asia, Korea is the only country where the Christian religion has become so successful. According to the Reverend Cho, Korea has

Chung-Dong First Methodist Church. Founded in 1898.

become the center for Christian missions to go forth to every part of the world to proclaim the Good News. At the present time this church sends 236 missionaries around the world.

Another interesting theory taught by the Full Gospel Church is based on the fact that among the 12 tribes of Israel in the Old Testament there was one tribe called "Dan." Now many Korean theologians believe that Dan-Gun, who was the founder of Korea, might be a member of the tribe of Dan. Dan is the given name and Gun means

"King." According to Reverend Cho, many other similarities can also be perceived between the cultures of ancient Israel and ancient Korea.

During the last 20 years of Christian history in Korea, one of the unique developments has been the so-called Minjoong Theology. "Minjoong" means "popular" or "average people" and more precisely it refers to those who have no political, economic, or cultural privileges in society. Minjoong theology made pioneer efforts in the search for a de-westernized and truly Korean Christianity

movement. Its founders came to realize that Christianity is not the same as Western culture and also not the same as democracy. The ministers preaching this version of Christianity sought to become friends of the ordinary people because Christ came to this world as a friend of all people. Christ preached for the salvation of all, including the poor, oppressed, and castaways. According to Minjoong teachings, he has given opportunities to all people so they can become children of God. Thus the Minjoong Theology in social and political themes reflects an understanding of the New Testament's teachings.

In many ways Korean Christianity is considered a modern miracle in the history of Christian missions. There are many historical, social, and political factors that account for these achievements. However, there are just a few elements which were the main forces in creating this miracle.

First of all, Korean Christians consider prayer and the philosophy of living with prayer as one of the most important articles of the Christian faith. Many Korean Christians begin their daily life at 4:00 A.M. with a dawn prayer meeting. The custom of the early dawn prayer meeting was begun in 1905 by Reverend Sun Joo Gil, who was one of the first evangelists in Korean Christian history. He also began the Great Holy Spirit Movement and started evangelical revivals throughout the country with emphasis on the early morning prayer meetings. In 1909, he began a 100,000-Soul-Salvation movement which led later on under Japanese occupation to the movement to keep the nation's cultural identity and secure independence from Japan. Thus, Reverend Gil laid the foundation of the modern Korean Christian revolution, and helped create the modern miracle of Korean evangelism.

Now most of Korea's churches emphasize early morning prayer meetings, and hold over-night prayer meetings and prayer and fasting meetings as well. Another interesting development is a "prayer institution," which is a center or camp for prayer located on a quiet mountain or in the country in beautiful surroundings. Such institutions are located throughout the country and are operated throughout the year. Many Christians visit them during the week-ends for meditation and prayer.

A second forceful factor in the development of the Korean churches was a Bible study movement which began in 1907 as a part of the Great Holy

Over-night prayer meeting and prayer institution.

Spirit Movement which had started a few years before. In early 1900, the Christians in Korea numbered only a few hundred, but during the first decade of the century the number rapidly increased to 9,400. The churches were faced with the immediate problem of providing quality education for the new Christians. The Bible study movement was developed not for the non-Christian but to provide those who were already Christians with spiritual enlightenment so that they would be enabled to witness effectively for Christ. The Bible study was implemented in the Sakyung Conference, "Sakyung" meaning literally "an earnest student of the Bible." In 1909, there were 800 Sakyung conferences functioning throughout the Korean Christian Churches.

On March 25th, 1915, Japan ordered Korea's churches to end all such movements because the Japanese government feared the Bible as a source of belief in liberty and freedom. The story of Moses leading Israel's struggle for independence from Egypt was considered a very dangerous influence on the Koreans. All the missionary schools were ordered to eliminate the teaching of the Bible from their curricula. Thus Bible study became an illegal activity and soon became an underground movement. This situation led to the development of the clandestine Family Bible Study program, which became very popular during the rest of the Japanese occupation. In 1916, Reverend Arch Campbell remembered one of these family Bible studies in his book *The Christ of the Korean Heart*: "A memory comes back to me. It is late on a crisp, cold night in December

128

Bible study meeting at office (left), Christian Radio Broadcasting service (center), T.V. evangelical broadcasting service (below).

1916, the little shops on both sides of the narrow streets of the mountain town in north Korea boarded up. Only a faint glow of yellow light seeps through an occasional paper covered door. From within a snug little home comes the muffled strains: '....Yesoo, Yesoo, Kweehan Yesoo...' ('Jesus, Jesus, precious Jesus...'). A little family of plainest people, like thousands of others, are having their family Bible study before stretching out on the heated floor for their well earned rest.... Today Jesus is in the hearts of a million people in this pitiful land, this land torn and wasted by war, a war not of their making, a war brought on by Godless greed and Western bungling, a war unequaled in history for destructiveness, misery and suffering. Jesus is here to give His sweet comfort, to supply strength for the heavy burdens, to bring the light of another world into the dark hovels, to impart the joy that the world cannot take away, to breathe the peace that passeth all understanding and to give songs in the night.''

Later, the Family Bible Study movement grew into a bigger movement, with the Bible study group meetings held in Christian neighborhoods, and this broke new ground for further developments. Today, Korean Christian Churches offer regular Bible study courses both in Sunday School and on weekdays, and they offer college and correspondence Bible study courses and disciple training courses as well.

Thirdly, Korean churches have always emphasized the work of missions or the evangelical movement. Their missionary object has been to carry salvation to the ends of the earth as Christ commanded in Acts 1:8. From the beginning of the Korean church evangelical work has been considered to be the most important function of the church. But a real evangelical movement was not begun until 1907, when the Reverend Sun Joo Gil began such a movement in P'yŏngyang, North Korea. This evangelical work led to the 100,000-Soul Salvation Movement that spread throughout the country. At the end of World War II and Korean liberation from Japan, Korea had about 3,000 Christian churches. Forty years later the number of Christian churches had increased to 30,000, a tenfold increase. Every year, on the average, 750 new churches were built.

Finally, the Korean church has involved itself a great deal with social services. As early as 1885, the first American missionary group started modern schools in Korea. They also established hospitals, orphanages, and homes for the poor

130

Myongdong Cathedral in Seoul, was build in 1898.

to improve social conditions. During the Japanese occupation, Christianity began the independence movement. Later, during the war with North Korea, the churches provided shelter for the homeless and the poor, and built 694 social institutions to help war refugees. During the nation's reconstruction period in the 1960s, the churches supported moral standards and advocated a democratic system of government and basic human rights. The Korean church emphasized not only the importance of individual salva-

tion but the need for the improvement of society as well. Thus the church participated in movements to protect the poor from various social injustices. In 1970, the Minjoong Theology developed from Korean Christianity stressing the hope of salvation for the poor, oppressed, and forgotten people. The Minjoong movement's ministers started churches for factory workers in slum areas and fostered the industrial evangelical movement. During the 1970s, Korea's churches also provided the poor with free medical check-

ups, free baby-sitting services, adult education, cultural lectures, and various other counseling services. Now Korean Christanity represents the social conscience of the nation, because the Christian churches' members have proved to be friends of the common people. Christians in Korea see themselves as called to serve the afflicted and oppressed and to answer to the groans of the man beaten, robbed, and left on the roadside.

On August 15, 1989, The World Alliance of Reformed Churches and the International Congregational Council, headquartered in Geneva, Switzerland, held their Twenty-second General Assembly meeting in Seoul, Korea. These organizations combined have churches in 82 nations with 70 million members, and this General Assembly meeting is held every seven years. This particular meeting was the first ever held in Asia, since the initiation of such meetings in 1877.

The theme for the 22nd General Assembly was, "Who do you say I am?" from Matthew 16:15. This theme involved discussion of three subthemes. The first was the need for a common witness of the faith. In order to carry out the missionary programs, the Assembly's leaders taught, there should be a common witness on such matters as South Africa's apartheid policies, the need for respect for human rights, and the threats to

Youido Plaza Easter Sunday early morning worship service.

peace and justice world wide. The second sub-theme involved the missions and the unity that the Reformed Churches pledged themselves to endeavor to strive for, in order to make contributions to the Ecumenical Movement. Lastly, the sub-theme of preserving justice and peace, dealt with the need for active social and political participation in their nation's affairs on the part of the member churches.

This meeting was a very important historic event for Korean churches because it was not only a landmark affair in being the first meeting on the Asian continent, but was also a recognition of the modern miracle of the Korean Christian Church.

Here is a list of Korean Christian Churches around the world, according to their number in various nations:

Nations	Churches	Nations	Churches
U.S.A.	3,000	Ivorycoast	1
Canada	81	Germany	29
Brazil	29	France	2
Argentina	12	England	4
Paraguay	6	The Netherlands	4
Gabon	1	Philippines	1
		Japan	65

133

D. Women's Liberation

In the traditional society of Korea, the woman's role was confined to the home. Women were required to learn the Confucian virtues of subordination and endurance, while being denied opportunities to participate in political and social functions. Their major role was to give birth to offspring so that the family line might continue unbroken, and women served to maintain the order of the family under the large family system. In terms of both social status and hierarchy, women were inferior to men. Regardless of the social stratum they belonged to, traditional social institutions and the custom of avoiding the opposite sex did not permit women to become involved in non-family affairs.

The situation began to improve, however, thanks to the education of women which followed the opening of the country to the outside world in the 1880s. Educated women engaged in the arts, in teaching, and in religious work, as well as in enlightening fellow women.

The self-awakening of women led to their national awakening under Japanese colonial rule, and women took part in the Independence Movement with no less vigor and determination than the men. A woman's liberation movement calling for expanded rights for women also began to emerge.

With the promulgation in 1948 of the Constitution guaranteeing equal rights for both sexes, women began to enjoy equality of treatment by the law. Having been given the franchise to vote, and the right to be elected to office, and to assume public duties, women were able to participate in the country's major policy decision-making. Unlike their Western counterparts, who acquired the franchise after long struggles, Korean women were merely given suffrage, a legal basis from which they could participate in social affairs.

Thanks to the successful implementation of five five-year economic development plans and the Saemaŭl (New Community) Movement since the 1960s, Korea has achieved remarkable economic growth. Export-oriented industries required a large female labor force. As the society diversified and the educational level of women was elevated, demand for skilled and professional women increased.

Despite the increase in the number of women engaged in social and economic activities, it has not been easy to resolve women's problems arising from conflicts with traditional values and institutions. With this in mind, the government established the Korean Women's Development Institute to carry out research and other projects designed to improve the status and welfare of women. In 1985, the government incorporated into the Sixth Five-Year Social and Economic Development Plan a master plan for the development of women and guidelines for the elimination of sex discrimination.

Women's education in ancient times was confined to the home. Formal education was allowed only to men, while women were given the duties of looking after work at home and bearing children to maintain the family line.

Instructions for Housewives, written by Queen Sohye of the Chosŏn Kingdom to provide edification for the women of the country, enumerates a code of conduct for housewives based on Confucian norms of the traditional society, calling upon women to become affectionate mothers and good-natured wives.

As Western civilization began to exert influence in the country in the 1880s, concepts of modern education started to take root, and attention was paid to the education of women as well as men. *Tongnip Shinmun (Independence News)*, the first newspaper of the country, published in 1896 by the Independence Club in Seoul, called on the government several times to recognize the importance of women's education and to establish girls' schools.

School education for women originated in the Ewha Haktang, Korea's first school for women, which was inaugurated in 1886 with the enrollment of only one girl student. Confucian culture and a national isolation policy that dominated Korean society at that time rendered it difficult to establish and operate girls' schools. American Christian missionaries, however, managed to set up a number of girls' middle schools such as

Chŏngsin and Paewha Girls' Schools in Seoul and Sungui Girls' School in P'yŏngyang.

It was after the Political Reform in 1894 that Korea established public schools under a new school system. The political reform recognized the need for education for women but the school decree made provisions for male schools only. The Adoration Society, founded in September, 1898, with the objective of establishing and operating a girls' school financed by membership fees, published in the month of its founding, "A Letter on Girls' School Facilities." This document is considered the nation's first "Declaration of Rights" for women with respect to education in that it was aimed not only at establishing a girls' school, but also at attaining equal rights for both sexes.

Hansŏng Girls' High School, the nation's first public school for women, was established in Seoul in 1908. In April of the same year, the government promulgated the Girls' High School Decree stipulating its objective to be "to teach high school education, skills, and arts essential for women." This was the nation's first legal provision for women's education since private education had started in Korea.

The Constitution of the Republic of Korean prescribes that "all citizens shall have the right to receive equal education in accordance with their capabilities." Thus, one of the basic rights of citizens is to be accorded educational opportunities irrespective of sex, age, or class.

The average number of years of education in Korea in 1980 was registered at 8.67 years for males and 6.63 years for females. The six-year primary school course has been compulsory since 1949 when the Education Law was passed. More than 90 percent of Korea's children, both boys and girls, who were eligible for schooling were enrolled in primary school as early as the 1960s.

The ratio of primary school graduates advancing to middle school was 92.6 percent for girls and 96.4 percent for boys in 1980. The ratio of middle school graduates entering high school in the same year stood at 62.2 percent for girls and 74.4 percent for boys, showing a significant discrepancy between male and female advancement. The ratio of high school graduates entering college and university in 1983 was 35.8 percent for females and 40.3 percent for males. Of those students who succeeded in entering college and university in the 1986 summer semester, women accounted for 26 percent of the total.

Among students attending four-year college courses, subjects of learning preferred by women are different from those chosen by their male counterparts. Majors preferred by co-eds in 1983 in order of preference were: teaching, language and literature, sciences, arts, and social sciences. Teaching accounted for 27.7 percent. The order of preference for male college students was engineering, which accounted for 31.5 percent, followed by social sciences, language and literature, and teaching. As in Western countries, the number of female teachers in Korea has increased. This reflects changes in social and family structure and increased participation by women in the nation's social activities. The percentage of women teachers in 1983 stood at 41.3 percent in primary schools, 36.3 percent in middle schools,

1988 Female Students of College and Universities by Department

In persons

	Enrollments	Graduation	Entrance
Total	270,343	58,706	70,577
Humanities	69,430	14,942	17,986
Social sciences	44,033	9,163	11,835
Natural sciences	63,892	11,390	19,488
Arts & Physical education	35,888	7,515	9,189
Medical science & Pharmacy	13,962	2,758	2,890
Teaching Profession	43,138	12,938	9,189

The Ewha
Women's
University
founded
in 1886.

1988 Summary of Teachers

In persons

	Male	Female
Kindergarten	854	12,224
Elementary school	69,823	62,704
Middle school	44,808	32,622
High school	63,779	17,360
Junior college	5,015	1,747
Junior Teachers college	586	94
College & University	24,957	4,928

1988 Status of Female High School Graduates

In persons

	Total	Entered to higher school	Employed	Unemployed	Unknown
High school (General)	184,013	92,599	26,038	28,068	37,308
High school (Vocational)	131,275	10,359	100,040	10,972	9,874
Junior College	41,162	2,652	23,236	9,341	5,933
Teachers' College	4,179	7	3,079	791	302
College & University	58,704	2,994	17,464	25,883	12,363
Graduate school	4,135	291	2,292	920	632

19.3 percent in high schools and 17.1 percent in colleges. These figures represent a sharp increase over the previous two years, but it is to be noted that the number of female teachers dwindles as the level of education at which they teach advances.

To correct this situation, it is desirable that more women be promoted to administrative positions of responsibility, that measures be worked out to reduce the current male dominance at higher educational institutions, and that sex discriminative content and expressions in curricula be eliminated. Strong efforts are required to provide both sexes with equal opportunities in education and employment.

To cope with the rapid changes taking place in the country's highly industrialized society while recognizing the limits of school education, life-long education has been promoted in recent years. Non-formal education was institutionalized under the Non-Formal Education Law passed in December, 1982, which guarantees citizens life-long opportunities for education so that they may develop their respective capabilities and talents.

In an effort to meet an increasing demand for skilled manpower in the wake of industrialization in the 1970s, technical schools and technical high schools provide education and training in over 40 areas of skill. Girls account for 15.5 percent of the enrollment in technical high schools and for more than half of the enrollment in advanced technical schools. At schools attached to industries, girls account for 98 percent of the enrollment. This clearly reflects the burning zeal for education on the part of women whenever opportunities are available.

Most popular in women's non-formal education in urban areas is general education. Various institutes are engaged in providing such formal education. They include educational departments attached to women's organizations, public welfare facilities, educational institutes operated by the media, college institutes, primary schools, secondary schools, community development centers and institutes run by public libraries. Non-formal educational programs for women consist of skills (54 percent), population and family life (19 percent), languages, national spirit and culture (18 percent), and services for others (10 percent).

Women's Halls in some big cities and provincial capitals conduct programs designed to improve the education of women so that they may elevate their social standing and contribute more to the nation's social development. Since 1975,

the Labor Ministry has operated educational programs for working women in areas with a large number of workers. In such programs the Korean language, Korean history, music, labor laws, the Saemaŭl (New Community) and Korean culture are taught. Educational programs designed to elevate the social consciousness of women are also provided by organizations and religious groups.

Non-formal education for women in rural areas centers on women's guidance programs. Emphasis is given in educational activities conducted by rural women's societies to subjects designed to heighten cultural standards, to solve rural problems, to improve the mode of life, to teach family planning, and to develop better sanitation methods. Guidance in such activities is provided by the Ministry of Health and Social Affairs,

1988 Summary of Economically Active Female Population (15 Years old and over)

In thousand persons

	Total	Economically active		Not Economically Active	Labour force participation rate
		Employed	Unemployed		
Total	15,308	6,770	120	8,418	45%
Farm household	2,829	1,642	7	1,180	58.3%
Non-farm household	12,479	5,128	113	7,238	42%

the Office of Rural Development, the National Federation of Agricultural Cooperatives, and the Family Planning Society.

Women's participation in social activities today is more active than ever before, especially in economic areas. It is a well-known fact that the remarkable economic growth Korea has achieved in the past two decades is due in large part to the female labor force in the manufacturing sector. Women are expected to make an even greater contribution in future economic development in view of the changing structure of industry and employment.

The economically active persons among the nation's female population showed a sharp increase from 26.8 percent in 1960 to 45.7 percent in 1975, but fell to 38.4 percent in 1980 and 33.9 percent in 1983. That women's participation in economic activities, following a tremendous rise up to 1975, declined in the latter half of the 1970s is attributable to the recession that hit the country in the wake of the oil crisis.

Women's economic participation is much greater in rural areas than in urban areas. The figures in 1983 stood at 51.8 percent in the rural areas and 37.9 percent in the urban areas. In the rural areas not only did the percentage of economically active women increase sharply in general, but that of women in their 30's and above showed a marked increase. This indicates that the rural areas suffered a shortage in their labor force as the males and young girls migrated to the cities and industrial areas, and the gap created thereby was filled by middle-aged housewives.

1988 Female Employment by Occupation and Age Group

In thousand persons

Age Group	Total	15-19	20-24	25-29	30-34	35-39	40-44	45-49	50-54	55-59	60+
Whole Occupation Totel Employment	6,770	367	1,067	833	843	769	695	721	594	414	467
Pro., Tech, & Related	414	111	134	110	53	32	22	21	15	6	10
Adm. & Managerial	8	—	—	—	1	1	1	2	1	1	1
Clerical workers	763	127	406	144	42	19	13	7	4	1	—
Sales workers	1,143	28	100	132	178	180	146	146	108	64	61
Service workers	1,101	31	82	124	166	165	176	155	99	62	41
Agri., Forestry & Fishermen	1,548	6	24	79	123	152	153	242	253	220	296
Production, Transport & Labourers	1,793	164	321	244	280	220	184	148	114	60	58

141

1988 Employment of Female Graduates by Occupation

	General High school	Vocational High school	Junior College	Teachers' College	College & University	Graduate School
Employed of Graduates	26,038	100,040	23,236	3,079	17,464	2,292
Pro., Technical & Related workers	1,088	2,627	11,797	3,079	8,005	1,564
Administrators & Related workers	802	3,500	752	—	832	102
Clerical & Related workers	5,911	56,483	4,412	—	4,091	251
Sales workers	3,676	10,278	1,345	—	806	12
Service workers	3,424	9,696	2,672	—	1,308	126
Agri., Forestry & Fishing workers	493	927	102	—	78	7
Production workers, Driving machinerians & Drivers	9,146	14,423	858	—	151	1
Others	957	—	—	—	—	—
Occupation not Adequately Defined	528	2,093	1,295	—	2,187	225
Military servicemen	13	4	3	—	6	4

In cities, on the other hand, the participation of married women in economic activities has shown a gradual upturn. A number of factors are believed to be responsible for this phenomenon. First, women are receiving education for more years than before, so that they are not starting to work at such a young age and the gap generated thereby is filled by middle-aged women. Second, increased living standards have prompted housewives to earn money to supplement their husband's incomes. They now enjoy more leisure time at home, due to the availability of electronic household appliances, and they wish to use it constructively. Third, women have a stronger desire to take part in social activities and are better able to adapt themselves to jobs than their predecessors.

Women job holders in 1983 accounted for 34.0 percent of the total number of people employed. Some 39.8 percent of women workers were engaged in primary industry, 19.1 percent in secondary industry, and 41.1 percent in tertiary industry. The largest portion of women workers are employed in tertiary industry. The percentage of females employed in primary industry is still high, but has declined in recent years, and the same is true in the manufacturing sector. About 80 percent of female workers in the manufacturing sector are employed by textile, clothing, electric and electronic industries, which have led the nation's exports since the 1970s. While women aged 14 to 24 accounted for 53.9 percent of the female labor force in the manufacturing industries in 1983, women of 30 years of age and above represented 84.3 percent of the female labor force in the rural areas. This shows a contrasting trend of younger female workers working in manufacturing and older workers in farming and fishing. This phenomenon is again accounted for by the fact that young females in the rural areas have moved to the manufacturing industries concentrated in the cities.

The clerical area saw a conspicuous increase in women workers from 1970 through the 1980s. The portion of female workers accounted for 33.3 percent of the total labor force in this area, which represented 8.6 percent of the whole female work force in 1983.

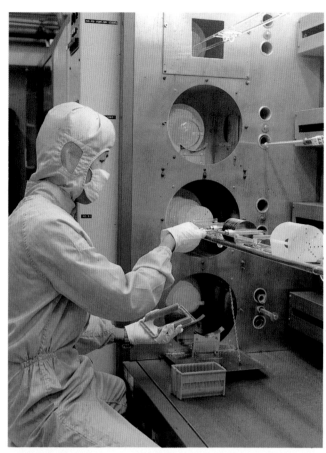

1988 Female Workers' Reasons for Working

In percentage

		Family Supporter	Help with Family Finances	Unpaid Family Workers	Utilization of Ability	Practical Experience	Enjoyment	Public Benefits	Others	Total
Whole Country		21.4	33.7	24.6	11.3	5.8	2.5	0.5	0.2	100
By Educational Attainment	Middle school graduates	19.2	46.3	21.6	5.3	4.0	3.2	0.2	0.1	100
	High school graduates	13.5	33.6	12.5	21.5	15.2	2.7	0.9	0.1	100
	College & University graduates	6.0	13.9	6.6	57.7	9.5	3.2	2.9	0.1	100
By Marital Status	Never Married	13.8	24.6	4.0	31.3	22.8	1.8	1.5	0.3	100
	Married	14.2	41.3	35.5	5.5	0.5	2.6	0.2	0.1	100
By Age Group	15-19	9.2	33.2	4.9	22.1	27.6	1.2	1.2	0.7	100
	20-29	10.9	32.1	11.6	26.7	14.9	2.6	1.1	0.1	100
	30-39	17.3	44.0	26.9	7.6	0.7	3.0	0.4	0.1	100
	40-49	29.1	36.0	29.7	3.0	0.5	1.4	0.2	0.2	100
	50-59	33.2	24.7	36.4	2.6	0.5	2.5	0.1	0.1	100

The percentage of female employees in professional, technological, and administrative jobs increased from 1.5 percent in 1960 to 4.2 percent in 1983. This indicates that the level of education acquired by women has been upgraded due to their increased educational opportunities. Of female employees engaged in professional and technological jobs, women of 20 to 29 years of age accounted for 61.2 percent in 1983. Women 20 to 24 years of age and mostly unmarried accounted for 63.9 percent of the women engaged in clerical work. It is thus presumed that women of higher education are employed in professional and skilled jobs. On the other hand, women engaged in administrative and supervisory positions are mainly 30 years old or above and have had more experience.

The level of education acquired by women who work has seen a great improvement in recent decades. In 1960 women employees who had graduated from middle and high schools accounted for only 2.7 percent and 2.0 percent of the total female work force respectively. The ratio of women employees having graduated from middle and high schools jumped to 33.0 percent in 1980. Female employees who had graduated from a two-year junior college increased from 0.4 percent in 1960 to 3.1 percent in 1980.

As for the marriage status of women employees, married and unmarried women are nearly equal in the professional and skilled labor force, but married women account for 88.1 percent of those in administrative and supervisory positions. In contrast, unmarried women constitute an absolute majority in clerical and manufacturing positions. Married women employees have increased by 12.6 percent on the average per annum since 1977.

Korean women's occupation structure by age shows a pattern closely related to childcare. Working women with infants are burdened with the dual work of doing a job and caring for a home. To maintain female employment without interruption and to ease the excessive burden on married women employees, it is necessary to expand nursery facilities at the work place. With this in mind the government has incorporated a master plan for women's development in the forthcoming Sixth Five-Year Social and Economic Development Plan launched in 1987. Envisaged under the master plan for women's development are the establishment of nursery facilities at job sites and the introduction of a babycare work suspension system under which female employees with infants may leave their jobs for some time to rear their infants and then return to their jobs.

146

Studies are also under way for the expanded employment of women on a part-time basis. If such social and institutional support were provided, women would be able to function as a more specialized and stable labor force in a wide range of fields and could make further contributions to their society and country.

Women in Korea have come a long way. They are no longer confined to the house but are participating in the policy-making processes of the government, in the legal profession, in education, in the high-tech industries, in business and in the arts. There is no doubt that the traditional contribution of women in Korean society will be further translated into new roles which will enable them to fully apply their potential and participate even more actively in the social, economic and political development of the country.

PART FIVE
The Taekwondo Movement

A. The Nature of Taekwondo

Tae-kwon-do is a martial art that uses physical, mental, and spiritual training to develop great physical strength for the purpose of cultivating Benefits to All Mankind character.

This martial art was developed as a form of self-defense in Korea over 2,000 years ago. "Tae" means kicking or techniques of using the feet, "Kwon" means punching or techniques of using the hands, and "Do" means discipline or enlightenment. Thus, one can say that it is an art of kicking and punching through disciplined training. It is the philosophy of Taekwondo that all of its movements are based on the instinct of self-defense which will lead from negative to positive actions and will lead the self to evolve into a higher self. Taekwondo techniques involve both the quick actions of Karate and the circular patterns of Kungfu. Further, they emphasize moral perfection through discipline. Thus, Taekwondo's objectives are aimed at gaining both physical strength and moral power through self-realization, which is achieved through implementing the teachings of the philosophy of Benefits to All Mankind.

Taekwondo is a martial art that does not require any weapons. Besides developing physical strength and mental health, it provides the joy of art. Through various motions of the hands and feet, and the constant practicing of these motions, one may become like a dancer who is required to learn many techniques, careful motions, and precise timing. Also, like the professional dancer who has a traditional but individualized style, practitioners of this sport are enabled to understand the beauty of art.

Taekwondo requires rigid mental discipline. Practitioners begin their exercises with meditation and finish with meditation. Their ultimate goal is to attain a spiritual state of perfect selflessness. Because of this ideal, they are required to repeat certain techniques or movements over and over again, enabling them to repeat actions without any hesitation. Meditation is also a source of focusing power; it requires a great deal of concentration in order to achieve a state of absolute selflessness. Focusing power is that which can bring all the physical and mental energies to concentrate upon one particular object. Like a streak of lightning, it unleashes all one's energy with explosive suddenness, as an instinctive reaction, without self-consciousness.

Taekwondo, in martial arts as a way of stressing moral awareness and the improving of one's life in every respect, reveals its basis in the philosophy of Benefits to All Mankind. The teaching of the Hwarangdo during the Shilla Kingdom in 540 A.D. was a good example of this training. Historians agree, in fact, that Taekwondo originated from the Hwarangdo. The guiding principles of the Hwarangdo knights were loyalty, filial duty, trustworthiness, valor, and justice. These characteristics are all essential components of the philosophy of Benefits to All Mankind. The Hwarangdo also inculcated a spirit of harmony and unity in the youth undergoing its discipline and taught them a flexible approach to social relationships.

There is another approach to understanding Taekwondo, based on analyzing each letter in its spelling. The first letter, "T," represents "think-

ing." This is the first requirement, or practice, in beginning an exercise. Through many hours of meditation one learns the Taekwondo way of thinking. Before any action one must learn to clearly think things through. To effectively react in self-defense, one must think clearly, think nobly, and act nobly. To fully understand the beautiful responses required of one in threatening situations takes much time. Thinking can prevail over the difficulty and obscurity of the object and at the same time refresh the mind with new discoveries, thereby extending the bounds of apprehension and as it were enlarging its strategies. Above all, only the thinking process will bring one self-realization.

The next letter, "A," stands for "action." After thorough thought to one's object, action should follow. The thinking process will be worth nothing if one does not act. Action may not always bring a good result but there will certainly be no good result without action. Only actions give strength that extends through all of one's physical, mental, and spiritual being. Taekwondo is a philosophy of action, as well as of thought, and every step in its training looks toward action.

The next letter, "E," suggests the "elegance" of rhythmical movements. Elegance is something more than ease, more than a freedom from awkwardness and restraint. It implies a precision, a polish, and a sparkling which is disciplined and spirited, yet delicate. Action based on firm discipline will produce the most elegant movements. The Taekwondo artist's clear thinking, high purpose, firm resolve, dauntless spirit, and determination, elegantly express themselves in his demeanor and attitude. Elegance is also a name for the transference of thought and spirit from one heart to another, no matter how it is done. The power of elegance is great when it has developed along with self-discipline.

The fourth letter, "K," refers to Taekwondo's original birth place, Korea. It was born and developed in the Korean tradition and culture. All of its structure, language, character, and teachings are related to Korea's spirit which is based on the philosophy of Benefits to All Mankind. Therefore, this traditional martial art is uniquely Korean.

The next letter, "W," can be conceived of as a reference to "will", that is, as a reference to character in action. In the schools of Taekwondo, when a person falls, he is bidden to get up again and to go on practicing day by day until he has acquired the strength or will to succeed. Whenever the will commands, the whole person will respond. The general of a large army may be defeated, but one cannot defeat the determined will of a student of Taekwondo. We cannot be held to what is beyond our strength and means, because at times the action and execution may not be in our power, but there is nothing that is really in our own power except the will. Every student ultimately stamps his value on himself. The goals we set for ourselves are sometimes given to us by others, but the student of Taekwondo is made great or little by his own will. In the exercise of his will, the student has to strive constantly to improve himself.

The next letter, "O," represents "order". A sense of order produces sanity and peace of mind, and helps ensure the health and security of the body. As the support beams are to a house, and as the bones are to the body, so is order to Taekwondo's discipline. The student who has a talent for order will be right in his judgment and considerate or conscientious in his action. Order is a lovely nymph, the child of beauty and wisdom, and her attendants are comfort, neatness, and activity. She is always to be found when sought for and never appears so lovely as when contrasted with her opposite, disorder. Order means light and peace, inward liberty and free command over one's self. Good order is the foundation for discipline. Taekwondo is a systematic martial art that depends upon tradition. All of its history, philosophy, and techniques are transmitted from master to disciple. The master has the responsibility to deliver these traditions to the disciple. Therefore disciples have to show their master respect and obey his teaching. From the beginning of each exercise, the student must create order in his mind, then put it into his body and finally in his action.

The next letter, "N," symbolizes "nature." One cannot impose his will on nature, but must first ascertain what the will of nature is. Sympathy with nature is a part of Taekwondo's teaching because nature is a friend to truth, honesty, compassion, honor. Nature gives to every time and season some beauties of its own and from morning to night presents a succession of changes so gentle and subtle that one can hardly mark their progress. In the same way, learning the techniques of Taekwondo to progress toward self-realization is equivalent to learning the laws of one's own nature. Whatever one is by nature,

Taekwondo teaches one to keep it intact, with emphasis on never deserting one's own talent. One is taught to be what nature intended and to develop fully one's own potential. Nature is also studied as an aspect of the natural order, and one learns to act according to nature, whose rules are few, plain, and most reasonable. Members of the ancient Hwarangdo made a practice of visiting places of scenic beauty to develop a sense of appreciation of nature. Nature has always been man's best teacher. She unfolds her treasures to his search, and opens his eyes, mind, and heart. It is according to nature that a grain thrown into good ground brings forth fruit; it is also according to nature that sound teachings thrown into a good mind bring forth fruit. A beginning student of Taekwondo will start his training with unnatural motion, but through long and hard discipline, he will learn to perform beautiful, natural motions.

The next letter is "D," representing one of the most important elements of the philosophy, the need for "defense." All sports consider a good defense to be the best offense, but Taekwondo puts even greater emphasis on defense. The secret of success is to know how to defend yourself; in Taekwondo the secret of the student's success is that he is a disciplined person and can control himself. Without learning the basic rules, all other training is good for nothing. One of the most important but most difficult things for a powerful mind to understand, is to know how to control itself. Thus Taekwondo's discipline involves not only defending oneself, but also involves controlling oneself in abstaining from a combative spirit and from anger. The master of Taekwondo is not a master of the skill of attacking but of the skill of defense. The outstanding leaders of Taekwondo always discourage fighting even if humiliation is the result.

The last letter "O," refers to "oneness." All the characters described before have to come together in a oneness or unity in order to make a perfect student of Taekwondo. Each one has its own importance, but they are all related to each other. Each one complements another, and in order to finalize one's training in Taekwondo, he must learn to put together all these characteristics to make one complete whole. He must harmonize all the things represented by these characters in himself in order to develop a more perfect inner unity.

There are many admirable systems in Taekwondo, but the following describes a few areas which have proven to be most effective for one's training.

As a whole body exercise, Taekwondo involves both physical and mental discipline. Through this training, the practitioner of Taekwondo can defend himself from any sudden attacks and can also develop coherent, clear mental powers and cultivate his character. In turn he will finally achieve self-confidence and courage.

Physically, this exercise will help one to develop more symmetrical growth within the whole body as he develops muscular strength and skillful techniques. Besides creating great strength, the discipline activates circulation of the blood and will finally result in dynamic physical health.

Mentally this training will result in higher self-esteem and will also influence one's attitude toward his entire way of life, by providing him with a fresh outlook on life in general.

Stress keeps building up in a person through living in today's highly complicated society. This environment increases our anxieties and fears, causing withdrawal. These things accumulate in one's mind, creating a great handicap to one's physical and mental growth, as well as causing misbehavior or creating anti-social attitudes. Taekwondo requires adherence to very strict rules and very hard physical and mental discipline, so that its students can overcome various stresses while building healthy minds to conquer their anxieties and fears.

Socially, students of Taekwondo learn high standards of moral behavior. They learn the principles and characteristics of the philosophy of Benefits to All Mankind. There never was any heart truly great and generous that was not also benevolent, full of charity, sympathy, understanding, and compassion. Taekwondo masters also teach the guiding principles of the Hwarangdo which are loyalty, filial duty, trustworthiness, valor and justice. The purpose of the training is to develop the student's mind and character so that he will be enabled to contribute his talents to bettering society. Leadership qualities are also taught to all the Taekwondo students. Students are considered as social leaders whose destiny is to become models for other people. They are also taught to show respect for the laws of the land and to show other exemplary social attitudes.

There are theories that this training will help cure or alleviate various psychological, physical, or mental problems, such as depression, phobias, anxiety, hyper-activity, heart disease, high blood pressure, thyroid disease, obesity, tremors, hyper-thyroid condition, overeating, smoking, and alcoholism.

Dr. James B. Free, who is now a Taekwondo student, tells of his experience in the March, 1987 *Taekwondo Times*. He begins by saying that "I was 52, looked 62 and felt 82. I was seventy-five pounds overweight, had very high blood pressure, gastric ulcers, and had experienced one heart attack. I took thyroid pills, gastritis pills, sleeping pills, tranquilizers and heart rate pills. I indulged in alcohol and cigarettes. I was twice divorced and chronically fatigued. I had spent four years in psychiatric sessions for depression and anxiety; was a sexually impotent husband and a neglectful father. My work was going downhill and my interest in living was nil. I was obese, sloppy, miserably unhappy. I huffed and puffed from the mere exertion of removing my shoes. I despised my life and myself. I wanted to die."

In April, 1986, five months after he started his martial arts training, Dr. Free took a treadmill test, which measures the condition of the heart and circulatory system. The treadmill test showed that his health was perfectly normal. His blood pressure was down to 120/80 and he had lost weight down to 195 pounds, having at that time lost 64 pounds.

Dr. Free continues, "Ten months have passed. I work out six days a week. Most of the other students only three, some even less. My doctor has told me to stop my thyroid, blood pressure, and heart pills. I don't need them. Without much thinking about it I simply dropped sleeping pills and tranquilizers, alcohol and cigarettes out of my life with no withdrawal pangs or craving. I awaken every morning filled with enthusiasm for the day. I warm up, do some stretching, go into the guest room; a heavy bag hangs where a bed once was. I go to the hospital, stopping occasionally to kick a tree or brick wall to release the Ki that flows all day. My patients wonder who this new man is. My sons, also Taekwondo students, are proud that their schoolwork is so much better."

B. The Roots of Taekwondo

The Koguryo's wall painting in the burial chamber of the Tomb of Dancers, a scene of two men who are about to start the Taekyun's game (below), the Sokkuram Grotto Shrine, built in 751, has images of guardsman which are portrayed in positions very much resembling Taekyun's basic defense and attack postures (right).

All the historical documentation confirms that Korean martial arts began during the Three Kingdoms period (57 B.C.-A.D. 668). As a training course for warriors and as one of the traditional games, the Taekyun discipline of this period was similar to the classical model of Taekwondo today in its style and techniques. Also known at this time by another name, the Subakhi, it was adopted as a military training requirement. Especially during the Harvest Moon Festival, which is similar to Thanksgiving Day in America, all the tribes got together to hold the Taekyun or Subakhi contest among themselves. Sometimes they held the exhibition games before the kings.

In various wall paintings in the royal tomb at P'yŏngyang, there is much evidence of the flourishing of martial arts during the Koguryŏ Kingdom (37 B.C.-A.D. 668). Pictures which were popular during this era provide proof of the practice of the Taekyun. Among the Koguryŏ's wall paintings in the burial chamber of the Tomb of Dancers, there is a scene of two men who are about to start the Taekyun's game. Also in the Three Rooms burial chamber of the tomb, there is in the third room on the west wall a drawing of warriors exercising at Taekyun. These paintings provide a strong evidence that Taekyun was

already a popular sport at that time. According to anthropological studies, these paintings were drawn sometime before the sixth century around A.D. 520. This is about one hundred years earlier than the Kwonbup, which is considered the first occurrence of martial arts training in China.

The Koguryŏ Kingdom attached great importance to a strong national defense policy and founded a military academy called the "Sunbae." The Sunbae was an institution designed to train and educate military leaders and superior warriors by developing good character. The students of the Sunbae had strong martial arts training but particular emphasis was given to mental and physical discipline. One facet of its training was teaching the ability to control one's breathing. The masters of the Sunbae considered breathing control as the basis for all physical and mental training.

One of the most impressive developments in the Shilla Kingdom was the Hwarang, a unique system of training young men. The Hwarang or "Flower of Youth Corps," acquired education consisting of both academic and military skills. Hwarang warriors trained in the martial art called Hwarangdo, which many historians consider to be the historical origin of the systematically organized training now called Taekwondo. There

is much historical evidence found in Kyŏngju City, the capital of the Shilla Kingdom. Both the Sŏkkuram Grotto Shrine, built in 751, and the Punhwangsa Pagoda, built in 634, have images of guardsmen which are portrayed in positions very much resembling those of present-day Taekwondo's basic defense and attack postures.

During the Koryŏ Kingdom (918-1392), Taekyun was developed as a popular military training system, and was refined in its techniques and organization. According to the *History of the Three Kingdoms*, written by Busik Kim in 1145, it was called "Subakhi," meaning "Master of Hands," and there were many recorded performances in front of kings at the palaces. Several kings promoted some of the masters of Subakhi to very high offices in military posts. Also during this period the military draft system was begun, and Subakhi was an important element of military training.

There are also records of Buddhist influence on the development of Taekwondo during this period. Buddhism was the national religion of the Koryŏ Kingdom and Subakhi was a part of Buddhist discipline for mental and physical excercises. Thus, during attacks by foreign powers, even monks participated in the national defense efforts. There were also demonstrations of Subakhi in

Buddhist religious ceremonies such as Yunduenghi and Palkwanhi.

Taekwondo was not only popular for military training, but also became one of the popular national sports during this kingdom. There are many records indicating that people of Koryŏ watched the demonstrations of Taekwondo during various national festivities. Also during this kingdom, Subakhi was developing many additional techniques, such as Kwŏnbup, Kwŏnbuk, and Subyuk or Taekyun.

At the beginning of the Chosŏn Kingdom (1392-1910) Subakhi was developed further and was used by the military as a basic requirement for military personnel; that is, as a screening tool to determine a candidate's suitableness for military employment. Subakhi also became a popular sport throughout the country and prizes were awarded for its various competitions.

In *Journeys Through The Eastern Nation*, prepared by King Sŏng Jong (1469-1494), there are records of Subakhi competitions between the Choong Chung and Julla districts which were held every year on July 15th. The government also selected high military officers on the basis of Subakhi training. The first book on the martial arts was published in 1790 with the title, *Common Martial Arts Book*; it was written by Dukmu

The Pre-world Games, International Taekwondo Championship 1985.

Lee and Jaga Park. In this book for the first time, the authors put together the descriptions of basic techniques of Subakhi, which emphasizes the movement of the hands, and the basic techniques of Taekyun, which stresses the uses of the feet. More importantly, for the first time in Taekwondo history, this book described its basic principles and 38 basic postures and techniques. The instructions recorded there are very similar to the techniques of present-day Taekwondo.

In 1592, Japan launched an invasion of Korea. The Shogun Toyotomi Hideyoshi's forces were equipped with firearms acquired from the West. In less than three weeks he had caputered Seoul, and Korea's national existence was at stake. Then Buddhist monks courageously rose up in defense of the nation. Equipped with Taekwondo, they organized the Buddhist National Salvation guerrilla teams to fight against the Japanese military. The Buddhist spirit for national salvation materialized not only as the driving force of patriotism, but also as the fighting spirit behind the effective resistance to the Hideyoshi invasion. Korean patriots rose in all parts of the country and used guerrilla warfare to defeat the Japanese army in battle after battle with their arms the art of Taekwondo. The Japanese were finally driven back to their own shores.

During the most recent Japanese occupation the practice of both Subakhi and Taekyun was prohibited because these activities could stimulate the spirit of national patriotism. The Japanese made every effort to erase any trace of Korean national identity, even to the extent of forbidding use of the Korean language and of burning all the books written in Korea.

To replace the nation's traditional martial arts, the Japanese government tried to force Korean citizens to learn Karate and Gongsudo.

After Korea's liberation from Japan on August 15, 1945, the traditional culture of Korea was revived again. Those who had continued their practice of the Taekwondo in secret now began to organize again for systematic training. However, an interesting new development in 1947 was the Dangsudo, which was a mixture of the traditional Taekyun and the more recently introduced Gongsudo or Karate from Japan. The Dangsudo did not last very long because of its Japanese origin.

In 1954, after so many changes through five thousand years of Korea's history, Taekwondo finally became firmly established with the current name. Since the early 1960s there have been many new developments. Even though Korean military training already required Taekwondo

Taekwondo finally became a demonstration sport in the 24th Seoul Olympics in 1988

discipline, it began to be adopted for the general public's recreational and general physical exercises. Another development was that more scientific studies began to examine the mental, physical, and biological aspects of Taekwondo.

In 1963, Taekwondo was adopted as one of the national medal sports and also became part of the physical education classes throughout the nation.

During the Vietnam War, Korea sent to South Vietnam 40,000 troops who were trained in Taekwondo. The Korean military power of Taekwondo was demonstrated to the watching world during the war. It was used in military combat very successfully for defeating the enemy in battle after battle. Because of the publicity given to it during the Vietnam War, Taekwondo began to spread internationally and now ranks as the world's most popular martial art.

At the present time, in 1988, Korea has about 3,500,000 Taekwondo students, with 50,000 black belt holders. There are 2,000 Taekwondo masters in 120 nations serving as instructors and there are 30 million students throughout the world.

Kukgiwŏn is the headquarters of the World Taekwondo Federation (WTF) which is located in Seoul, Korea. The WTF was officially approved as the world's controlling body of the sport by the International Olympic Committee in 1980.

There have been seven world championships since 1973. The first two and the seventh were held in Seoul. The United States, West Germany, Ecuador, and Denmark have hosted the other four.

The 1985 Seventh World Championship attracted 776 participants from 63 countries. Korea won seven of eight divisions, which is typical of its performance in all the world championships.

In 1986, Taekwondo was adopted as a regular event in the 10th Asian Games, and the Korean athletes again demonstrated their dominance of the sport by winning seven of eight gold medals. Taekwondo finally became a demonstration sport in the 24th Seoul Olympics in 1988. This exposure heightened its popularity around the world. One of the opening ceremonies of the Seoul Olympics was a demonstration of Taekwondo which was received with wild enthusiasm not only by the audience at the Olympic stadium but by the fifty million people watching the televised events throughout the world. Furthermore, the International Olympic Committee meeting in Seoul gave approval for Taekwondo to be a regular Olympic sport for the 25th Olympic Games at Barcelona in 1992.

PART SIX

The 24th Seoul Olympiad 1988

The Korean sports movement opened a bright, new chapter on September 30, 1981, when Seoul was successful in its bid to host the 1988 Summer Olympic Games. The International Olympic Committee (IOC), meeting in Baden-Baden, West Germany, selected Seoul in a 52 to 27 vote over the Japanese city of Nagoya. Korea would be the second Asian nation to host the Olympics, following Japan, which had hosted the Games in 1964.

The ambitious idea of hosting the olympic Games was first conceived in 1971 when the nation initiated construction of massive sports facilities with an eye to hosting both the 1986 Asian Games and the Olympics. Seoul's success in winning the bid for the Olympics is solid proof of international recognition of Korean athletic capacity and potential, and it serves as a wonderful incentive for the youth of the nation.

Two months before the final vote, IOC members and the leaders of various international sports federations returned from a trip to Seoul full of enthusiasm for the sports facilities being built. The selection of Korea as an Olympic site is also significant in that the Republic overcame a serious political handicap as a divided nation. North Korea made strenuous eforts to undermine Seoul's bid, but the Republic successfully overcame this obstacle. In contrast to North Korea's deceitful maneuverings, Seoul officials made it clear that holding the Olympics in Seoul could lead to the promotion of better relations with the North.

Furthermore, the Korean sports leaders repeatedly emphasized President Chun Doo Hwan's remarks that the Seoul Olympics would be absolutely apolitical and that the doors to the Olympics were open to all IOC member countries in accordance with the Olympic principle of universal participation, regardless of racial, religious, or political differences. In line with this, Korean athletics are based on the firm belief that sports are important in the development of physical fitness and that, above all, they should lead to the promotion of friendship and good will among all nations.

The fifth General Assembly of the Association of National Olympic Committees (ANOC) was held in Seoul in April, 1986, with 152 of the 161 ANOC member countries attending. The participation by such a record number of countries, including most Communist and nonaligned nations with which Korea has no formal diplomatic relations, was a strong indication that the 24th Olympics would be able to rise above the political barriers that have often marred the Olympic Movement.

In the summer of 1988 some 13,000 athletes and officials from 161 countries were in Seoul for the Olympics, competing in 23 sports, two of which, tennis and table tennis, were new additions. The games were held from September 17 to October 2, 1988, a period that included three weekends and two Korean national holidays. At the same time, the Seoul Olympic Organizing Committee (SLOOC) scheduled a cultural festival that matched the games in grandeur and significance. This provided Korea a rare opportunity to show the world its own culture and art treasures and gave the peoples of the participating countries a chance to share theirs as well. These events helped the world make progress toward greater international understanding and friendship.

The World Peace Gate, a commemorative monument to the Seoul Olympic Games, stands at the entrance to the Olympic Park, the site of many sports facilities as well numerous sculptures created by artists from around the world.

A. The Opening Ceremonies of the Seoul Olympics

At 10:00 A.M. on September 17, 1988 the 24th Summer Olympiad, which had as its theme the slogan, "Beyond All Barriers," raised its splendid curtain at the Han River in the "Land of Morning Brightness." Unlike the previous three Olympic Games, the Seoul Olympics were a testament to the breaking of barriers, to friendship and harmony. The flowers displayed in the opening ceremony were meant to disclose the soul of a nation in which is embodied the spirit of the Beneficial Man. The ceremony, under a beautiful autumn blue sky, was witnessed by 100,000 spectators and a television audience of 50 million around the world.

Barriers of race, religion, and ideology can divide the world, but in 1988 the world leaped the barriers. In Seoul, Korea, mankind came together as one. As the barriers came down, new hope arose and new buds sprouted to cover the painful scars of division. Like the day heaven sent the sun's first rays, the Seoul Olympics prefigured a new dawn for the world.

Act I.
The Kang Sang Jae or River Worship Ceremony

The stage was set for the 24th Games of the Olympiad, as powerful waters of the Han River carried the Olympic spirit, which had captured the world, toward the Olympic stadium. Since the Han is Seoul's link to the five oceans and six continents, it is appropriate that mankind's grand festival of harmony began there. The dragon drum ship led an inspiring armada of 160 vessels from the Yŏngdong Bridge toward the stadium. As the 160 boats reached the stadium, the huge native drum was carried inside, where its mesmerizing beat would sound out a tribute to the Olympics. The world was divided by various

boundaries, waterways, mountains, and ideologies. However, like a river which can pass through any boundaries and finally reach the ocean, 13,600 athletes from 160 nations, numbers which set Olympic records, came to Korea, crossing these religious and ideological boundaries in the high spirit of harmony and progress. As the 160 ships on the Han River were converging to the main stadium, from various directions these scenes were shown on a giant scoreboard screen at the stadium with accompanying music played by Korea's traditional orchestras. At this moment about 100,000 blue and white balloons were released representing the eastern and western nations participating. According to Korean tradition blue represents the East and white represents the West.

Act II.
The Hemagi or
The Greeting of
Morning Brightness

The second act of the opening ceremony had four different scenes including the Sabyukgil (The Way to Early Dawn), the Yong-go Hangyul (The Dragon Drummer Parade), the C'hŏn-gi-in (The Heaven-Earth-Men), and T'aecho-ye Bit (The First Beams of the New World). This four-part act represented the new beginning of the world. It was a form of opening

prayer for the Olympic Games to ask
heaven for divine guidance for the
games' success. For the ceremony
there was beautiful dancing by 100
drummer girls.

Act II, Part 1.

The Sabyukgil or The Way To Early Dawn

At the beginning the stage was nearly empty, which meant that in the beginning of the world there was nothing. Then suddenly there came a new beginning, represented by the morning brightness. Drummer soldiers—1,200 of them—wearing the traditional white, blue, red, and yellow costumes entered the stadium from the north and south gates to open the way for the sun. They separated, going in four directions toward the east, the west, the north and the south, centering

themselves around the group of flag girls. These girls observed the sacred ritual of greeting the sun. Then they made way for the dragon drummer procession which had started from the Han River earlier.

The stadium was then no mere structure of concrete and green field. It was transformed to represent the ritualistic passage of dawn and a new awakening for all mankind and all the earth. It was like the first day of creation once again. On this cleansed and virgin land, the young people of the world had the opportunity to observe the rite of vowing eternal harmony to one another and commitment to progress for all mankind.

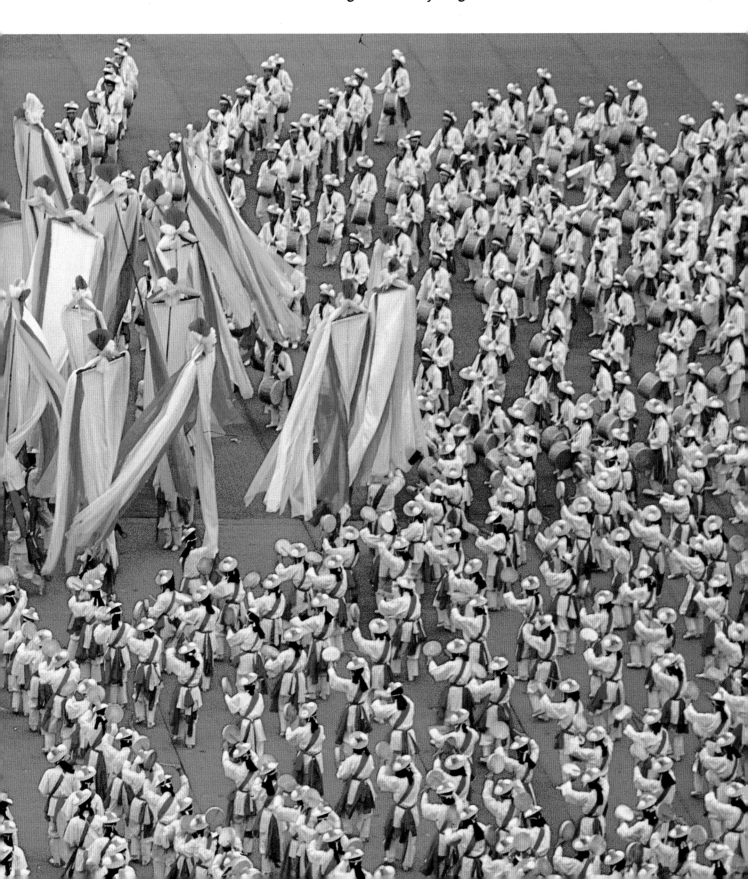

Act II, Part 2.
The Yong-Go or Dragon Drummer Procession

Then the Dragon Drummer parade entered the stadium from the north gate with a thunderous drumming sound. The dragon drum, two meters in diameter and the largest ever made in the world, was made especially for this occasion. The sound of the drums had a rhythm like a human pulse. This was a drum of life, a drum of rhythm, a drum of 13,600 athletes' pulses which signified the steps of five billion people marching together in hope of a better tomorrow. Patterned after the Chosŏn Kingdom royal procession, the dragon drum procession had the drum taking the traditional place of the royal carriage.

The procession moved toward the towering world's tree, or cosmic tree, which, based on Korean folk tales, stood 29 meters high. It represents the very axis of the universe and symbolizes the three orders of heaven, earth, and man.

The Gaesue or the "world's tree" was to form a bridge between earth and heaven. When the dragon drummers reached the tree of the world there was silence for a moment and then when the drummer struck three times, the sun at the top of the tree of the world was released. This meant that finally the sun had risen to the sky, which celebrated the harmony of heaven, earth, and man.

Suddenly the world's tree was transformed into the Olympic Holdrin in which would burn an inspiring flame that represented a new dawn for mankind and that would light up the world for the sixteen days to come.

172

Act II, Part 3.

The C'hŏn-gi-in or the Heaven-Earth-Man

Under the bright morning sun in the green pasture without divisions or walls the 44 Korean fairies and 44 Greek fairies met between heaven and earth. This represented the East and West becoming one and trying to build a harmonious new world. Then 88 fairies, who symbolized the 1988 Olympics, were seen dancing together to celebrate the union. Then a thousand-member choir and orchestra joined in the music of "In the Beginning of the New World."

Act II, Part 4.
The T'aec'ho-ye Bit or the First Beams of the New World

This scene began when 1,625 modern dancers rose up from the stadium ground to form a perfect circle. Now the first light of the new sun was shining bright in the main stadium. Then dancers spelled out WELCOME to the entire world with light traditional background music in the pentatonic scale. Next they moved into positions to form the five Olympic rings and the Seoul Games logo. Mr. Roh Tae Woo, President of the Republic of Korea, and the First Lady entered the stadium followed by Mr. Antonio Samaranch, President of the International Olympic Committee.

The Olympic Athletes March In

The 13,600 athletes were led into the stadium by the 300 flag girls of middle school age, who were holding flags blazoned with the Olympic emblem. Then 73,000 pitch-pipes which had been placed on the audience seats started playing simultaneously. These pitch-pipes sounded the four basic harmony tones, Doh (low), Mi, Sol, Doh (high). This added the harmony of sound to the audio-visual effects.

Starting with the nation of Greece, 160 nations' athletes marched in by the order reflected in the native Korean language alphabet, the "Hangŭl." It was a one hour and seventeen minute procession in which athletes wore the most colorful of their country's traditional costumes.

When each team entered the stadium, information about the country and the size of the Olympic team was flashed on the scoreboard. In one section of the stands spectators revealed colored cards in unison to depict the country's flag.

Mr. Se-jick Park, President of the Seoul Olympic Organizing Committee, gave a brief welcome speech and introduced Mr. Antonio Samaranch, President of the International Olympic Committee, who congratulated the organizers and the people of South Korea for all they had done.

Then, Mr. Roh Tae Woo, President of the Republic of Korea, stated, "Now I declare the opening of the 24th International Olympic Games in Seoul, Korea."

Many firecrackers were set-off and various card-actions were started in the stadium including formation of the symbols for "Harmony and Progress."

During the raising of the Olympic Flag, 103 members of an old order military band, wearing traditional colorful dress like they once used for the King's procession, led the Olympic flag holder, a gold medalist from Korea. This band's instruments consisted of gongs, fiddles, drums, shell trumpets, oboes, and flutes. While the Olympic flag was being raised the Olympic hymn was sung and played by the choir and orchestra. When the Olympic flag reached the top of the pole, suddenly 2,400 white doves were released to symbolize the world's hope for peace and freedom! These doves had been raised by a specialist over a four year period for this occasion. Simultaneously five jets were flying high above, trailing colored smoke and forming it into the shape of the five Olympic rings.

179

The Lighting Of The Sacred Fire

The Olympic sacred fire was started by the sun at 10:00 A.M. on August 23, 1988 from the original Olympic altar in Geece. On August 27, at 11:00 A.M., the Olympic fire arrived at one of the fairest islands of Korea. Then it passed through 61 cities during the next 22 days to arrive at last at Seoul.

As it entered the stadium of the Olympics, the sacred fire was carried by a national hero, the history-making gold medalist Mr. Gee Chung Shon. In 1936, at the Berlin Olympic Games, Mr. Shon was a marathon runner who had been forced to run with the Japanese national flag on his uniform. When he approached the final finishing line, with much pain in his face he tried to cover with his hand the Japanese flag on his chest. Now at 75 years of age, this time he proudly entered the stadium with the Korean flag on his chest. It was quite a moving moment to watch this gold medalist and national hero running like a happy child.

After Mr. Shon had run half the course he passed the torch to Miss Chunae Lim, a three time gold medalist. This represented the participation of the old and young generations and men and women in the final running.

When Miss Lim reached the 100-foot torch base, she was met by three representatives of the common people, a school teacher, a student, and an athlete, who ignited the fire.

A flight of jets flew over the stadium, producing smoke in the five Olympic colors. It was a spectacular sight, evocative of the blessing of heaven upon the games.

Oaths by Athletes and Judges

Two representatives from the athletes a women and a man, each holding an Olympic flag in the left hand and with the right hand raised, said "We will participate in these Olympic Games with the true spirit of sportsmanship to the honor and prestige of our teams and will respect and follow the Olympic Games' rules." And one representative from the judges gave an oath: "We will respect and follow the Olympic Games rules and carry out our duties for fairness and safety according to the true Olympic spirit of sportsmanship."

The Korean National Anthem was led by the choir and orchestra and sung by the audience.

The athletes marched out promptly through both the north and south gates.

Act III.
The Joun-Nal or The Happy Days

After the sacred ritual of greeting the sun, as on the first day of creation, another inspiring scene unfolded, a scene of a time gone by when all people on earth lived happily in peace. Eight hundred dancers expressed the joy of the earthly community, while suggesting the mystery of heaven, in offering prayers for heaven's blessings. The granting of these blessings was represented by 76 skydivers who came flowing to the earth during the ceremony.

Eight hundred high school girls wearing the traditional blue and white dresses participated in this scene, which consisted of three different dances: the Kangbok or the supplication to heaven for blessing; the C'hail C'hum or the Sunshade Dance; and the Wha Kwan-mu or the Coronet Dance.

Act III, Part 1.
The Kangbok or the Supplication To Heaven for Blessing

As the dancers were praying for the heavenly blessing, there were answers from the sky. These were 76 parachutists forming the Olympic sign in the sky. The crowd held its breath as the parachuters dropped from a height of 4,000 meters to land precisely within the stadium, which looked like a flower vase from the sky. Like flowers falling on the Olympic ceremonies as a form of heavenly blessing, the parachuters came gently to the earth in the stadium.

Act III, Part 2.
C'hail C'hum or the Sunshade Dance

As soon as the parachutists landed, they began opening their sunshades. It has long been a tradition in Korea that sunshades are set up whenever festivities such as special worship services, wedding ceremonies, parties, or funerals take place. The colorful sunshades wav-

ing in the wind were like blessings from heaven, representing the happy days and excitement of the festivities of the Olympics.

Act III, Part 3.
The Whakwan-Mu or the Coronet Dance

As the parachutes and the sunshades left the scene, the flower crown dance was performed, reminiscent of the beginning of human history when there was harmony between heaven and earth.

The beauty and grace of the flower crown dance was the finest example of the traditional Korean dance; its culmination had a calming affect on the audience and set the atmosphere for the performances to come.

This last act was the highlight for the dances representing earth's happy days. Whakwan-mu is a highly disciplined royal palace dance. The costumes and headdresses were those used for the Chosŏn Kingdom's traditional royal dances. Colors were mixed among the basic five and the elegance and refinement of the Korean traditional royal dances were displayed. In a way this dance gave solemnity and ceremonial tone while providing a calm, tranquil mood in the audience. It ended with the formation of the Korean national flower, the Rose of Sharon.

The dancers were clad in the brilliant colors traditional to the Chosŏn Kingdom, seen today in old Korean paintings. In reds, blues and striped cloth, the colors swirled around and came together to form flowers, clouds, and rivers.

Act IV.
The
Confusion

But then the wondrous era of peace passed and a dark era of confusion plunged the world into discord and strife.

Suddenly good feeling and harmony were replaced with disagreements and conflicts. This was to show how evil spirits are always tempting or are jealous of mankind's happy times. Good and evil, love and hate, creation and destruction were dramatized to show how mankind is once again facing confusion about his values and ideals, to show how ideological cultural, and racial conflict are creating great tensions. The 841 dancers participating in this dance and wearing various versions of 160 different traditional face masks, represented 60 countries involved in the Olympics.

The 841 traditional masks moved about in a chaotic manner; there were masks of war, of starvation and disease, and of devils and gods in conflict with each other. Good and evil, love and hate, creation and destruction, confrontation and divisions, the barriers that can divide mankind, were also represented above the audience in twenty huge balloon masks encircling the stadium roof. These were meant to add to the overwhelming scene of utter confusion. In the midst of this rampage by dancers wearing the masks of violence, drug mania, pollution, nuclear weapons, adn disease, a hell fire erupted.

188

Act V.
Beyond All Barriers

In the middle of the confusion there came 1,008 Taekwondo students ranging from primary school age to high school age, who wore white martial arts dress. Even as the earth is one despite its many boundaries and walls, these Taekwondo students were showing the power of their wills to break down all the barriers in order to build a new, harmonious world. Taekwondo is a Korean traditional martial art that places emphasis on defensive measures taught through discipline, self-control, and physical as well as mental development.

Over one boundary after another, Taekwondo students defeated all the conflicts among the nations. They started with a small formation, attempting to break a piece of board and then the formations grew bigger and bigger. Finally they formed a small mountain and broke through. Their actions were so beautiful that they seemed like a piece of calligraphy in the air. They showed the power of mental discipline, the power instilled in the heart through meditation, and the power of the Korean spirit, which is Benefits to All Mankind. Their Taekwondo power seemed to be coming from harmonious and gentle hearts because there was such perfect unison in their dancing.

The "Beyond All Barriers" scene was in complete contrast with the confusion of the previous scene so that it gave a positive image after the negative one and a reverse of order after confusion as if one were coming out to a cool pleasant pasture from a muggy city environment. The dancers appeared to be moving man's history from the dark wilderness to a bright new world.

191

Act VI.
The Silence

There was only a deep silence after the Taekwendo students had made the stadium clean again, because they picked up everything on the grounds when they left. Every movement was stopped and there was emptiness on the ground. Earth was waiting for a new birth. The world where there are no barriers was like a new life starting, quietly breaking the silence. The new life was represented by a little boy (named Tae Woong Yun, eight years old, in the second grade at Seoul Jam-Yuen Elementary School) entering the stadium rolling in front of himself an iron hoop. The round hoop represented the round world or the shining new earth where the new hope for a better future was rolling forward.

This exemplified a typical oriental approach in that most oriental arts are centered on a single object, such as a single plum blossom serving as the focal point in a whole print. So one little child in the whole stadium arena seemed like a typical Korean classical print.

This scene showed a world of new hope, full of dreams and emotions. The round hoop represented the harmonious world and was a symbol of the Olympics. This also symbolized the way the games served as a link between the old generations and the future generations of children. Thus this hoop was rolling from the old, inharmonious past toward the new, harmonious future. The little boy, Tae Woong Yun, was born on September 30, 1981 the date the International Olympic Committee (IOC) voted for Korea to be the site of the 1988 Summer Olympic Games.

Act VII.
The New Sprouts

Next appeared the new sprouts, the buds that could grow into a bright new future. As soon as Tae Woong disappeared from the stadium, 1,200 children, all of whom were also born in September 1981 entered the stadium. They were all engaged in typical children's play and games. Jumping rope, playing shuttle cog and cat's cradle, the children at play were a nostalgic reminder to the world of the innocence of youth. The play of natural lively children represented the infancy of art. They were fresh and pure, full of hope and peaceful. They had no enemies or barriers and appeared to be true democrats. They were playing in the child's eternal world of imagination and feeling, lifted above the limitations of time and space. This scene gave the watching world that sense of joy that is experienced mostly in observing small children and the spontaneity of their smiles. Appropriately, the involvement of thousands of children epitomized a basic premise of the Games: that our world's future lies with its youth.

Act VIII.
The Harmony

At last the world was shown to be embraced by the tremendous elation of harmony, as 1,450 college students were next seen, participating in a "GO" game which is one of the famous traditional folk games in Korea. Not winning or losing, but achieving harmony between the negative and positive principles was the ultimate goal of this game. Even in the intense battle the two top circles were contracted and the combatants became friends, showing men's need for love and harmony.

The Go Game saw villagers divided into teams of blue (Yin) and red (Yang) confronting each other with the enormous rope knots known as "Coy." The objective, however, was not winning the competition. The climax of the game was shown in the achievement of harmony and unity. The teams crashed into each other, not to destroy but to merge.

The Coy is made of a soft shrub, proving that the strength that can bring harmony to the world can even come from the softness of straw. It is the same kind of strength Koreans wished to display at the Olympic Games.

Now the sprouts had grown and become energetic youths. Using sound and motion effects, the game appealed to the audience with a very powerful image of the youthful energy of Korea. This scene was designed to show the harmony of Yin and Yang in Korean philosophy as the traditional reconciliation was achieved. Here was the ultimate symbolism at the Games of reunification.

195

Act IX.
The One World

Finally the world was seen as becoming one. Under the beautiful bright morning sun, families of the world entered the stadium hand-in-hand. The first group who entered the stadium were dressed as the national flowers of the nations where previous Olympic Games were held. The next group represented the animals which were mascots in previous Olympic Games. Then about six hundred dancers from twelve nations entered, representing the six continents.

Now beyond all barriers the world had become one family, as represented by the family of national flowers, from 78 countries, and by the animal family, represented by famous Olympic mascots.

All the participants in the opening ceremony flooded into the arena, from the East, West, South and North, to form a human family.

Less than 40 years earlier, young people of the world had fought each other, armed with weapons and different ideologies. Today, they were gathered on the same land hand in hand sharing love, passion and dreams. Koren dancers mingled with folk dancers from around the world. Korean spectators sang and embraced their guests. Hand in hand the people of the world were joined. They sang:

Let us not hate each other.
Let us not deceive each other.
Let us not argue with each other.
Only with love, let us build one
  family of the world.
The world of plants
The world of animals
The world of peoples
Only with love, Let us build one
  family of the world.

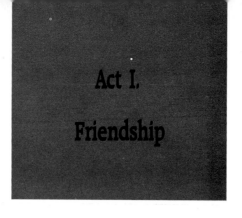

Act I.

Friendship

View the empty grounds....
in 'a full-capacity stadium.
The Emille bell began to ring
heralding the opening of the
closing ceremony.

The Emille bell has a long-lingering sound epitomizing the farewell expression. The bell, the largest and most beautifully resonant bell in the country, was cast in 770. It has a height of 3.33 meters and a diameter of 2.27 meters. To cast such a huge bell many Buddhist monks had to make a tour of the country to raise funds. According to tradition, one of the monks who traveled from house to house thoughout the country knocked at the gate of a destitute farmer. To the visiting monk, the matron of the house said that, being so poor, she had nothing to contribute but an infant daughter. The monk wrote down what the woman offered in his donation book.

Later when the casting of the bell was begun it was decided that a human sacrifice was necessary. In the history of Buddhism there were many human sacrifices made in order to make most holy the items of worship. So the infant daughter of the destitute farm woman was brought and thrown into the pot of melted copper. The bell was finally cast and responded to being struck with a mournful tolling which reminded one of a baby crying "emille..., emille...." Hence the name of the bell became "Emille" (meaning "Mommy").

The athletes of the world had run more swiftly, aimed higher and grown stronger than ever before and now reached for their dreams as they embraced one another and the games came to a close. The time of parting was at hand and although it was a moment of sadness, there was also the joy of knowing they would meet again. So fittingly, the closing ceremony began with a joyous dance, celebrating the priceless, bountiful friendship the world had reaped from the Games.

It has been a Korean custom, as well as one reserved by many other people, that when a friend departs, the ones remaining behind come out and wave their hands while the departing person will look back with a returning wave. A long-lingering round of the Emille bell at the closing ceremonies gave one the feeling of missing departed ones. This typical expression of friendship was the basis of the closing ceremonies.

Now was the time for farewell after fierce and intense competition among the world record 13,600 athletes assembled from 160 nations. Though they were competitors, they had a chance to share their fellowship, and now they had to say goodby with a promise that they would hope to see one another in Barcelona, Spain, after four years.

This friendship program began with Western ribbon gymnastics and the Korean "Sangmo" or "circle play," accompanied by the tradi-

tional farmer's musical instruments. Like an Olympic mascot, the Hodori or baby tiger on top of the farm dancers' hat trailed long white ribbons with which the dancers made a circle. This was an expression that the East and the West all share a common feeling of friendship and love.

The distinctive character of this scene was clearly seen in the beautiful curved line formed by the one ribbon. One could hear the ringing of the Emille bell with its long lingering sound and see at the same time the beauty of the long curved ribbon. The music was also complemented with the sounds of many traditional percussion instruments. The ribbon gymnastics and the circle play mingled very well and harmonized their effects.

The Athletes' Grand Entrance

Led by 150 flag carriers, the athletes poured into the stadium with the tension of competition gone. These were unforgettable moments for these young people from around the globe.

Raising Three National Flags

By the Olympic Charter, the Greek national flag was raised as the national anthem of Greece was played. Next, in the middle, the Korean national flag was raised to the accompaniment of the Korean national anthem. Finally, the flag of Spain, the next Olympic site, was raised, while the Spanish national anthem played.

Act II, Part 1.

Building
The Bridge

Magpies were busy building a new bridge for the lovers who were separated between heaven and earth. This act was based on a folk tale of Korea. The couple's love for each other was so great that even the birds were touched, and the magpies were helping to build a bridge for this couple to meet each other every 7th of July.

Seven hundred and fifty dancers or magpies were seen entering the stadium from the North and South gates. They made an S-letter formation through the athletes to represent a bridge. The lovers could have only a very brief meeting and had to quickly depart because the bridge was not able to hold them very long. Thus this scene showed a sorrowful, heart-rending moment of farewell, but it promised hope.

As the moon rose, the Korean legend of Uta Bridge was staged, using cymbals and fan dancers to represent mystical sights and sounds. The men with cymbals and the women with fans merge and divide, experiencing the joy of meeting and the sorrow of parting.

Act II, Part 2.
The Light and Sound

Like a Milky Way with an elegant curve of light the famous fan and cymbals dance was performed by dancers wearing traditional dress. This act showed harmony between the fans and cymbals and the light and sound. The cymbals and fans symbolized man and woman. Further, they showed the harmonizing of the two extremes of positive and negative as a principle of nature.

Act III.

The Sailing Ships

About 569 dancers and actors wearing Buddhist monks' robes were next seen, as they moved like sailing ships through the athletes of the world. They held 160 flags representing the 160 nations who had participated in the 1988 Olympics as they went sailing out of the stadium. As farewell music eleven ballad singers sang the famous "Shim-Chŏng" song based on a very sad folk tale. The story of Shim-Chŏng is one that deals primarily with the theme of filial piety, one of the most highly regarded virtues of Korea. A girl named Shim Chŏng sold herself to a group of fishermen in order to raise money for her blind father. The fishermen were going to use Shim Chŏng for offering to the sea. This sorrowful scene enhanced the mood of nostalgic farewell among the athletes. Using various lights, the sailing ships appeared to be sailing in the peaceful ocean like a littering Milky Way. On a gentle night without any anxiety over winning or losing, all the athletes now felt sadness at parting.

A melancholy boat song from Shim Chŏng signaled the performance entitled "Parting Ships." The Olympic Stadium field represented the sea and the stadium the port of parting.

The blue flags carried by the dancers and the Buddhist robes they wore became the lapping waves of the sea and the farmers' flags became the sails. As the oars were pulled, a visionary farewell scene was created in an adaptation of a Korean folk play.

At the opening ceremony the world had witnessed mankind

gathering at the Olympic Stadium from the Han River. Now it was time to board those boats again to return to the homelands.

The Declaration of Closing

Mr. Se-jick Park, Chairman of the Seoul Olympic Organizing Committee, gave the closing remarks and introduced Mr. Antonio Samaranch, President of the International Olympic Committee. Mr. Samaranch said: "I give the greatest thanks to the President, Mr. Roh, to the Korean people, to the city of Seoul and to the Olympic Organizational Committee. Also, I would like to give thanks to all the athletes, the audiences, the reporters, and all of the staffs who participated in running the Olympics so successfully and safely. Now I declare the closing of the 24th Seoul Olympics and I hope to see you all at Barcelona, Spain, in 1992."

212

The Olympic Flag Transfer

Mr. Yong-rae Kim, mayor of Seoul, handed over the Olympic flag to Mr. Samaranch. Mr. Samaranch gave the Olympic flag to Mr. Pascual Maracal, who is the mayor of Barcelona, Spain.

Next, there were thirty members of the Seoul City dancing group who came into the stadium with another thirty members of the Barcelona dancing team. The Seoul dancing group performed the traditional "Changgo" or "hourglass drum dance." This drum has been one of the most frequently used accompaniments for most forms of traditional Korean music. The thick skin on the left side is struck with the palm and produces a soft, low sound and the thin skin of the right side is struck with a bamboo stick which produces a hard, crisp sound. The Barcelona dancing team performed

one of their traditional folk dances called "Saradna" in which all the dancers held hands and formed a circle.

The Lowering of the Olympic Flag and the Extinguishing of the Olympic Sacred Fire

While the Olympic song was being played and sung by the orchestra and choir, the Olympic flag was lowered and carried out by eight Korean gold medalists. Meanwhile the Olympic sacred fire was allowed to expire. The stadium became completely dark and then five guns fired.

Act IV. V.

The Farewell Wishes and The Adieu

As the Olympic flame was extinguished, the stadium fell into complete darkness and tranquility ruled while the melancholy Taegŭm or flute music started playing, breaking the quietness in the stadium. The dance afterwards expressed farewell wishes to all for a safe journey home. These dance also dramatized a closing prayer of thanksgiving for the successful Olympics as well as of hope for further blessing of the Olympics in the future.

Then the dark stadium turned into a dazzling sky of shining stars, as the spectator's hopes soared aloft on red and blue lanterns. Eight hundred

high school students who wore traditional children's costumes participated in the lantern dancing. They held the blue and red lanterns of the type formerly used for guidance down a dark country road. They were symbolic of guiding all the world guests to a safe return home. The background music was a famous folk song "Arirang." Next all the athletes joined in the lantern dance. They all sang the Arirang song in unison while holding hands and forming various circles symbolizing the world's one family.

In a final gesture of friendship, Seoul's mascot, Hodori, or the baby tiger rose toward the night sky with Barcelona's Colby, their arms around each other. Fireworks spectacularly illuminated the sky. Hodori and Colby went on their way while performers and athletes joined in the Korean group dance as they moved hand-in-hand. The peoples of the earth were joined in a tight circle.

Act VI.

The Going Home

Now 160 ships departed from the Han River. The scene duplicated the beginning of the ceremony, but in reverse, as the ships now symbolized the last prayer to God to take care of all the athletes and take them safely home.

The curtain of the 24th Seoul Olympics was drawn at the Han River where the 160 ships were seen sailing away, led by the ship which held 600 blue and red lanterns. Each ship had one Olympic torchlight which was lighted before the extinguishing of the main Olympic flame.

Each ship was going back to its homeland with the Seoul Olympic spirits, Harmony and Progress, based on the philosophy of Benefits of All Mankind. Through the Han River the spirits of Harmony and Progress were spreading out all over the world. In the meantime Hodori and Colby were going up to the sky and the second scene of these sailing ships led by hundreds of lanterns showed the care Koreans have taken to promote the welfare of all mankind. These scenes were displayed very dramaticlly both with horizontal and vertical effects. With these lights of harmony and progress, all the world's athletes were sailing back across their countries various boundaries and barriers like a river winding its way to join the ocean of the world.

The outstanding dedication of the men and women behind the games, the devoted service of volunteer workers and Korea's citizens, and the clear autumn sky all contributed to make this 24th summer games a memorable event. The triumph of Seoul, one which could hardly have been predicted, was now reaching its final moment. The golden curtain was about to come down.

The Seoul Olympics which began on the Han were closing at the same place, as the vessel carrying more than 600 red and blue lanterns sailed downstream, symbolic of peoples returning to their homelands. But the water of the river moves endlessly and returns; nothing ever really begins or ends on this eternal river.

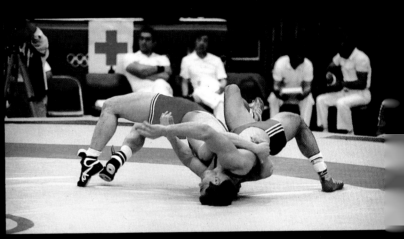

Highlights of the 24th Olympics

Mr. David Miller, correspondent for *The London Times*, best summed up by the significance of the Seoul Olympics by saying, "We saw them (the Koreans) for what they are: tranquil yet with an inner strength, graceful yet energetic, moulded by ancient dynasties, yet ambitiously modern.

South Korea these days is dramatically successful, but the opening ceremony in Seoul gave us not assertiveness or aggression, but gentleness. The people are determined yet poetic; their pageant was a picture of history, color and elegance. For three hours, on a morning when the gods graced Seoul with sun and an autumn blue sky, the emphasis was not on achievement, which is as much a part of the South Korean story as it is of the Olympic Games, but on harmony and friendship.

As Seoul, 5000 years old, opened the Games with a display that was a triumphal celebration of its new international recognition, it simultaneously captured that mystic, indefinable quality that is the essence of the Olympics, man's shared experience of nature, and of his personal efforts, with his fellow men." (September 19, 1988, p. 44)

While the athletes of the world were in burning fierce competition, various international cultural festivities were held nearby at the Han River. Included among them were the 1988 Seoul International Folk Festival, which had 600 participants from twelve countries; the Han River International Jazz Festival, the International Traditional Culture and Food Festival; which had twenty nations participating; the Novel Calligraphy contest, the International Chess Games; a Kite Flying Contest, and an Outdoor International Fashion Show.

One other special festivity was the Floating Lantern Festival at the Han River. This was a form of tribute to the Olympics by the Buddhists. The lanterns were of yellow and lavender colors which symbolized the lotus flowers that represent Buddhism. There were 70,000 lanterns floating, making a splendid embroidery along the river during the nights. Thus the thousands of

A Commemorative stand at the Olympic Park in Seoul, the site of numerous sculptures created by artists from around the world.

Florence Griffith Joyner (front page),
Greg Louganis (left) and a medalist of
the women gymnastics.

viewers felt as if they were watching unseasonable lotus flowers bloom during the autumn nights.

In many ways the 24th Seoul Olympics may be remembered as one of the best in Olympic history because there had been so many obstacles to be overcome by the Korean hosts, along with the 13,600 athletes from 160 nations, and the nearly 5,000 coaches and officials. A great number of Korean volunteers worked very hard to carry out the daily tasks, and about 20,000 students ranging from primary school children to college students participated in the opening and closing ceremonies. There were also 7,000 English-speaking Korean housewives who served as volunteer house-maids for the Olympic Village.

According to the results of the contests, the champion country was the Soviet Union, and to the surprise of the United States, East Germany came in second, with the United States taking third place. Also providing somewhat of a surprise was the fact that more smaller nations were winners than ever before. Fifty-one nations won medals, which is an Olympic record for the number of nations represented among the winners. Korea, to every nation's surprise, won 33 medals which made its ranking fourth in the entire competition. Also 31 nations, more than ever before, won gold medals; about 30 world records

and scores of new Olympic standards were established. According to Mr. Samaranch, the I.O.C. president, "The '88 Olympics were the best and the most universal Olympic Games in history."

In the 1988 Summer Olympics, Florence Griffith Joyner of the United States introduced herself to the world and surprised everyone by setting an Olympic record at 100 meters, a world record at 200 meters, and by winning a gold medal in the 4×100 relay and a silver medal in the 4×400 relay.

Greg Louganis showed the world another side of the American spirit. Diver Louganis, seeking a matching set of golds for the pair he won at the 1984 Los Angeles Games, led the competitions until his head hit the springboard on his ninth dive, a reverse 21/2 somersault in the pike position. He received a score of just 6.3 for that dive, but made a dramatic comeback with a superlative performance in his next dive, scoring the highest total of the tournament at 87.12. In a magnificent display of artistry and courage, Louganis overcame pain, self-doubt and a sleepless night to stamp the games with one of its most stirring performances when he captured the springboard diving gold medal. In Seoul, Louganis also won his second straight gold medal in platform diving with a brilliant come-from-behind finish.

225

Some Negative Aspects of the Games and Media Coverage

Even though the Seoul Games brought a record number of nations together again after political divisions lasting for 16 years, some controversies occurred concerning drug use by the athletes. The 88 Olympics also made a record with one of the biggest drug use revelations in Olympic history.

Ben Johnson, the Canadian sprinter, was disqualified from the games for using anabolic steroids. Johnson's world record in one of the games' hottest contests, the men's 100-meter dash, was fueled by the drugs. Nine other athletes, including two gold medalists from the Bulgarian weightlifting team, a Hungarian weightlifting silver medalist, and a British judo bronze medalist were also stripped of their prizes because of drug use. Five other non-medalists tested positive for substances ranging from caffeine to diuretics. Mr. Robert Boy, chief medical officer of the U.S. Olympic Committee said, "Steroid use is pretty rampant. My only surprise is that johnson got caught. These athletes have good information on how to mask drugs."

There was also some degree of anger among some members of the Interntional Olympic Committee that the United States teams pranced through the opening ceremony, mugging for the cameras and holding signs. They were seen by some as an unruly, wild gang. Two gold medalists from the United States were arrested for theft, and a track star was arrested after kicking the door of a taxi.

Negative coverage by the NBC television network so outraged many among the host nation that many Koreans jeered the American athletes and applauded their opponents from any other country. Many Koreans felt that most American athletes were behaving as if they were masters in an occupied country and were showing no respect for their hosts. The negative coverage on Korea's social issues by NBC at a time of international festivities for which an entire nation had devoted itself and had prepared strenuously for, for eight years, was thought of as a humiliating experience. One Korean citizen expressed it this way, "They came to our party as our guests. How they could talk about our daughters being prostitutes, selling our children and our black markets, etc...."

In particular, the charge that Korea was selling its children overseas angered not only Koreans, but many Americans. In this area we are dealing with children and their innocent lives but NBC treated it as if it were a matter of exporting "goods." Korean society still emphasizes a great deal the blood related family and Koreans are still not accustomed to adopting orphans. Also, many of these children under consideration were fathered by American G.I.'s. Is it better for these children to remain in an orphanage or to go to a family where they will be loved and have better opportunities? Because of the damaging NBC coverage the Korean government has implemented steps to stop sending Korean orphans to the United States. This in turn has upset a great number of Americans because there are over three hundred organized groups of parents who have adopted Korean children and who promote opportunities for Korean orphans to have a better life.

Overall, however, the 24th Seoul Olympics were very successful. As Mr. Juan Antonio Samaranch said, "I feel the Olympic movement is the real winner. We showed the world the Olympics were possible in Seoul. The Games went on."

Bibliography

KOREA-GENERAL

American Chamber of Commerce in Korea. Living in Korea. 1987. 35.00 (ISBN 0-686-23876-1). A M Newman.

Bland, John O. China, Japan & Korea. facsimile ed. LC 77-160959. (Select Bibliographies Reprint Ser). Repr. of 1921 ed. 32.00 (ISBN 0-8369-5826-8). Ayer Co Pubs.

Butler, Lucius A., compiled by. Films for Korean Studies. LC 77-86325. (Occasional Paper: No. 8). 167p. 1978. pap. 6.00x (ISBN 0-917536-12-6). UH Manoa CKS.

Center for Korean Studies Staff. Korean Studies, Vol. I. (Korean Studies). 284p. 1977. pap. text ed. 13.50x (ISBN 0-8248-0560-7). UH Pr.

Fu-Chen & Byung-Nak, Song. The Saemaul Undong: The Korean Way of Rural Transformation. (Working papers Ser.: No. 79-9). 23p. 1979. pap. 6.00 (ISBN 0-686-78258-5, CRD036, UNCRD). UNIPUB.

Fukuda, Tsuneari, ed. Future of Japan & the Korean Peninsula. Jahng, K., tr. from Japanese. LC 78-71337. (Illus.). 1978. 14.40x (ISBN 0-930878-14-0). Hollym Int'l.

Grad, Andrew J. Modern Korea. 1979. Repr. of 1944 ed. lib. bdg. 24.00x (ISBN 0-374-93226-3, Octagon). Hippocrene Bks.

Hazard, B. H., ed. Korean Studies Guide, LC 74-9394. (University of California, Institute of Asiatic Studies Ser). (Illus.). 220p. 1975. Repr. of 1954 ed. lib. bdg. 35.00x (ISBN 0-8371-7662-X, MAKS). Greenwood.

Hoare, James & Pares, Susan. Korea: An Introduction. (Illus.). 180p. 1988. pap. text ed. 12.95 (ISBN 0-7103-0299-1). Routledge Chapman & Hall.

Kang. T. W. Is Korea the Next Japan? Understanding the Structure, Strategy & Tactics of America's Next Competitor. 256p. 1988. 19.95 (ISBN 0-02-916692-6). Free Pr.

Korean Report, Pt. 1: A Critical Review of the Saemaul Movement in the Republic of Korea with Special Reference to the Concept of Basic Needs. (Working Papers Ser.: No. 79-13). 25p. 1979. pap. 6.00 (ISBN 0-686-78237-2, CRD021, UNCRD). UNIPUB.

Korean Report, Pt. 2: A Study on Basic Minimum Needs at the Micro-Area Level in the Republic of Korea. (Working Papers Ser.: No. 79-14). 88p. 1979. pap. 6.00 (ISBN 0-686-78238-0, CRD022, UNCRD). UNIPUB.

Lee, Yong-Sook, et al, eds. Teaching about Korea: Elementary & Secondary Activities, 226p. (Orig.). 1986. pap. 15.95 (ISBN 0-89994-309-8). Soc Sci Ed.

Lie, Hiu. Die Mandschu-Sprachkunde in Korea. LC 70-635028. (Uralic & Altaic Ser: Vol. 114). (Illus.). 275p. (Orig.). 1972. pap. text ed. 16.00x (ISBN 0-87750-162-9.). Res Ctr Lang Semiotic.

McCann, David R., et al, eds. Studies on Korea in Transition. LC 78-67859. (Occasional Papers: No. 9). 245p. 1979. pap. 8.00x (ISBN 0-917536-13-4). UH Manoa CKS.

McCormack, Gavan & Selden, Mark, eds. Korea, North & South: The Deepening Crisis. LC 78-4503. 1978. 12.50 (ISBN 0-85345-448-5). Monthly Rev.

Methodological Evolution & Issues of Regional Development Planning in Korea: Country Report: Republic of Korea. (Working Papers Ser.: No. 76-3). 78p. 1976. pap. 6.00 (ISBN 0-686-78483-9, CRD085, UNCRD). UNIPUB.

Morse, Ronald A., ed. Korean Studies in America: Options for the Future. LC 83-13996. 164p. (Orig.). 1983. cloth 33.25 (ISBN 0-8191-3408-2); pap. text ed. 16.25 (ISBN 0-8191-3409-0). U Pr of Amer.

Occasional Papers, 2 pts. Incl. Parental Encouragement & College Plans of High School Students in Korea. Yang, Choon & Won, George.; Gains & Costs of Postwar Industrialization in South Korea. Lim, Youngil. 51p. 1973. pap. 3.50 (ISBN 0-917536-00-2). UH Manoa CKS.

Osgood, Cornelius. The Koreans & Their Culture. LC 51-271. (Illus.). Repr. of 1951 ed. 108.80 (ISBN 0-8357-9523-3, 2015843). Bks Demand UMI.

Rhee, Kyu-Ho. To the Young Korean Intellectuals. LC 81-84201. (Illus.). 197p. 1981. 14.95x (ISBN 0-930878-24-8). Hollym Int'l.

Steenson, Gary. Coping with Korea. (Coping with Ser.). 160p. 1987. 29.95x (ISBN 0-631-15033-1); pap. 9.95 (ISBN 0-631-15622-4). Basil Black well.

Steinberg, David I. The Republic of Korea: Economic Transformation & Social Change. (Profiles-Nations of Contemporary Asia Ser.). 160p 1988. text ed. 34.50 (ISBN 0-86531-720-8) Westview.

Young, An-Jae. New Dimensions of Small Town Development: A Case Study of Five Lower-Order Centres in Korea. (Working Papers Ser.: No. 78-11). 27p. 1978. pap. 6.00 (ISBN 0-686-78487-1, CRD099, UNCRD). UNIPUB.

KOREA-BIBLIOGRAPHY

Courant, Maurice A. Bibliographie Coreenne, Tableau Litteraire De la Coree, 4 vols in 3. (Incl. suppl). Repr. of 1894 ed. Set. 177.00 (ISBN 0-8337-0692-6) B Franklin.

Kim, An-Jae. Urban Development Strategies in the Republic of Korea: An Evaluation. (Working Papers Ser.: No. 74-4). 21p. pap. 6.00 (ISBN 0-686-78263-1, CRD042, UNCRD). UNIPUB.

Koh, Hesung Chun & Steffens, Joan, eds. Korea: An Analytical Guide to Bibliographies. LC 70-125119. (Bibliographies Ser.). 352p. 1971. 25.00x (ISBN 0-87536-241-9). HRAFP.

*Miller, E. Willard & Miller, Ruby M. The Third World: South Korea & North Korea: A Bibliography. (P 2500). 32p. 1988. 8.75 (ISBN 1-55590-950-7, P 2500). Vance Biblios.

Shulman, Frank J., compiled by. Doctoral Dissertations on Japan & on Korea, 1969-1979: An Annotated Bibliography of Studies in Western Languages. LC 82-13563. 400p. 1982. 35.00x (ISBN 0-295-95895-2); pap. 14.95x (ISBN 0-295-95961-4). U of Wash Pr.

Silberman, Bernard S. Japan & Korea: A Critical Bibliography. LC 82-11841. 120p. 1982. Repr. of 1962 ed. lib. bdg. 35.00x (ISBN 0-313-23594-5, SIJK). Greenwood.

—Japan & Korea: A Critical Bibliography. LC 62-11821. pap. 33.50 (ISBN 0-317-10731-3, 2055366.) Bks Demand UMI.

KOREA-CIVILIZATION

Haboush, Jahyun K. A Heritage of Kings: One Man's Monarchy in the Confucian World. (Studies in Oriental Culture: No. 21). 304p. 1988. 32.50 (ISBN 0-231-06656-2). Columbia U Pr.

Hyde, Georgie D. South Korea: Education, Culture & Economy. LC 87-34908. 320p. 1988. 49.95 (ISBN 0-312-01666-2). St Martin.

Morse, Ronald A., ed. Wild Asters: Explorations in Korean Thought, Culture & Society. LC 86-32595. 94p. (Orig.). 1987. lib. bdg. 22.75 (ISBN 0-8191-6116-0, Pub. by Woodrow Wilson Int'l. Ctr); pap. text ed. 11.50 (ISBN 0-8191-6117-9, Pub. by Woodrow Wilson Int'l. Ctr.) U Pr of Amer.

KOREA-DESCRIPTION AND TRAVEL

Adams, Edward B. Korea Guide, (Illus.). 1979. pap. 12.00 (ISBN 0-89860-026-X). Eastview.

—Korea Guide. rev. ed. LC 77-670017. (Illus.). 392p. 1983. pap. 19.50 (ISBN 0-8048-1466-X, Seoul Int'l. Publishing House). C E Tuttle.

—Korea's Kyongju. LC 79-670108. (Illus.). 379. 1979. pap. 18.20 (ISBN 0-8048-1414-7, Pub. by Seoul Int'l. Publishing House). C E Tuttle.

Bartz, Patricia M. South Korea. (Illus.). 1972. 49.95x (ISBN 0-19-874008-5). Oxford U Pr.

Cho Chung, Kyung, et al. The Korea Guidebook, 1988. 1988. pap. 16.95 (ISBN 0-317-62308-7). HM.

*Chough, Marine Geology of Korean Seas. 157p 1988. text ed. 44.00 (ISBN 0-13-556390-9). P.H.

Chung, Kyung C., et al. Korea Guidebook, 1987. 1987. pap. 14.95 (ISBN 0-395-44092-0). HM.

Compact Guide to Korea. 72p. 1987. pap. 3.50 (ISBN 0-941009-02-5). Hollym Corp. Pubs.

Cox, Keller & Frazier, Raymond L. Buck; a Tennessee Boy in Korea. 1982. 9.95 (ISBN 0-9610818-0-5); pap. 4.95 (ISBN 0-9610818-1-3). Chogie Pubs.

Crowther, Geoff. Korea: A Travel Survival Kit. (Illus.). 224p. (Orig.). 1988. pap. 8.95 (ISBN 0-86442-021-8). Lonely Planet.

Current, Marion E. Looking at Each Other. (Illus.). 96p. 1983. pap. 4.55 (ISBN 0-8048-1415-5, Pub. by Seoul Int'l. Publishing House). C E Tuttle.

Facts about Korea. 292p. 1987. pap. 9.95 (ISBN 0-941009-03-3). Hollym Corp. Pubs.

Fodor's Korea. (Illus.). 160p. 1983. pap. 8.95 traveltex (ISBN 0-679-00968-X). McKay

Fodor's '89 Korea. 1988. pap. 11.95 (ISBN 0-679-01667-8, Fodor). McKay.

Harrap Limited Staff, ed. Korea. 1986. pap. 49.75X (ISBN 0-245-54016-4, Pub. by Harrap Ltd. England). State Mutual Bk.

Hollym Publishers Staff, ed. Compact Guide to Korea (Illus.). 78p. 1986. pap. 4.95 (ISBN 0-89346-269-1). Heian Int'l.

Hooser, Mike. Jet-Setters' Guide to Korea. (Illus.). 657p. (Orig.). 1988. pap. 13.00 (Pub. by Seoul Int'l. Tourist Korea). C E Tuttle.

Insider's Guide to Korea. (Illus.). 192p. 1987. pap. 12.95 (ISBN 0-935161-69-4). Hunter Pub. NY.

Insight Guides Staff. Korea. (Illus.). 378p. 1983. o.p. 18.95 (ISBN 0-13-516633-0); pap. 16.95 (ISBN 0-13-516641-1) P-H.

Joo, Myong-do K. Korean Traditions. (Illus.). 130p. 1981. 18.20 (ISBN 0-8048-1412-0, Pub. by Seoul Int'l. Publishing House). C E Tuttle.

Korea, the Land of Morning Calm. (Asian Guides Ser.). 1988. pap. 9.95 (ISBN 0-8442-9715-1, Passport Bks). Nat'l. Textbk.

Kowalczyk, Robert. Morning Calm: A Journey Through the Korean Countryside. 2nd ed. (Asian Photos Ser.). (Illus.). 60p. 1983. pap. 14.95 (ISBN 0-933704-47-X). Dawn Pr.

Kwan-jo, Lee, photos by. Rhapsody in Nature: Korean Countryside. (Illus.). 120p. 1985. 20.00 (ISBN 0-8048-1433-3, Pub. by Seoul Int'l. Tourist Korea). C E Tuttle.

Kyung Cho, Chung, et al. Korea Guidebook, 1989. (Illus.). 528p. 1988. pap. 16.95 (ISBN 0-395-48678-5). HM.

Lanier, Alison R. Update-South Korea. LC 80-83919. (Country Orientation Ser.). 1982. pap. text ed. 27.50 (ISBN 0933662-33-5). Intercult Pr.

Lee, Chong-Sik. Korea: Land of the Morning Calm. (Illus.). 1988. 34.95 (ISBN 0-87663-693-8). Universe.

McCune, Shannon. Korea's Heritage: A Regional & Social Geography. LC 56-6087. (Illus.). 264p. 1956. 20.00 (ISBN 0-8048-0351-X). C E Tuttle.

McNair, Sylvia. Korea LC 85-23273. (Enchantment of the World Ser.). (Illus.). 127p. (gr. 5-6). 1986. PLB 23.93 (ISBN 0-516-02771-9). Childrens.

Michaud, Sabrina & Michaud, Roland. Korea: A Jade Paradise. (Illus.). 144p. 1981. casebound 45.00 (ISBN 0-86565-020-9). Vendome.

Nilsen, Robert. South Korea Handbook. Morris, Mark, ed. (Illus.). 586p. (Orig.). 1989. pap. 14.95 (ISBN 0-918373-20-4). Moon Pubns CA.

Rucci, Richard B., ed. Living in Korea 3rd, rev. ed. (Illus.). 244p. 1984. pap. 18.00 (ISBN 0-8048-1424-4, Pub. by Seoul Int'l. Publishing House). C E Tuttle.

Seoul. (Times Travel Library). (Illus.). 104p. (Orig.). 1988. pap. 10.95 (ISBN 1-55650-090-4). Hunter Pub NY.

Tourist Map of Korea 32p. 1987. pap. 3.50 (ISBN 0-941009-06-8). Hollym Corp. Pubs.

Winchester, Simon. Korea. (Illus.). 224p. 1988. 17.95 (ISBN 0-13-516626-8). Prentice Hall Pr.

Yoo, Yushin. Korea the Beautiful: Treasures of the Hermit Kingdom. LC 86-83328. (Illus.). 226p. 1987. 24.95 (ISBN 0-942091-01-9). Golden Pond Pr.

KOREA-ECONOMIC CONDITIONS

Adelman, Irma & Robinson, Sherman, Income Distribution Policy in Developing Countries: A Case Study of Korea. LC 76-14269. xx, 346p. 1978. 37.50x (ISBN 0-8047-0925-4). Stanford U Pr.

Adelman, Irma, ed. Practical Approaches to Development Planning: Korea's Second Five-Year Plan. LC 69-19467. 320p. 1969. 32.50x (ISBN 0-8018-1061-2). Johns Hopkins.

Aghevli, Bijan B. & Marquez-Ruarte, Jorge. A Case of Successful Adjustment: Korea's Experience During 1980-84. (Occasional Papers: No. 39). 34p. 1985. pap. 7.50 (ISBN 0-939934-51-5). Int'l Monetary.

Bartz, Patricia M. South Korea. (Illus.). 1972. 49.95x (ISBN 0-19-874008-5). Oxford U Pr.

Bridges, Brian. Korea & the West. 1987. 12.95 (ISBN 0-7102-1110-4, Pub. by Routledge UK). Routledge Chapman & Hall.

Brown, Gilbert T. Korean Pricing Policies & Economic Development in the 1960s. LC 73-8121. pap. 84.00 (ISBN 0-317-19886-6, 2023086). Bks Demand UMI.

'Cho, Lee-Jay & Kim, Yoon H., eds. Economic Development in the Republic of Korea: A Policy Perspective. 750p. 1989. 67.50x (ISBN 0-8133-7773-0). Westview.

Cole, David C. & Lim, Youngil. The Korean Economy: Issues of Development. LC 79-620015. (Korean Research Monograph Ser.: No. 1). pap. 22.50 (ISBN 0-317-27747-2, 2019466). Bks Demand UMI.

Cole, David C. & Park, Yung C. Financial Development in Korea, 1945-1978. (Harvard East Asian Monographs: No. 106). 340p. 1983. text ed. 17.50 (ISBN 0-674-30147-1). Harvard U Pr.

Corey, Kenneth E. Qualitative Planning Methodology: An Application in Development Planning Research to South Korea & Sri Lanka. (Working Paper Ser.: No. 3). 23p. 1985. 3.00 (ISBN 0-913749-08-7). U MD Inst.

Dee, Philippa S. Financial Markets & Economic Development: The Economics & Politics of Korean Financial Reform. 180p. 1986. lib. bdg. 53.50x (ISBN 3-16-345087-3, Pub. by J C B Mohr BRD). Coronet Bks.

Hamilton, Clive. Capitalist Industrialization in Korea. LC 85-8997. (WVSS on East Asia Ser.). 260p. 1985. pap. text ed. 30.50x (ISBN 0-8133-7069-8). Westview.

Hong, Wontack. Factor Supply & Factor Intensive of Trade in Korea. 251p. 1976. text ed. 12.00x (ISBN 0-8248-0539-9). UH Pr.

—Trade, Distortions & Employment Growth in Korea. 410p. 1979. 17.50x (ISBN 0-8248-0678-6, Korea Devel. Inst.). UH Pr.

—Trade, Growth, & Income Distribution: The Experience of the Republic of Korea. (Working paper Ser.: No. 3). 84p. 1981. 5.00 (ISBN 0-318-16160-5). Overseas Dev. Council.

Hong, Wontack & Krueger, Anne O., eds. Trade & Development in Korea. 253p. 1975. text ed. 12.00x (ISBN 0-8248-0536-4). UH Pr.

Hyde, Georgie D. South Korea: Education, Culture & Economy. LC 87-34908. 320p. 1988. 49.95 (ISBN 0-312-01666-2). St. Martin.

Jones, Leroy & Sakong, Il. Government, Business, & Enterprenuship in Economic Development: The Korean Case. (East Asian Monographs: No. 91). 1979. 17.50x (ISBN 0-674-35791-4). Harvard U Pr.

Jung, Kim D. Mass-Participatory Economy: A Democratic Alternative for Korea. 94p. (Orig.). 1985. lib. bdg. 19.75 (ISBN 0-8191-4920-9, Ctr Int'l Affairs Harvard Univ.); pap. text ed. 8.50 (ISBN 0-8191-4921-7). U Pr. of Amer.

Kim, Chungsoo. Evolution of Comparative Advantage: The Factor Proportions Theory in a Dynamic Perspective. 125p. 1983. lib. bdg. 52.00x (ISBN 3-16-344621-3, Pub. by J C.B Mhr BRD). Coronet Bks.

Kim, Kyong-Dong. Man & Society in Korea's Economic Growth: Sociological Studies. 226p. 1979. text ed. 16.00x (ISBN 0-8248-0965-3, Pub. by Seoul U Pr). UH Pr.

Korea: Development in a Global Context. 292p. 1984. 15.00 (ISBN 0-8213-0459-3, BK 0459). World Bank.

Korea: The Management of External Liabilities. (Country Study Ser.). 112p. 1988. 6.50 (ISBN 0-8213-1026-7, BK1026). World Bank.

Kubo, Yuji, et al. Multisector Models & the Analysis of Alternative Development Strategies: An Application to Korea. (Working Paper: No. 563). 52p. 1983. 6.95 (ISBN 0-8213-0174-8, WP 0563). World Bank.

Kuznets, Paul W. Economic Growth & Structure in Republic of Korea. LC 76-45407. (Illus.). 1977. 30.00x (ISBN 0-300-02019-8). Yale U Pr.

Lim, Youngil. Government Policy & Private Enterprise: Korean Experience in Industrialization. LC 81-84218. (Korea Research Monographs: No. 6). 1981. pap. 4.00x (ISBN 0-912966-36-X). IEAS.

Lindauer, David. Labor Market Behavior in the Republic of Korea: An Analysis of Wages & Their Impact on the Economy. (Working Paper Ser.: No. 641). 94p. 1984. 6.95 (ISBN 0-8213-0380-5, WP 0641). World Bank.

Luedde-Neurath, Richard. Import Controld & Export-Oriented Development: A Reassessment of the South Korean Case. (Special Studies on East Asia). 250p. 1985. pap. text ed. 29.50x softcover (ISBN 0-8133-7080-9). Westview.

Mason, Edward S. The Economic & Social Modernization of the Republic of Korea. (Harvard East Asian Monographs: Vol. 92). 500p. 1980. 20.00x (ISBN 0-674-23175-9). Harvard U Pr.

Merrill, John. D.P.R. Korea: Politics, Economics & Society. (Marxist Regimes Ser.). 220p. 1987. 35.00 (ISBN 0-86187-424-2, Pub. by Pinter Pubs UK); pap. 12.50 (ISBN 0-86187-425-0). Columbia U Pr.

'Michell, Tony. From a Developing to a Newly Industrialised country: The Republic of Korea, 1961-82. International Labour Office Staff, ed. (Employment, Adjustment & Industrialisation Ser.: No. 6). vi, 180p. pap. 21.00 (ISBN 92-2-106396-8). Int'l Labour Office.

Moskowitz, Karl, ed. From Patron to Partner: The Development of U.S.Korean Business & Trade Relations. LC 83-48028. 256p. 1984. 28.00x (ISBN 0-669-06837-3).Lesington Bks.

'Pal-Yong Moon & Bong-Soon Kang. Trade, Exchange Rate, & Agricultural Pricing Policies in the Republic of Korea. (Comparative Studies: The Political Economy of Agricultural Pricing Policy). 326p. 1989. 19.95 (ISBN 0-8213-1211-1, BK1211). World Bank.

Pares, Susan. Korean Western Culture in Contrast Crosscurrents. (Illus.). 188p. 1985. pap. 5.00 (ISBN 0-8048-1429-5, Pub. by Seoul Int'l Tourist Korea). C E Tuttle.

Park, Chong Kee Social Security in Korea: An Approach to Socio-Economic Development. 1975. text ed. 10.00x (ISBN 0-8248-0537-2). UH Pr.

Park, Chong Kee, ed Essays on the Korean Economy: Vol. III—Macroeconomic & Industrial Development in Korea. 424p. 1981. text ed. 15.00x (ISBN 0-8248-0754-5). UH Pr.

—Essays on the Korean Economy: Vol. IV—Human Resources & Social Development in Korea. 383p. 1981. text ed. 15.00x (ISBN 0-8248-0755-3). UH Pr.

Park, W.H. & Enos, J. L. The Adoption & Diffusion of Imported Technology: The Case of Korea. 224p. 1985. 55.00 (ISBN 0-7099-2030-X, Pub. by Croom Helm UK). Routledge Chapman & Hall.

Repetto, Robert, et al. Economic Development, Population Policy & Demographic Transition in the Republic of Korea. (Harvard East Asian Monographs: No. 93). 200p. 1981. text ed. 16.50x (ISBN 0-674-23311-5). Harvard U Pr.

Shinohara, Miyohei, et al. Japanese & Korean Experiences in Managing Development. (Working Paper Ser.: No. 574). 98p. 1984. 6.95 (ISBN 0-8213-0233-7, WP 0574). World Bank.

Suh, Sang Chul. Growth & Structural Changes in the Korean Economy, 1910-1940. (Harvard East Asian Monographs: No. 83). 1978. 15.00x (ISBN 0-674-36439-2). Harvard U Pr.

Westphal, Larry E. Ecports of Capital Goods & Related services from the Republic of Korea. (Working Paper ser.: No. 659). 64p. 1984. 6.95 (ISBN 0-8213-0310-4, WP 0659). World Bank.

Westphal, Larry E. & Rhee, Yung W. Korean Industrial Competence: Where It Came From. (Working Paper: No. 469). 76p. 1981. 5.00 (ISBN 0-686-36176-8, WP-0469). World Bank.

Whitehill, Arthur M., ed Doing Business in Korea: Challenge in the Morning Calm. 144p. 1987. 34.50 (ISBN 0-89397-276-2). Nichols Pub.

Wijnbergen, S. Van. Short-Run Macro-Economic Adjustment Policies in South Korea: A Quantitative Analysis. LC 82-8408. (World Bank Staff Working Papers: No. 510). (Orig.). 1982. pap. 10.95 (ISBN 0-8213-0000-8, WP0510). World Bank.

World Bank Staff. Korea: Managing the Industrial Transition, Vol. 1-Conduct of Industrial Policy O-S equal O-P. 1987. 12.00 (ISBN 0-8213-0887-4, BK0887). World Bank.

—Korea: Managing the Industrial Transition, Vol. 2-Selected Topics & Case Studies. 1987. 12.95 (ISBN 0-8213-0893-9, BK0893). World Bank.

—Korea: Problems & Issues in a Rapidly Expanding Economy. LC 76-17238.(A World Bank Country Economic Report Ser). (Illus.). 296p. 1976. 22.95x (ISBN 0-8018-1864-8). Johns Hopkins.

Yung Whee Rhee, et al Korea's Competitive Edge: Managing Entry into World Markets. LC 84-47956. 176p. 1984. text ed. 22.95x (ISBN 0-8018-3266-7). Johns Hopkins.

Yusuf, Shahid & Peters, Kyle, Capital Accumulation & Economic Growth: The Korean Paradigm. LC 85-648. (Staff Working Paper: No. 712). 64p. 1985. 6.95 (ISBN 0-318-11951-X, WP0712). World Bank.

KOREA-ECONOMIC POLICY

*Alam, M. Shahid. Governments & Markets in Economic Development Strategies: Lessons from Korea, Taiwan, & Japan. 1989. lib. bdg. 39.95 (ISBN 0-275-92935-3, C2935). Praeger.

KOREA-FOREIGN RELATIONS

Barnds, William J., ed. The Two Koreas in East Asian Affairs. LC 75-27379. 216p. 1976. 30.00x (ISBN 0-8147-0988-5). NYU Pr.

*Barnett, Angele. How to Understand Our Relationship with Korea. 77p (Orig.). 1988. pap. text ed. 11.95 (ISBN 0-925421-00-6). Amer Intercultural.

Bayard, Thomas O. & Young, Soo-Gil, eds. Economic Relations Between the United States & Korea: Conflict or Cooperation? LC 88-8257. (Special Report Ser.: No. 8). 192p. (Orig.). 1989. pap. 12.95 (ISBN 0-88132-068-4). Inst Int'l Eco.

Bermudez, Joseph. North Korean Special Forces. 160p. 1988. 60.00 (ISBN 0-7106-0528-5). Janes Info Group.

Bird, Isabella L. Korea & Her Neighbours. (Pacific Basin Bks.). 400p. (Orig.). 1985. pap 14.95 (ISBN 0-7103-0135-9, Kegan Paul). Routledge Chapman & Hall.

—Korea & Her Neighbours, 2 vols. in 1. LC 85-52348. (Illus.). 664p. 1986. pap. 11.50 (ISBN 0-8048-1489-9). C E Tuttle.

Bridges, Brian. Korea & the West. 1987. 12.95 (ISBN 0-7102-1110-4, Pub. by Routledge UK). Routledge Chapman & Hall.

*Burnett, Scott S., ed. Korean-American Relations: Documents Pertaining to the Far Eastern Diplomacy of the United States, Vol. III: The Period of Diminishing Influence, 1896-1905. LC 51-1111. 320p. 1989. text ed. 24.00x (ISBN 0-8248-1202-6). UH Pr.

Chiu, Hungdah & Downen, Robert, eds. Multi-System Nations & International Law, International Status of Germany, Korea & China. LC 81-85785. (Occasional Papers-Reprints Series in Contemporary Asian Studies, No. 8-1981). 203p. (Orig.). 1981. pap. text ed. 5.00 (ISBN 0-942182-44-8). Occasional Papers.

*Chung-In Moon, et al. Alliance under Tension: The Evolution of South KOrean-U.S. Relations. 229p. 1988. text ed. 35.00x (ISBN 0-8133-0835-6). Westview.

Clough, Ralph N. Embattled Korea: The Rivalry for International Support. 418p. 1987. 29.95 (ISBN 0-317-60082-6). Westview.

Dam, Kenneth, ed. Korea at the Crossroads. 72p. 1987. pap. 4.95 (ISBN 0-87609-027-7). Coun Foreign.

Deuchler, Martina. Confucian Gentlemen & Barbarian Envoys: The Opening of Korea, 1875-1885. LC 76-57228. (Royal Asiatic Society Ser). 324p. 1978. 27.50x (ISBN 0-295-95552-X). U of Wash Pr.

Fukuda, Tsuneari, ed. Future of Japan & the Korean Peninsula. Jahng, K., tr. from Japanese. LC 78-71337. (Illus.). 14.40x (ISBN 0-930878-14-0). Hollym Int'l.

Ha, Young-Sun. Nuclear Proliferation, World Order, & Korea. 221p. 1979. text ed. 16.00x (ISBN 0-8248-0966-1, Pub. by Seoul U Pr). UH Pr.

*Hinton, H. C., et al. The Changing Requirements for Korean Security: The Next Ten Years. (Institute for Foreign Policy Analysis Ser.). 84p. 1988. pap. text ed. 9.95 (ISBN 0-08-036727-5, Pub. by Pergamon-Brasseys). Pergamon.

Kearney, Adrienne A, et al. South Korea: The Politicization of Trade Policy. 170p. Date not set.

pap. text ed. 50.00 (ISBN 1-55813-017-9, HI-3836-P). hudson Inst.

Koh, Byung C. The Foreign Policy Systems of North & South Korea. LC 82-23807. 296p. 1984. lib. bdg. 40.00 (ISBN 0-520-04805-9). U of Cal Pr.

Koo, Youngok & Sung-Joo Han. The Foreign Policy of the Republic of Korea. LC 84-1841. (Studies of the East Asian Institute, columbia University). 304p. 1984. 29.50x (ISBN 0-231-05882-9). Columbia U Pr.

Kwak, tai-Hwan & Chay, John, eds. U.S.-Korean Relations, 1882-1982. 433p. 1983. lib. bdg. 36.00x (ISBN 0-86531-608-2). Westview.

Lee, Yur-Bok & Patterson, Wayne, eds. One Hundred Years of Korean-American Relations, 1882-1982. LC 84-24040. 202p. 1986. 24.95 (ISBN 0-8173-0265-4). U of Ala Pr.

Morley, James W. Japan & Korea: America's Allies in the Paific. LC 81-4196. (Illus.). 152p. 1981. Repr. of 1965 ed. lib. bdg. 35.00x (ISBN 0-313-23033-1, MOJK). Greenwood.

Moskowitz, Karl, ed. From Patron to Partner: The Development of U.S.Korean Business & Trade Relations. LC 83-48028. 256p. 1984. 28.00x (ISBN 0-669-06837-3). Lexington Bks.

Nam, Joo-Hong. America's Commitment to South Korea: The First Decade of the Nixon Doctrine. (LSE Monographs in International Studies). (Illus.). 256p. 1986. 39.50 (ISBN 0-521-26765-X). Cambridge U Pr.

Park, Choon-Ho & Pae, Jae S. Korean International Law. (Korean Research Monographs: No. 4). 53p. 1982. pap. 4.00x (ISBN 0-912966-40-8). IEAS.

Park, Jae K. & Koh, Byung C., eds. The Foreign Relations of North Korea: A New Perspective. LC 87-13269. 490p. 1987. 39.50 (ISBN 0-8133-0569-1). Westview.

Sakamoto, Yoshikazu. Korea As a World Order Issue. (Working Papers: No. 3). 1978. pap. 2.00 (ISBN 0-911646-07-8). World Policy.

Scalapino, Robert A. The United States & Korea: Looking Ahead. (The Washington Papers: Vol. VII, No. 69). 88p. (Orig.). 1979. Pub. by CSIS). U Pr of Amer.

Scalapino, Robert A. & Lee, Hongkoo, eds. Korea U. S. Relations: The Politics of Trade & Security. (Research Papers & Policy Studies: No. 25). 256p. (Orig.). 1989. pap. 17.00 (ISBN 1-55729-005-9). IEAS.

—North Korea in a Regional & Global Context. LC 85-81190. (Korea Research Monograph: No. 11). xviii, 404p. (Orig.). 1986. pap. 20.00 (ISBN 0-912966-82-3). IEAS.

Stueck, William W., Jr. The Road to Confrontation: American Policy Toward China & Korea, 1947-1950. LC 80-11818. (Illus.). ix, 326p. 1981. pap 10.95x (ISBN 0-8078-4080-7). U of NC Pr.

Sung-joo, Han & Myers, Robert J., eds. Korea: The Year 2000. LC 87-22712. (Ethick & Foreign Policy Ser.: Vol. 5). (Illus.). 284p. (Orig.). 1988. lib. bdg. 30.00 (ISBN 0-8191-6668-5, Carn Counc Intrntl); pap. text ed. 16.75 (ISBN 0-8191-6669-3). U Pr of Amer.

Sunoo, Harold H. America's Dilemma in Asia: The Case of South Korea. LC 78-24029. 224p. 1979. 22.95x (ISBN 0-88229-357-5). Nelson-Hill.

Swartout. Robert R., Jr. Mandarins, Gunboats, & Power Politics: Owen Nickerson Denny & International Rivalries in Korea. LC 79-22242. (Asian Studies at Hawaii: No. 25). 1980. pap. text ed. 10.75x (ISBN 0-8248-0681-6). UH Pr.

Yung Whee Rhee, et al. Korea's Competitive Edge: Managing Entry into World Markets. LC 84-47956. 176p. 1984. text ed. 22.95x (ISBN 0-8018-3266-7). Johns Hopkins.

KOREA-HISTORY

see also Korean War, 1950-1953

Behl, Roy, et al. Public Finance During the Korean Modernization Process. (Harvard East Asian Monographs: No. 107). 1985. text ed. 15.00x (ISBN 0-674-72233-7, Pub. by Coun East Asian Stud). Harvard U Pr.

Billings, Peggy. Fire Beneath the Frost. LC 83-16525. (Illus.). 88p. (Orig.). 1984. pap. 5.95 (ISBN 0-377-00135-X). Friendship Pr.

Bird, Isabella L. Korea & Her Neighbours, 2 vols. in 1. LC 85-52348. (Illus.). 664p. 1986. pap. 11.50 (ISBN 0-8048-1489-9). C E Tuttle.

Bohm, Fred C. & Swartout, Robert R., Jr., eds. Naval Surgeon in Yi Korea: The Journal of George W. Woods. LC 84-80605. (Korea Research Monographs: No. 10). (Illus.). 137p. (Orig.). 1984. pap. text ed. 6.00x (ISBN 0-912966-68-8). IEAS.

Choe Ching Young. The Rule of the Taewon'gun, 1864-1873: Restoration in Yi Korea. LC 73-183975. (East Asian Monographs Ser: No. 45). 1972. pap. 11.00x (ISBN 0-674-78030-2). Harvard U Pr.

Choi, Woonsang. Korea: A Chronology & Fact Book. (World Chronology Ser.). 1983. lib. bdg. 8.50 (ISBN 0-379-16319-5). Oceana.

Choy, Bong-Youn. Korea: A History. LC 73-147180. (Illus.). 1971. 21.50 (ISBN 0-8048-0249-1). C E Tuttle.

Clark, Donald N. Christianity in Modern Korea. LC 86-9092. (Asian Agenda report: No. 5). 70p. (Orig.). 1986. lib. bdg. 14.25 (ISBN 0-8191-5384-2, Pub. by the Asia Soc); pap. text ed. 5.25 (ISBN 0-8191-5385-0). U Pr of Amer.

Covell, Jon C. Korea's Cultural Roots. (Illus.). 122p. 1984. 19.95 (ISBN 0-89346-222-5). Heian Int'l.

Covell, Jon C. & Covell, Alan C. Korean Impact on Japanese Culture: Japan's Hidden History. LC 83-81484. (Illus.). 112p. 1984. 19.50x (ISBN 0-930878-34-5). Hollym Int'l.

Cumings, Bruce. The Two Koreas. LC 84-81643. (Headline Ser.: 269). (Illus.). 80p. 1984. 4.00 (ISBN 0-87124-092-0). Foreign Policy.

Cumings, Bruce, ed. Child of Conflict: The Korean-American Relationship 1945-1953. LC 82-48871. (Publications on Asia of the School of International Studies: No. 37). 352p. 1983. 25.00x (ISBN 0-295-95995-9). U of Wash Pr.

De Bary, William T. & Haboush, Jahyun K., eds. The Rise of Neo-Confucianism in Korea. 512p. 1985. 45.00x (ISBN 0-231-06052-1). Columbia U pr.

Deuchler, Martina. Confucian Gentlemen & Barbarian Envoys: The Opening of Korea, 1875-1885. LC 76-57228. (Royal Asiatic Society Ser.). 324p. 1978. 27.50x (ISBN 0-295-95552-X). U of Wash Pr.

Ginsburgs, George K. & KIm, Roy U. calendar of Diplomatic Affairs Democratic People's Republic of Korea 1945-1975. 1977. 27.50 (ISBN 0-918542-00-6). Symposia Pr.

Goodrich, Leland M. Korea: A Study of U. S. Policy in the United Nations. LC 78-24120. 1979. Repr. of 1956 ed. lib. bdg. 35.00x (ISBN 0-313-20825-5, GOKO). Greenwood.

Griffis, William E. Corea, the Hermit Nation. rev., 9th, enl. ed. LC 74-158615. Repr. of 1911 ed. 37.50 (ISBN 0-404-02916-7). AMS Pr.

Grpta, Alka. U. N. Peacekeeping Activities in Korea: A Study of India's Role, 1947-1953. 1977. 11.00x (ISBN 0-88386-850-4). South Asia Bka.

Haboush, Jahyun K. A Heritage of Kings: One Man's Monarchy in the Confucian World. (Studies in Oriental Culture: No. 21). 304p. 1988. 32.50 (ISBN 0-231-06656-2). Columbia U Pr.

Halliday, Jon & Cumings, Bruce. Korea: The Unknown War. LC 88-42717. (Ills.). 224p. 1988. 19.95 (ISBN 0-394-55366-7). Pantheon.

Han, Woo-Keun. The History of Korea. Mintz, Grafton K., ed. Lee, Kyung-Shik, tr. from Korean. (Illus.). 546p. 1971. (Eastwest Ctr); pap. text ed. 11.95 (ISBN 0-8248-0334-5). UH Pr.

Heinl, Robert D. Victory at High Tide: The Inchon-Seoul Campaign. 16.95 (ISBN 0-405-13282-4). Ayer Co Pubs.

Henthorn, william E. History of Korea. LC 75-143511. 1971. 17.00 (ISBN 0-02-914460-4); pap. text ed. 11.95 (ISBN 0-02914610-0). Free Pr.

Hong, Wontack & Krueger, Anne O., eds. Trade & Development in Korea. 253p. 1975. text ed. 12.00x (ISBN 0-8248-0536-4). UH Pr.

Hwang, In K. The Korean Reform Movement of the 1880's: Transition in Intra-Asian Relations. LC 78-290. 1978. text ed. 16.25 (ISBN 0-87073-974-3). Schenkman Bks Inc.

—One Korea via Permanent Neutrality: Peaceful Management of Korean Unification. 200p. (Orig.). 1986. text ed. 18.95 (ISBN 0-87047-017-5). Schenkman Bks. Inc.

Kang, Wi J. Religion & Politics in Korea under the Japanese Rule. LC 86-18262. (Studies in Asian Thought & Religion: Vol. 5). 1987. lib. bdg. 39.95x (ISBN 0-88946-056-6). E Mellen.

Kim, Edward. Facts about Korea. (Illus.). 230p. 1986. pap. 9.95 (ISBN 0-89346-268-3). Heian Int'l.

Kim, Jeong-Hak. The Prehistory of Korea. Pearson, Richard J. & Pearson, Kazue, trs. from Japanese. 8248-0552-6). UH Pr.

Kim, Joungwon A. Divided Korea: The Politics of Development, 1945-1972. LC 74-24936. (East Asian Monographs: No. 59). 330p. 1975. text ed. 21.00x (ISBN 0-674-21287-8). Harvard U Pr.

Kim, Key-Hiuk. The Last Phase of the East Asian World Order: Korea, Japan, & the Chinese Empire, 1860-1882. LC 77-83106. (Center for Japanese Studies, UC Berkeley: No. 16). 1979. 40.00x (ISBN 0-520-03556-9). U of Cal Pr.

Kim, Richard E. Lost Names: Scenes from a Boyhood in Japanese-Occupied Korea. 224p. (YA) 1988. 14.95 (ISBN 0-87663-678-4). Universe.

Kirkbride, Wayne A. DMZ: A Story of the Panmunjom Axe Murder. 2nd ed. LC 84-80059. (Illus.). 137p. 1984. 9.95x (ISBN 0-930878-40-X). Hollym Int'l.

Knox, Donald. The Korean War: Pusan to Chosin: An Oral History. LC 85-8567. (Illus.). 512p. 1985. 24.95 (ISBN 0-15-147288-2). HarBraceJ.

Lee, Ki-Baik. A New History of Korea. Wagner, Edward W. & Schultz, Edward J., trs. from Korean LC 83-246. (Harvard-Yenching Institute Ser). (Illus.). 474p. 1984. text ed. 25.00x (ISBN 0-674-61575-1) Harvard U Pr.

—A New History of Korea. Wagner, Edward W. & Schultz, Edward J., trs. from Korean. LC 83-246. (Harvard-Yenching Institute Publications). (Illus.). 516p. 1988. pap. text ed. 12.95 (ISBN 0-674-61576-X). Harvard U Pr.

Lum, Peter. Six Centuries in East Asia: China, Japan & Korea from the 14th Century to 1912. LC 72-12582. (Illus.). 288p. 1973. 22.95 (ISBN 0-87599-183-1). S G Phillips.

McKenzie, Frederick A. Korea's Fight for Freedom. LC 76-111784. Repr. of 1920 ed. 19.45 (ISBN 0-404-04137-X). AMS Pr.

'Michell, Tony. From & Developing to a Newly Industrialised Country: The Republic of Korea, 1961-82. International Labour Office Staff, ed. (Employment, Adjustment & Industrialisation Ser.: No. 6). vi, 180p. (Orig.). 1988. pap. 21.00 (ISBN 92-2-106396-8). Intl Labour Office.

'Nahm, Andrew C. Korea: Tradition & Transformation; A History of the Korean People. LC 86-81681. 583P. 1988. 44.50 (isbn 0-930878-56-6). Hollym Int'l.

Nahm, Andrew C.A Panorama of Five Thousand Years: Korean History. rev. ed. LC 81-84202. (Illus.). 125p. 1983.22.50x (ISBN 0-930878-23-X). Hollym Int'l.

—A Panorama of Five Thousand Years: Korean History. (Illus.). 126p. 1984. 19.95 (ISBN 0-89346-248-9). Heian Int'l.

Rees, Davis. Short History of Modern Korea. (Illus.). 216p. 1988. 16.95 (ISBN 0-87052-575-1). Hippocrene Bks.

'Robinson, Michael E. Cultural Nationalism in Colonial Korea, 1920-1925. LC 88-18804. 240p. 1989. 25.00 (ISBN 0-295-96600-9). U of Wash Pr.

Sandusky, Michael C. America's Parallel. LC 83-61934. (Illus.). 487p. 1983. 19.95 (ISBN 0-913513-00-8). Old Dominion Pr.

Song Minako I. & Matsui, Masato, eds. Japanese Sources on Korea in Hawaii. LC 79-55927. (Occassional Papers: No. 10). 151p. (Orig.). 1980. pap. 8.00 (ISBN 0-917536-14-2). UH Manoa CKS.

Swartout, Robert R., Jr. Mandarins, Gunboats, & Power Politics: Owen Nickerson denny & International Rivalries in Korea. LC 79-22242. (Asian studies at Hawaii: No. 25). 1980. pap. text ed. 10.75x (ISBN 0=8248-0681-6). UH Pr.

Tai sung An. North Korea in Transition: From Dictatorship to Dynasty. LC 82-15866. (Contributions in Political Science Ser.: No. 95). xi, 212p. 1983. lib. bdg. 35.00 (ISBN 0-313-23638-0, ANK/). Greenwood.

U.S. Congress, Senate Committee on Foreign Relations. The United States & the Korean Problem, Documents, 1943-1953. LC 72-38089. Repr. of 1953 ED. 20.00 (ISBN 0-404-56962-5). AMS Pr.

Wagner, Edward W. The Literati Purges: Political Conflict in Early Yi Korea. LC 74-21777. (East Asian Monographs: No.58). 200p. 1975. text ed. 20.00x (ISBN 0-674-53618-5). Harvard U Pr.

KOREA-JUVENILE LITERATURE

Athby, Gwynneth. A Family in South Korea. (Families the World over Ser.). (Illus.). 32p. (gr. 2-5). 1987. 8.95 (ISBN 0-8225-1675-6). Lerner Pubns.

Burkholder, Ruth C. Won Gil's Secret Diary. LC 83-16529. (Illus.). 14p. (Orig.). (gr. 1-3). 1984. pap. 4.95 (ISBN 0-377-00138-4). Friendship Pr.

Farley, Carol. Korea: A Land Divided. LC 83-7789. (Discovering Our Heritage Ser.). (Illus.). 144p. (gr. 5 up). 1983. PLB 12.95 (ISBN 0-87518-244-5). Dillon.

Haskins, Jim. Count Your Way Through Korea. (Count Your Way Bks.). (Illus.). 24p. (gr. 1-4). 1989. 10.95 (ISBN 0-87614-348-6). Carolrhoda Bks.

'Lerner Publications, Department of Geography Staff., South Korea in Pictures. (Visual Geography Ser.). (Illus.). 64p. (gr. 5 up). 1989. PLB 9.95 (ISBN 0-8225-1868-6). Lerner Pubns.

Lye, Keith. Take a Trip to South Korea. (Take a Trip to Ser.). (Illus.). 32p. (gr. 1-6). 1985. PLB 10.90 (ISBN 0-531-10012-X). Watts.

Moffett, Eileen. Korean Ways. (Illus.). 55p. (gr. K up). 1986. 9.00 (ISBN 0-8048-7013-6, Pub. by Seoul Intl Tourist Korea). C E Tuttle.

North Korea. (Let's Visit Places & Peoples of the World Ser.). (Illus.). (gr. 5 op). 1988. 13.95 (ISBN 0-7910-0157-1). Chelsea Hse.

KOREA-POLITICS AND GOVERNMENT

Adams, Edward B. Palaces of Seoul. 2nd, rev. ed. LC 72-77238. (Illus.). 220p. 1982. pap. 13.00 (ISBN 0-8048-1416-3, Pub. by Seoul int'l Publishing House). C E Tuttle.

Athevli, Bijan B. & Matquez-Ruarte, Jorge. A Case of Successful adjustment: Korea's Experience During 1980-84. (Occasional Papers: No. 39). 34p. 1985. pap. 7.50 (ISBN 0-939934-51-5). Int'l Monetary.

An, Tai Sung. North Korea: A Political Handbook. LC 83-16307. (Illus). 294p. 1983. lib. bdg. 45.00 (ISBN 0-8420-2205-8). Scholarly Res Inc.

Atia Watch staff. Human Rights in Korea. 364p. 1986. 15.00 (ISBN 0-938579-74-6). Fund Free Expression.

Brandt, Vincent S. A Korean Village Between Farm & Sea. LC 73-162857. (East Asian Ser: No. 65). (Illus.). Repr. of 1971 ed. 50.80 (ISBN 0-8357-9163-7, 2017013). Bks Demand UMI.

Bridges, Brian. Korea & the West. 1987. 12.95 (ISBN 0-7102-1110-4, Pub. by Routledge UK). Routledge Chapman & Hall.

Brown, Gilbert T. Korean Pricing Policies & Economic Development in the 1960s. LC 73-8121. pap. 84.00 (ISBN 0-317-19886-6, 2023086). Bks Demand UMI.

Chong-Sik Lee, ed. & tr. from Korean. Materials on Korean Communism, 1945-1947. LC 77-80003. (Occasional Papers: No. 7). 268p. 1977. pap. 6.00x (ISBN 0-917536-11-8). UH Manoa CKS.

'Haas, Michael, ed. Korean Reunification: Alternative Pathways. 176p. 1989. lib. bdg. 39.95 (ISBN 0-275-93148-X, C3148). Praeger.

Hinton, Harold C. Korea under New Leadership: The Fifth Republic. 304p. 1983. lib. bdg. 36.95 (ISBN 0-275-91006-7, C1006); pap. 16.95 (ISBN 0-275-91571-9, B1571). Praeger.

Hyung Wook Kim & Park, Saul. Korean CIA Chief's Testimony-Revolution & idol, Vol. 1: Story Behind Korean May 16 Revolution & Anti-Revolution. 304p. (Orig., Korean.). 1984. pap. text ed. 15.00 (ISBN 0-911987-00-2). Korean Independent.

—Korean CIA Chief's Testimony-Revolution & Idol, Vol. 3: Secret Story of Chung Hee Park Era. 345p. (Orig., Korean.). 1984. pap. 15.00 (ISBN 0-911987-02-9)., Korean Independent.

Jones, Leroy & Sakong, Il. Government, Business, & Entrepreneurship in Economic Development: The Korean Case. (East Asian Monographs: No.91). 1979. 17.50x. (ISBN 0-674-35791-4). Harvard U Pr.

Ju, Woo J. Human Rights & Democracy in Korea. 160p. 1988. 11.95 (ISBN 0-8062-3312-5). Carlton.

Jung, Kim D. Mass-Participatory Economy: A Democratic Alternative for Korea. 94p. (Orig.). 1985. lib. bdg. 19.75 (ISBN 0-8191-4920-9, Ctr Int'l. Affairs Harvard Univ); pap. text ed. 8.50 (ISBN 0-8191-4921-7). U Pr of Amer.

Kim, Chong L. & Kihl, Young W. Representation & Legislative Culture in Constituencies: A Study of Linkage Forths in Korea, No. 13. LC 83-620939. 30p. 1983. write for ingo. U Iowa law.

Kim, Chong-Lim & Pai, Seong-Tong. Legislative Process in Korea. (The Institute of Social sciences Korean Studies Ser.: No. 3). 343p. 1981. text ed. 18.00x (ISBN 0-8248-0933-5). UH Pr.

Kim, Chong Lim, et al. The Legislative Connection: The Politics of Representation in Kenya, Korea & Turkey. LC 83-20725. (Duke Press Policy Studies). (Illus.). xvii, 237p. 1984. 39.75 (ISBN 0-8223-0534-8). Duke.

Kim, Hak-Joon. The Unification Policy of South & North Korea: A Comparative Study. 341p. 1984. text ed. 18.00x (ISBN 0-8248-0964-5, Pub. by Seul U Pr). UH Pr.

'Kim, Ilpyong J. & Kihl, Young W., eds. Political Change in South Korea. LC 88-11069. 263P. 1988. text ed. 27.95x (ISBN 0-943852-60-9, Pub. by PWPA). Paragon Hse.

Kim, Jong-Min. Politik in Suedkorea zwischen Tradition und Fortschritt: Krisensequenzen in einem Schwellenland. (European University Studies: No. 31, Vol. 31). (Ger.). 1983. 52.30 (ISBN 3-8204-5992-8). P Lang Pubs.

Kim, Se-Jin. Politics of Miltary Revolution in Korea. LC 71-123101. (Illus.). xv, 239p. 1971. 22.50 (ISBN 0-8078-1168-8). U of NC Pr.

Kwak, Tae-Hwan, et al, eds. Korean Reunification: New Perspectives & Approaches. 525p. 1985. 46.00 (ISBN 0-8133-0217-X). Westview.

Lee, Chong-Sik. Japan & Korea: The Political Dimension. LC 85-5455. (Publication Ser.: 318). (Illus.). xiv, 234p. 1985. lib. bdg. 24.95x (ISBN 0-8179-8181-0). Hoover Ins't Pr.

Lee, Hahn-Been. Korea: Time, Change & Administration LC 67-28036. (Illus.). 253p. 1968.

14.00x (ISBN 0-8248-0072-9, Eastwest Ctr). UH Pr.

Lim, Youngil. Government Policy & Private Enterprise: Korean Experience in Industrialization. LC 81-84218. (Korea Research Monographs: No. 6). 1981. pap. 4.00x (ISBN 0-912966-36-X). IEAS.

McCormack, Gavan, et al, eds. Korea, North & South: The Deepening Crisis. LC 78-4503. 1980. pap. 5.50 (ISBN 0-85345-531-7). Monthly Rev.

McCune, George M. Korea Today. LC 82-20290. xxi, 372p. 1982. Repr. of 1950 ed. lib. bdg. 48.50x (ISBN 0-313-23446-9, MCKT). Greenwood.

MacDonald, Donald S. The Koreans: Contemporary Politics & Society. 316P. 1988. 32.50 (ISBN 0-8133-0515-2). Westview.

Matray, Jamies A. The Reluctant crusade: American Foreign Policy in Korea, 1941-1950. LC 85-1079. 368p. 1985. text ed. 30.00x (ISBN 0-8248-0973-4). UH Pr.

Merrill, John. D.P.R. Korea: Politics, Economics & Society. (Marxist Regimes Ser.). 220p. 1987. 35.00 (ISBN 0-86187-425-0). Columbia U Pr.

'Merril, John. Korea: The Peninsular Origins of the War. LC 85-40990. (Illus.). 240p. 1989. 32.50x (ISBN 0-87413-300-9). U Delaware Pr.

'Nam. Koon W. South Korean Politics: The Search for Political Consensus & Stability. 384p. 1989. lib. bdg. 36.50 (ISBN 0-8191-7507-2). U Pr of Amer.

Oliver, Robert T. Syngman Rhee. LC 72-13864. (Illus.). 380p. 1973. Repr. of 1954 ed. lib. bdg. 35.00x (ISBN 0-8371-67590-0, OLSR). Greenwood.

Pae, Sung M. Testing Democratic Theories in Korea. 318p. 1986. lib. bdg. 30.50 (ISBN 0-8191-5379-6); pap. text ed. 16.25 (ISBN 0-8191-5380-X). U Pr of Amer.

Pak. Chi-Young. Political Opposition in Korea, 1945-1960. (The Institute of Social Sciences Korean Studies: No. 2). 251p. 1980. text ed. 18.00x (ISBN 0-8248-0932-7). UH Pr.

Palais, James B. Politics & Policy in Traditional Korea, 1864-1876. (East Asian Monographs). 288p. 1976. text ed. 22.00x (ISBN 0-674-19058-0). Harvard U Pr.

Park, Chong Kee. Social Security in Korea: An Approach to Socio-Economic Development. 1975. text ed. 10.00x (ISBN 0-8248-0537-2). UH Pr.

Reve, W. D. The Republic of Korea: A Political & Economic Study. LC 79-1979. Repr. of 1963 ed. lib. bdg. 35.00x (ISBN 0-313-21265-1, rerk). Greenwood.

'Robinson, Michael E. Cultural Nationaliam in Colonial Korea, 1920-19225. LC 88-18804. 240p. 1989. 25.00 (ISBN 0-295-96600-9). U of Wash Pr.

Sakamoto, Yoshikiazu. Korea As a World Order Issue. (Working Papers: No. 3). pap. 2.00 (ISBN 0-911646-07-8). World Policy.

Scalapino, Robert A. & Kim, Jun-Yop, eds. North Korea Today: Strategic & Domestic Issues. LC 82-8351. (Korea Research Monograph: No. 8). 371p. pap. 10.00 (ISBN 0-912966-55-6). IEAS.

Sohn, Hak-Kyu. Authoritarianism & Opposition in South Korea 272p. 1989. 67.50 (ISBN 0-415-03550-3). Routledge Chapman & Hall.

Suh, Dae-Sook. Kim II Sung: The North Korean Leader. (Studies of the east Asian Institute). (Illus.). 448p. 1988. 40.00x (ISBN 0-231-06572-8). Columbia U Pr.

Suh, Dae-Sook & Lee, Chae-Jin, eds. Political Leadership in Korea. LC 76-5480. (Publications on Asia of the Institute for Comparative & Foreign Area Studies: No. 27). 276p. 1976. 25.00x (ISBN 0-295-95437-X). U of Wash pr.

Sulivan, Hohn & Foss, Roberts, eds. Two Koreas-One Future? A Report Prepared for the American Friends Service Committee. Lc 86-30762. (Illus.). 176p. (Orig.). 1987. lib. bdg. 25.00 (ISBN 0-8191-6049-0, Pub. by Am Friends Serv); pap. text ed. 12.25 (ISBN 0-819-6050-4, Pub. by Am Friends Serv). U Pr of Amer.

Sunoo, Harold H. America's Dilemma in Asia: The Cast of South Korea. LC 78-24029. 224p. 1979. 22.9x (ISBN 0-88229-357-5). Nelson-Hall.

Weems, Beniamin. Reform, Rebellion & the Heavenly Way. LC 64-17267. (Association for Asian studies Monograph: No. 15). 122p. 1964. 7.95x (ISBN 0-8165-0144-0). U of Ariz Pr.

World Bank Staff. Korea: Managing the Industrial Transition, Vol. 1-Condust of Industrial Policy O-S equal O-P. 1987. 12.00 (ISBN 0-8213-0887-4, BK0887). World Bank.

Yersu, Kim. Cultural Policy in the Republic of Korea. (Studies & Documents on Cultural Policies). (Illus.). 50p. 1976. pap. 5.00 (ISBN 92-3-101384-X, UI30, UNESCO). UNIPUB.

Young Whan Kihl. Politics & Policies in Divided Korea: Regimes in Contest, 1845-1983. 330p. 1983. 42.50x (ISBN 0-86531-700-3); pap. text ed. 18.95X (ISBN 0-86531-701-1). Westview.

KOREA-RELIGION

Clark, Donald N. Christianity in Modern Korea. LC 86-9092. (Asian Agenda Report: No. 5). 70p. (Orig.). 1986. lib. bdg. 14.25 (ISBN 0-8191-5384-2, Pub. by the Asia Soc); pap. text ed. 5.25 (ISBN 0-8191-5385-0). U Pr of Amer.

Covell. Alan C. Ecstasy: Shamanism in Korea. LC 83-81487. (Illus.). 107p. 1983. 19.50x (ISBN 0-930878-33-7). Hollym Int'l.

De Bary, William T. & Haboush, Jahyun K, eds. The Rise of Neo-Confucianism in Korea. 512p. 1985. 45.00x (ISBN 0-231-06052-1). Columbia U pr.

'Grayson, James H. Korea: A Religious History. (Illus.). 336p. 1989. 65.00 (ISBN 0-19-826186-1). Oxford U Pr.

Kendall, Laurel & Dix, Griffin, eds. Religion & Ritual in Korean Society. LC 86-82390. (Korean Research Monograph: No. 12). xii, 223p. 1987. pap. 15.00x (ISBN 0-317-54483-7). IEAS.

Lee, Kwan-Jo. Search for Nirvana. (Illus.). 124p. 1984. 24.00 (ISBN 0-8048-1417-1, Pub. by Seoul Int'l Publishing House). C E Tuttle.

Nemeth, David J. The Architecture of Ideology: Neo-Confucian Imprinting on Chgju Island, Korea. (UC Publications in Geography: Vol. 26). (Orig.). 1988. pap. 42.00x (ISBN 0-520-09713-0). U of Cal Pr.

Palmer, Spencer J. Confucian Rituals in Korea. (Illus.). 270p. 1984. 30.00 (ISBN 0-89581-457-9). Jain Pub Co.

Young-chan Ro. The Korean Neo-Confucianism of Yi Yulgok. LC 87-12172. (SUNY Series in Philosophy). 160p. 1988. 39.50x (ISBN 0-88706-655-0); pap. 12.95x (ISBN 0-88706-656-9). State U NY Pr.

Yu, C. C. & Guisso, R. Shamanism: The Spirit World of Korea. LC 87-71271. (Studies in Korean Religions & Culture). 192p. 1988. 30.00 (ISBN 0-89581-875-2, Asian Human Pr); pap. text ed. 13.00 (ISBN 0-89581-886-8, Asian Human Pr). Jain Pub Co.

KOREA-SOCIAL CONDITIONS

Gendell, Murray. Stalls in the Fertility Decline in Costa Rica, Korea & Sri Lanka. (Working Paper: No. 693). 122p. 1985. 6.95 (ISBN 0-8213-0668-5, WP 0693). World Bank.

History & Prehistory in the National Park System & the National Historic Landmarks Program, 1987. 1226p. 1987. pap. 3.75 (ISBN 0-318-23438-6, S/N 024-005-01021-1). USGPO.

Kendall, Laurel. The Life & Hard Times of a Korean Shaman: Of Tales & the Telling of Tales. LC 87-19152. 168p. 1988. lib. bdg. 23.00x (ISBN 0-8248-1136-4); pap. text ed. 9.95x (ISBN 0-8248-1145-3). UH Pr.

KIm, Choong S. Faithful Endurance: An Ethnography of Korean Family Dispersal. LC 88-20487. 181p. 1988. 25.95x (ISBN 0-8165-1071-7). U of Ariz Pr.

Lee, Man-Gap. Sociology & Social Change in Korea. 341p. 1982. text ed. 18.00x (ISBN 0-8248-0937-8). UH Pr.

Lee, On-Jook. Urban-to-Rural Return Migration in Korea. 194p. 1980. text ed. 15.00x (ISBN 0-8248-0938-6) UH Pr.

MacDonald, Donald S. The Koreans: Contemporary Politics & Society 316p. 1988. 32.50 (ISBN 0-8133-0515-2). Westview.

Merrill, John. D.P.R. Korea: Politics, Economics & Society. (Marxist Regimes Ser.). 220p. 1987. 35.00 (ISBN 0-86187-424-2, Pub. by Pinter Pubs UK); pap. 12.50 (ISBN 0-86187-425-0). Columbia U Pr.

Palmore, James A, et al. Family Planning Accessibility & Adoption: The Korean Population Policy & Program Evaluation Study. LC 88-3761. (Papers of the East-West Population Institute: No. 108). xii, 125p. 1987. scholarly monograph 3.00 (ISBN 0-86638-106-6). EW Ctr HI.

Rhee, Yong-Pil. The Breakdown of Authority Structure in Korea in 1960: A Systems Approach. (The Institute of Social Sciences Korean Studies Ser.: No. 4). 130p. 1982. text ed. 14.00x (ISBN 0-8248-0936-X). UH Pr.

Sorensen, Clark W. Over the Mountains Are Mountains LC 87-6222. (Illus.). 208p. 1987. 25.00 (ISBN 0-295-96507-X). U of Wash Pr.

Whang, In-Joung. Management of Rural Change in Korea: The Saemaul Undong. (The Institute of Social Sciences Korean Studies Ser.: No. 5). 305p. 1981. text ed. 18.00x (ISBN 0-8248-0934-3). UH Pr.

KOREA-SOCIAL LIFE AND CUSTOMS

Beechman, Lenore. Song of the Soul: In Celebration of Korea. LC 83-15536. (Illus.). 38p. (Orig.). 1984. pap. 4.95 (ISBN 0-377-00137-6). Friendship Pr.

Center for Korean Studies Staff. Korean Studies, Vol. 4. 176p. 1982. 13.50x (ISBN 0-8248-0816-9). UH Pr.

Covell, Jon C. Korea's Cultural Roots. 6th ed. LC 83-81319. (Illus.). 132p. 1986. 19.50x (ISBN 0-930878-32-9). Hollym Int'l.

'De Mente, Boye. Korean Etiquette & Ethics in Business. 224p. 1988. pap. 14.95 (ISBN 0-8442-8522-6, NTC Bks). Natl Textbk.

Griffis, William E. Corea, the Hermit Nation. rev., 9th, enl. ed. LC 74-158615. Repr. of 1911 ed. 37.50 (ISBN 0-404-2916-7). AMS Pr.

Hesung, Chung Koh. Korean Family & Kinship Studies Guide. 568p. 150.00 (ISBN 0-317-34232-0, LC 80-81130). HRAFP.

Hong, Sawon. Community Development & Human Reproductive Behavior. 196p. 1979. text ed. 12.00x (ISBN 0-8248-0685-9, Korea devel Inst). UH Pr.

Howe, Russel W. The Koreans: Passion & Grace. LC 88-984. (Illus.). 272p. 1988. pap. 12.95 (ISBN 0-15-647185-X). HarBraceJ.

Janelli, Roger L. & Janelli, Dawnhee Y. Ancestor Worship & Korean Society. LC 81-51757. (Illus.). 248p. 1982. 27.50x (ISBN 0-8047-1135-6). Staman: Of Tales & the Telling of Tales. LC 87-19152. 168p. 1988. lib. bdg. 23.00x (ISBN 0-8248-1136-4); pap. text ed. 9.95x (ISBN 0-8248-1145-3). UH Pr.

Kim, Young-Pyoung. A Strategy for Rural Development: Saemaeul Undong in Korea. 1980. pap. 3.50 (ISBN 0-89249-032-2). Int'l Development.

Mason, Edward S. The Economic & Social Modernization of the Republic of Korea. (Harvard East Asian Monographs: Vol. 92). 500p. 1980. 20.00x (ISBN 0-674-23175-9). Harvard U Pr.

Michell, Tony. Simple Etiquette in Korea. 1985. 19.95x (ISBN 0-317-39119-4, Pub. by Norbury Pubns Ltd). State Mutual Bk.

Pares, Susan. Korean Western Culture in Contrast Crosscurrents. (Illus.). 188p. 1985. pap. 5.00 (ISBN 0-8048-1429-5, Pub. by Seoul Int'l Tourist Korea). C E Tuttle.

KOREA (DEMOCRATIC PEOPLE'S REPUBLIC)-CULTURAL POLICY

Sik, Chai Sin & Hun, Hyon Jong. Cultural Policy in the Democratic People's Republic of Korea. (Studies & Documents on Cultural Policies). (Illus.). 39p. 1980. pap. 5.00 (ISBN 92-3-101645-8, U991, UNESCO). UNIPUB.

KOREA (DEMOCRATIC PEOPLES REPUBLIC)

An, Tai Sung, North Korea: A Political Handbook. LC 83-16307. (Illus.). 294p. 1983. lib. bdg. 45.00 (ISBN 0-8420-2205-8). Scholarly Res Inc.

Barnds, william J., ed. The Two Koreas in east Asian Affairs. LC 75-27379. 216p. 1976. 30.00x (ISBN 0-8147-0988-5). NYU Pr.

Brun, Ellen & Hersh, Jacques. Socialist Korea: A Case Study in the Strategy of Economic Development. LC 76-1651. (Illus.). 432p. 1977. 16.50 (ISBN 0-85345-386-1). Monthly Rev.

Ginsburgs, george. calendar of Diplomatic Affairs, Demoncratic People's Republic of Korea, 1945-1975. Kim, Roy U., ed. LC 77-71677. 275p. 1977. lib. bdg. 25.00 (ISBN 0-379-20354-5). Oceana.

Stern, Thomas, ed. Republic of Korea 1984 Statistical Abstract, Vol. 1. (Illus.). 45p. (Orig.). 1984. pap. 4.50 (ISBN 0-317-06992-6). Korea Eco Inst.

KOREAN AIR LINES INCIDENT, 1983

Clubb, Oliver. KAL Flight 007: The Hidden Story. LC 84-62522. 174p. 16.95 (ISBN 0-932966-59-4). Permanent Pr.

Dallin, Alexander. Black Box: KAL 007 & the Superpowers. LC 84-24151. 180p. 1985. 22.50x (ISBN 0-520-05515-2); pap. 8.95x (ISBN 0-520-05516-0). U of Cal Pr.

Hersh, Seymour M. The Target Is Destroyed: What Really Happened to Flight 007 & What America Knew about It. LC 87-40074. 404p. 1987. pap. 4.95 (ISBN 0-394-75527-8, Vin). Random.

Johnson, R. W. Shootdown: Flight 007 & the American Connection. (Illus.). 544p. 1987. pap. 4.50 (ISBN 0-14-009474-1). Penguin.

Pearson, David. KAL 007—The Cover Up: Why the True Story Has Never Been Told. 1987. 19.45 (ISBN 0-671-55716-5). Summit Bks.

KOREAN ART
see Art, Korean

KOREAN BALLADS AND SONGS
see also Folk-Songs, Korean

KOREAN DRAMA

O Yong-jin, et al. Wedding Day & Other Korean Plays. The, Korean National Commission for UNESCO, ed. Slettland, G., et al., trs. from Korean. (Korean Novel, Plays, & Poetry Ser.: No. 2). xiii, 211p. 1983. 20.00 (ISBN 0-89209-013-8). Pace Intl Res.

KOREAN FOLK-SONGS
see Folk-Songs, Korean

KOREAN LANGUAGE

Abbreviated Russian-Korean Dictionary. 648p. (Rus. & Korean.). 9.95 (ISBN 0-686-97385-2, M-9055). French & Eur.

Chambers, Kevin. Korean Phrasebook. 96p. (Orig.). 1988. pap. 2.95 (ISBN 0-86442-606-9). Lonely Planet.

Chin-W Kim, ed. Papers in Korean Linguistics. 1979. pap. text ed. 14.50 (ISBN 0-917496-11-6). Hornbeam Pr.

De Mente, Boye. Korean in Plain English. 160p. 1987. pap. 7.95 (ISBN 0-8442-8521-8, Passport Bks). Natl Textbk.

Dictionary Korean-Chinese. 1274p. (Korean & Chinese.). 1978. 49.95 (ISBN 0-686-92316-2, M-9289). French & Eur.

Essence English-Korean Dictionary. 2731p. 1988. 44. 50x (ISBN 0-930878-79-5). Hollym Intl.

Essence Korean-English Dictionary. 2510p. 1988. 44. 50x (ISBN 0-930878-80-9). Hollym Intl.

Foreign Service Institute Staff. Korean, Vol. 1. 553p. 1980. incl. 18 audio cassettes 195.00x (ISBN 0-88432-047-2, Q800). J Norton Pubs.

—Korean, Vol. 2. 560p. 1980. incl. 16 audio cassettes 225.00 (ISBN 0-88432-048-0, Q850). J Norton Pubs.

Grant, Bruce. Guide to Korean Characters. 367p. 1982. 95.00x (Pub. by Collets (UK)). State Mutual Bk.

Grant, Bruce K. A Guide to Korean Characters: Reading & Writing Hangul & Hanja. 2nd ed. 367p. (Eng. & Korean.). 1982. 24.50 (ISBN 0-930878-13-1). Hollym Int).

Hong, Chai-Song. Syntaxe des Verbes de mouvement en Coreen Contemporain. LC 84-28391. (Lingvisticae Investigationes Supplementas: No. 12). sv, 309p. (Fr.). 1985. 48.00x (ISBN 90-272-3122-2). Benjamins North Am.

Hwang, Shin J. Discourse Features of Korean Narration. LC 85-61654. (Publications in Linguistics Ser.: No. 77). 200p. (Orig.). 1987. pap. 24.00x (ISBN 0-88312-002-X); microfiche (5) 10. 00 (ISBN 0-88312-418-1). Summer Inst Ling.

Jones, B.J. Korean Phrasebook. LC 87-82975. 200p. (Orig.). 1987. pap. 7.95x (ISBN 0-930878-20-5). Hollym Intl.

—Let's Learn Korean. 2nd rev. ed. LC 85-60068. (Illus.). 64p. 1985. 14.95x (ISBN 0-930878-41-8); cassette incl. Hollym Intl.

—Standard English-Korean Dictionary for Foreigners. Romanized ed. LC 81-84204. (Illus.). 386p. (Eng. & Korean.). 1982. pap. 8.95x (ISBN 0-930878-21-3). Hollym Intl.

Jones, B.J. & Rhie, Gene S., eds. English-Korean Practical Conversation Dictionary: All-Romanized. LC 83-81486. (Illus.). 658p. 1984. pap. 12.50 (ISBN 0-930878-22-1). Hollym Intl.

Kim, Nam-Kil. The Grammar of Korean Complementation. LC 83-63529. (Occasional Papers: No. 11). 162p. 1984. 12.00 (ISBN 0-917536-15-0). UH Manoa CKS.

Lee, H.B. Korean Grammar. 224p. 1989. 42.00 (ISBN 0-19-713606-0). Oxford U Pr.

Lee, Pong K. & Ryu, Chi S. Let's Talk in Korean. LC 78-72953. 312p. 1982. 7.95x (ISBN 0-930878-10-8). Hollym Intl.

Lee, Pong K. & Ryu, Chi Sik. Easy Way to Korean Conversation. 3rd, rev. ed. (Illus.). 78p. 1984. 14. 95x (ISBN 0-930878-17-5); cassette incl. Hollym Intl.

Lukoff, Fred. Spoken Korean. LC 73-17223. (Spoken Language Ser.). 370p. (gr. 9-12). 1975. pap. 10.00x Bk. 1, Units 1-12 (ISBN 0-87950-150-2); pap. 15. 00x Bk. 2, 305p. Units 13-30 (ISBN 0-87950-151-0); 6 dual track cassettes for bk. 1 65.00x (ISBN 0-87950-155-3); Bk. 1 & cassettes 75.00x (ISBN 0-87950-156-1). Spoken Lang Serv.

Martin, Samuel E. Korean in a Hurry: A Quick Approach to Spoken Korean. LC 60-8363. 1954. pap. 4.25 (ISBN 0-8048-0349-8). C E Tuttle.

Martin, Samuel E. & Lee, Young-Sook C. Beginning Korean. LC 86-50701. 608p. 1986. pap. 20.50 (ISBN 0-8048-1507-0). C E Tuttle.

Martin, Samuel E., et al. Korean-English Dictionary. (Linguistic Ser.). (Korean & Eng.). 1967. text ed. 95.00 (ISBN 0-300-00753-1). Yale U Pr.

Park, B. Nam & Kay, Chunghwa T. FSI Korean Basic Course, Units 19-47. 1975. pap. text ed. 15.00x (ISBN 0-686-10749-7); 16 cassettes 96.00x (ISBN 0-686-10750-0). Intl. Learn Syst.

Park, Francis Y. Speaking Korean, Bk. I. LC 84-80023. 489p. 1984. text ed. 18.00x (ISBN 0-930878-50-7). Hollym Intl.

—Speaking Korean, Bk. II. LC 84-80023. 559p. text ed. 34.50x (ISBN 0-930878-51-5). Hollym Intl.

Penton Overseas, Inc. Staff. Vocabulearn: Korean-English, Level I. Linguetheque of L.A., tr. 36p. 1986. incl. 2 cass 14.95 (ISBN 0-939001-50-0). Penton Overseas.

Vocabulearn: Korean English, Level II. Linguatheque of L.A., tr. 36p. 1987. incl. 2 cass. 14.95 (ISBN 0-939001-61-9). Penton Overseas.

Rhie, Gene S., ed. Standard Korean-English Dictionary for Foreigners: All Romanized. 394p. 1986. pap. 8.95 (ISBN 0-930878-49-3). Hollym Intl.

Rockwell, Coralie. Kagok: A Traditional Korean Vocal Form. I.C 72-87568. (D (Monographs), No. 3). (Illus.). 302p. (Orig.). 1972. pap. text ed. 7.50 (ISBN 0-913360-05-8). Asian Music Pub.

Rucci, Richard B. Korean with Chinese Characters. (Illus.). 146p. 1981. pap. 3.90 (ISBN 0-8048-1469-4, Seoul Intl Publishing House). C E Tuttle.

—Korean with Chinese Characters, No. 2. (Illus.). 130p. 1984. pap. 3.50 (ISBN 0-8048-1431-9, Pub. by Seoul Intl Publishing House). C E Tuttle.

Shin Ja Joo Hwang. Korean Clause Structure. (Publications in Linguistics & Related Fields Ser: No. 50). 1975. microfiche only 2.00x (ISBN 0-88312-101-8). Summer Inst Ling.

Song, Seok C. Explorations in Korean Syntax & Semantics. LC 82-83500. (Korean Research Monographs: No. 14). 384p. (Orig.). 1988. pap. 20 00x (ISBN 1-55729-000-8). IEAS.

Study English-Korean — Korean-English Dictionary. (Illus., Eng. & Korean.). 1987. 14.95 (ISBN 0-89346-300-0). Heian Intl.

Thorlin, Eldora & Henthorn, Taesoon. Everyday Korean. LC 71-183519. 192p. 1972. pap. 4.50 (ISBN 0-8348-0069-1). Weatherhill.

Woong, Hub, et al. The Korean Language. Korean National Commission for UNESCO, ed. (Korean Art, Folklore, Language, & Thought Ser.: No. 6). (Illus.). viii, 277p. 1983. 25.00 (ISBN 0-89209-019-7). Pace Intl. Res.

KOREAN LANGUAGE READERS

Chang, Sung-Un. Korean Newspaper Readings. 4.95 (IBSN 0-88710-042-2). Yale Far Eastern Pubns.

Chang, Sung-Un & Martin, Samuel E. Readings in Contemporary Korean. 4.95 (ISBN 0-88710-075-9). Yale Far Eastern Pubns.

Holt, D. & Holt, G. Korean at a Glance. (At a Glance Ser.). 236p. 1988. 6.95 (ISBN 0-8120-3998-X.) Barron.

KOREAN LITERATURE (COLLECTIONS)

Chung, Chongwha, ed. Korean Classical Literature: An Anthology. 200p. 1988. 25.00 (ISBN 0-7103-0279-7, Kegan Paul). Routledge Chapman & Hall.

Kim, Chong-un, ed. Postwar Korean Short Stories: An Anthology. 277p. 1983. text ed. 18.00x (ISBN 0-8248-0833-9, Pub. by Seoul U Pr). UH Pr.

Koh Chang-soo, tr. from Korean. Anthology of Contemporary Korean Poetry. 130p. 1988. 6.50 (Pub. by Seoul Intl Tourist Korean). C E Tuttle.

McCann, David R., ed. Black Crane, No. 1: An Anthology of Korean Literature. (Cornell University East Asia Papers: No. 14). 145p. 1977. 5.00 (ISBN 0-939657-14-7). Cornell East Asia Pgm.

—Black Crane, No. 2: An Anthology of Korean Literature. (Cornell University East Asia Papers: No. 24). 111p. 198. 5.00 (ISBN 0-939657-24-4). Cornell East Asia Pgm.

KOREAN LITERATURE— BIBLIOGRAPHY

Courant, Maurice A. Bibliographie Coreenne, Tableau Litteraire De la Coree, 4 vols in 3. (Incl. suppl). Repr. of 1894 ed. Set. 177.00 (ISBN 0-8337-0692-6). B Franklin.

Hesung Chun Koh, ed. Modern Korean Literature in English: A Bibliography. LC 85-81854. (Orig.). 1988. pap. text ed. write for info. (ISBN 0-910825-03-3). E Rock Pr.

Zong, In-sob. A Guide to Korean Literature. LC 82-84416. 296p. 1983. 22.00x (ISBN 0-930878-29-9). Hollym Intl.

KOREAN LITERATURE—HISTORY AND CRITICISM

Kim, Ilan-Kyo, ed. Studies on Korea: A Scholar's Guide. LC 79-26491. 458p. 1980. text ed. 27.50x (ISBN 0-8248-0673-5). UH Pr.

Lee, Peter H. Korean Literature: Topics & Themes. LC 64-19167. (Association for Asian Studies, Monographs & Papers: No. 16). pap. 37.80 (ISBN 0-317-10017-3, 2003443). Bks Demand UMI.

—Songs of Flying Dragons. LC 73-92866. (Harvard-Yenching Institute Monographs Ser: No. 22). 352p. 1975. text ed. 22.50x (ISBN 0-674-82075-4). Harvard U Pr.

Lee, Peter H., ed. Anthology of Korean Literature: From Early Times to the Nineteenth Century. LC 81-69567. 448p. 1981, pap. text ed. 12.00x (ISBN 0-8248-0756-1). UH Pr.

Sym, Myung-Ho. The Making of Modern Korean Poetry: Foreign Influences & Native Creativity. 354p. 1982. text ed. 18.00x (ISBN 0-8248-0935-1, Pub. by Seoul U Pr.). UH Pr.

KOREAN NATIONAL CHARACTERISTICS
see National Characteristics, Korean

KOREAN PAINTING
see Painting, Korean

KOREAN PAINTINGS
see Paintings, Korean

KOREAN POETRY— TRANSLATIONS INTO ENGLISH

Barkan, Stanley H., compiled by. South Korean Poets of Resistance. Ko Won, tr. LC 79-90037. (Cross-Cultural Review Ser.: No. 4). Illus., Korean & Eng.). 1980. 15.00x (ISBN 0-89304-606-X, CCC124); pap. 5.00x (ISBN 0-89304-607-8). Cross Cult.

Ko, Won. Contemporary Korean Poetry. LC 74 113487. (Iowa Translations Ser.). pap. 63.50 (ISBN 0-317-42170-0, 2025934). Bks Demand UMI.

Koh, Chang-soo, tr. Best Loved Poems of Korea: Selected for Foreigners. LC 83-81485. 128p. 9.95x (ISBN 0-930878-35-3). Hollym. Intl.

Lee, Peter H., ed. The Silence of Love: Twentieth-Century Korean Poetry. LC 80-21999. 367p. 1980. text ed. 17.95x (ISBN 0-8248-0711-1); pap. 8.95 (ISBN 0-8248-0732-4). UH Pr.

'Lee Sung-Il, tr. from Korean. & intro. by. The Wind & the Waves: Four Modern Korean Poets. 140p. (Orig.). 1989. pap. 12.00 (ISBN 0-89581-917-1, AHP Pbks). Jaion Pub Co.

Sun-ai, Lee & Luce, Don, eds. The Wish. LC 83-18480. (Illus.). 72p. (Orig.). 1984. pap. 6.95 (ISBN 0-377-00136-8). Friendship Pr.

KOREAN REUNIFICATION QUESTION (1945-)

Barnds, William J., ed. The Two Koreas in East Asian Affairs. LC 75-27379. 216p. 1976. 30.00x (ISBN 0-8147-0988-5). NYU Pr.

Sandusky, Michael C. America's Parallel. LC 83-61934. (Illus.). 487p. 1983. 19.95 (ISBN 0-913513-00-8). Old Dominion Pr.

KOREAN TALES
see Tales, Korean

KOREAN WAR, 1950-1953

Acheson, Dean. Korean War. 1971. pap. text ed. 2.95x (ISBN 0-393-09978-4). Norton.

—Korean War. 1971. pap. text ed. 2.95x (ISBN 0-393-09978-4). Norton.

Alexander, Vebin. Korea: The First War We Lost. (Illus.). 558p. 24.95 (ISBN 0-87052-135-7). Hippocrene Bks.

'America's Tenth Legion: X Corps in Korea, 1950. 1989. 24-95 (ISBN 0-89141-258-1). Presidio Pr.

The Arab-Israel War, the Chinese Civil War & the Korean War. LC 87-1159. (West Point Military History Ser.). 1987. 25.00 (ISBN 0-89529-322-6); pap. 18.00 (ISBN 0-89529-274-2). Avery Pub.

Atlas to the Arab-Israel Wars, the Chinese Civil War & the Korean War. (West Point Military History Ser.). 1987. pap. 20.00 (ISBN 0-89529-320-X). Avery Pub.

Berger, Carl. The Korea Knot, a Military-Political History. rev. ed. LC 86-22767. 255p. 1986. Repr. of 1964 ed. lib. bdg. 48.50x (ISBN 0-313-25281-5, BEKK). Greenwood.

Blair, Clay. The Forgotten War: America in Korea 1950-1953. 1146p. 1989. pap. 16.95 (ISBN 0-385-26033-4, Anchor Pr). Doubleday.

—The Forgotten War: American in Korean 1950-1953. LC 87-41095. 896p. 1987. 29.45 (ISBN 0-8129-1670-0). Times Bks.

Bradbury, William C. Mass Behaviour in Battle & Captivity: The Communist Soldier in the Korean War. Meyers, Samuel M., ed. LC 68-16705. pap. 101.80 (ISBN 0-317-08308-2, 2020034). Bks Demand UMI.

Condit, Doris M. The Test of War, Nineteen Fifty to Nineteen Fifty-Three. LC 84-601133. (History of the Office of the Secretary of Defense Set.: Vol. II). (Illus.). 700p. 1988. write for info. (ISBN 0-9620386-0-1). US Dept Defense.

Congressional Medal of Honor Library: The Names, The deeds—Korea. 1987. pa. 3.95 (ISBN 0-440-11518-3). Dell.

Cotton, James & Neary, Ian, eds. The Korean War in History. LC 87-4209. (Studies on East Asia). 184p. 1989. text ed. 45.00 (ISBN 0-391-03497-9). Humanities.

Cumings, Bruce. The Origins of the Korean War: Liberation & the Emergence of Separate Regimes. LC 80 8543. (Illus.). 552p. 1981. pap. 24.50x LPE (ISBN 0-691-10113-2). Princeton U Pr.

Cumings, Bruce, ed. Child of Conflict: The Korean-American Relationship 1945-1953. LC 82-48871. (Publications on Asia of the School of International Studies: No. 37). 352p. 1983. 25.00x (ISBN 0-295-95995-9). U of Wash Pr.

Edwards, R. Korean War. (Flashpoints Ser.). (Illus.). 80p. (gr. 7 up). Date not set. PLB 15.93 (ISBN 0-86592-036-2). Rourke Corp.

Foot, Rosemary. The Wrong War: American Policy & the Dimensions of the Korean Conflict, 1950-1953. LC 84-29305. (Cornell Studies in Security Affairs). 296p. 1985. 32.50x (ISBN 0-8014-1800-3). Cornell U Pr.

Gardener, Llyod C. The Korean War. LC 72-130383. (A New York Times Book Ser.). 1972. pap. text ed. 8.95 (ISBN 0-8129-6193-5, Dist. by M & B Fulfillment). Wiener Pub Inc.

Goodrich, Leland M. Korea: A Study of U.S. Policy in the United Nations. LC 78-24120. 1979. Repr. of 1956 ed. lib. bdg. 35.00x (ISBN 0-313-20825-5, GOKO). Greenwood.

Gough, Terrence J. United States Army Mobilization & Logistics in the Korean War: A Research Approach. LC 87-1781. (CMH Pub Ser.: No. 70-19). (Illus.). 134p. (Orig.). 1987. pap. 4.25 (S/N 008-029-00154-3). USGPO.

Goulden. J.C. Korea: The Untold Story of the War. 736p. 1983. pap. text ed. 14.95 (ISBN 0-07-023580-5). McGraw.

Grey, Jeffrey. The Commonwealth Armies & the Korean War. An Alliance Study. LC 87-367000. (War, Armed Forces & Society Ser.). 256p. 1988. 45.00 (ISBN 0-7190-2611-3, Pub. by Manchester Univ Pr). St Martin.

Hastings, Max. The Korean War. (Illus.). 416p. 1988. pap. 10.95 (ISBN 0-671-66834-X, Touchstone Bks). S&S.

Hoyt, Edwin P. The Pusan Perimeter: Korea LC 83-40539. (Illus.). 320p. 1984. 19.95 (ISBN 0-8128-2960-3). Scrbrough Hse.

Israel, Fred L., ed. Major Presidential Decisions. LC 80-22040. 850p. 1980. pap. 11.95 (ISBN 0-87754-218-X). Chelsea Hse.

Kaufman, Burton I. The Korean War. 1986. pap. text ed. 11.95 (ISBN 0-07-554665-5). McGraw.

—The Korean War: Challenges in Crisis, Credibility, & Command. LC 85-26222. 400p. 1986. 39.95 (ISBN 0-87722-418-8). Temple U Pr.

Kindead, Eugene. In Every War but One. LC 81-7014. 219p. 1982. Repr. of 1959 ed. lib. bdg. 35.00x (ISBN 0-313-23113-3, KIEW). Greenwood.

Knox, Donald. The Korean War: Pusan to Chosin: An Oral History. LC 85-8567. (Illus.). 512p. 1985. 24. 95 (ISBN 0-15-147288-2). HarBraceJ.

—The Korean War: Pusan to Chosin: An Oral History. (Illus.). 1987. pap. 10.95 (ISBN 0-317-56663-6, Harv). HarBraceJ.

—The Korean War: Uncertain Victory. Coppel, Alfred, ed. 672p. 1988. 29.95 (ISBN 0-15-147289-0). HarBraceJ.

*The Korean War Soldier at Heartbreak Ridge. (The Soldier Ser.). 48p. (gr. 5-6). 1989. PLB 10.95 Capstone Pr.

Kurland, Gerald. The Korean War. (Events of Our Times Ser.: No. 13). 32p. lib. bdg. 3.95 incl. catalog cards (ISBN 0-686-07222-7). SamHar Pr.

Lowe, Peter. The Origins of the Korean War. (Origins of Modern Wars Ser.). 240p. (Orig.). 1986. pap. text ed. 14.95 (ISBN 0-582-49278-5). Longman.

MacDonald, Callum A. Korea: The War Before Vietnam. LC 86-22943. 320p. 1987. 24.95 (ISBN 0-02-919621-3). Free Pr.

McFarland, Keith D. The Korean War: An Annotated Bibliography. LC 83-482-04, 600p. 1988. lib. bdg. 70.00 (ISBN 0-8230-9068-3). Garland Pub.

*Merrill, John. Korea: The Peninsular Origins of the War. LC 85-40990. (Illus.). 240p. 1989. 32.50x (ISBN 0-87413-300-9). U Delaware Pr.

Mesko, Jim. Armor in Korea. (Armor Special Ser.: No. 6038). (Illus.). 80p. 1983. 8.95 (ISBN 0-89747-150-4). Squad Sig Pubns.

Montross, Lynn & Montross, Ca. U.S. Marine Operations in Korea, 1950-53, 4 vols. 1988. Repr. of 1962 ed. Set. lib. bdg. 295.00x. Reprint Servs.

Mueller, John E. War, President & Public Opinion. LC 85-5352. (Illus.). 326p. 1985. pap. text ed. 14.25 (ISBN 8-8191-4649-8). U Pr of Amer.

O'Ballance, Edgar. Korea: Nineteen Fifty to Nineteen Fifty-Three. LC 85-14787. 172p. 1985. Repr. of 1969 ed. lib. bdg. 14.00 (ISBN 0-89874-885-2). Krieger.

Ridgway, Matthew B. The Korean War. (Quality Paperbacks Ser.). (Illus.). 360p. 1986. pap. 12.95 (ISBN 0-306-80267-8). Da Capo.

*Schaller, Michael. Douglas MacArthur. The Far Eastern General. (Illus.). 320p. 1989. 22.50 (ISBN 0-19-503886-X). Oxford U Pr.

Simmons, Robert R. The Strained Alliance: Peking, P'yongyang, Moscow & the Politics of the Korean Civil War. LC 74-4891. 1975. 10.95 (ISBN 0-02-928880-0). Free Pr.

Spanier, John W. Truman-MacArthur Controversy & the Korean War. 1965. pap. 7.95 (ISBN 0-393-00279-9, Norton Lib). Norton.

Spurr, Russell. Enter the Dragon: China's Undeclared War Against the U.S. in Korea, 1950-51. LC 87-18436. (Illus.). 384p. 1988. 22.95 (ISBN 1-55704-008-7). Newmarket.

Stairs, Denis. The Diplomacy of Constraint: Canada, the Korean War, & the United States. LC 72-95814. 1974. 35.00x (ISBN 0-8020-5282-7). U of Toronto Pr.

*Stanton, Shelby L. X Corps: The U.S. Tenth Corp. in Korea. 1989. 24.95. Presidio Pr.

Stokesbury, James L. A Short History of the Korean War. Cady, Howard, ed. LC 88-5229. (Illus.). 352p. 1988. 18.95 (ISBN 0-688-06377-2). Morrow.

*Stokesbury, James L. A Short History of the Korean War. 276p. 1990. pap. 12.95 (ISBN 0-68809513-5, Quill). Morrow.

Stone, I. F. The Hidden History of the Korean War, 1950-1951. (A Nonconformist History of Our Times Ser.). 368p. 1988. 17.95 (ISBN 0-316-81773-2); pap. 8.95 (ISBN 0-316-81770-8). Little.

Vatcher, William H., Jr. Panmunjom: The Story of the Korean Military Armistice Negotiations. LC 72-14001. (Illus.). 322p. 1973. Repr. of 1958 ed. lib. bdg. 22.50x (ISBN 0-8371-6743-4, VAPA). Greenwood.

—Panmunjom: The Story of the Korean Military Armistice Negotiations. LC 72-14001. (Illus.). 322p. 1973. Repr. of 1958 ed. lib. bdg. 22.50x. (ISBN 0-8371-6743-4, VAPA). Greenwood.

Westover, John G. Combat Support in Korea, No. LC 54-13365. (CMH Pub.: United States Army in Action Ser.: No. 22-1). (Illus.). 266p. (Orig.). 1986. pap. 7.50 (ISBN 0-318-21651-5, S/N 008-029-00149-7). USGPO.

Whiting, Allen S. China Crosses the Yalu: The Decision to Enter the Korean War. LC 68-13744. x. 219p. 1960. 30.00x (ISBN 0-8047-0627-1); pap. 8.95 (ISBN 0-8047-0629-8). Stanford U Pr.

KOREAN WAR, 1950-1953— AERIAL OPERATIONS

Blunk, Chester L. Every Man a Tiger: The 731st USAF Night Intruders Over Korea. (Illus.). 128p. 1987. pap. 9.95 (ISBN 0-89745-087-6). Sunflower U Pr.

Futrell, Robert E. United States Air Force in Korea: 1950-1953. rev. ed. LC 81-60776. 843p. 1983. 18.00 (ISBN 0-318-11837-8, S/N 008-070-00488-7). USGPO.

Hallion, Richard P. The Naval Air War in Korea. LC 85-62097. (Illus.). 250p. 1986. 22.95 (ISBN 0-933852-47-9). Nautical & Aviation.

—The Naval Air War in Korea. 432p. 1988. pap. 3.95 (ISBN 0-8217-2267-0). Zebra.

*Kohn, Richard H. & Harahan, Joseph P., eds. Air Interdiction in World War II, Korea, & Vietnam. 104p. 1986. 4.75 (ISBN 0-912799-35-8). Off Air Force.

Kohn, Richard H. & Harahan, Joseph P., eds. Air Superiority in World War II & Korea. (USAF Warrior Studies). (Illus.). 116p. (Orig.). 1983. pap. 4.75 (ISBN 0-912799-00-5). Off Air Force.

*Robinson, Anthony. Nightfighter: A Concise History of Nightfighting Since 1914. (Illus.). 144p. 1988. 24.95 (ISBN 0-7110-1757-3; Pub. by Ian Allen). Motorbooks Intl.

Stewart, James T. & Gilbert, James, eds. Airport: The Decisive Force in Korea. LC 79-7298 (Flight: Its First seventy-Five Years Ser.). (Illus.). 1979. Repr. of 1957 ed. lib. bdg. 25.00x (ISBN 0-405-12204-7). Ayer Co. Pubs.

KOREAN WAR, 1950-1953— CAMPAIGNS

*Appleman, Roy E. Disaster in Korea: The Chinese Confront MacArthur. LC 88-28133. (Military History Ser.: No. 11). (Illus.). 464p. 1989. 35.00 (ISBN 0-89096-344-4). Tex A&M Univ. Pr.

Appleman, Roy E. East of Chosin: Entrapment & Breakout in Korea, 1950. LC 86-22184. (Military History Ser.: No. 2). (Illus.). 416p. 1987. 28.50 (ISBN 0-89096-283-9). Tex A&M Univ. Pr.

Appleman, Roy E., ed. United States Army in the Korean War, South to the Naktong, North to the Yalu (June-November 1950) LC 60-60043. (Center of Military History Publication: No. 20-2). (Illus.). 841p. 1986. Repr. of 1961 ed. 25.50 (ISBN 0-317-59467-2, S/N 008-029-00079-2). USGPO.

Cowdrey, Albert E. United States Army in the Korean War: Medic's War. (CMH Pub. Ser.: 20-5). (Illus.). 409p. 1987. text ed. 21.00 (ISBN 0-318-23533-1, 008-029-00147-1). USGPO.

Heinl, Robert D., Jr. Victory at High Tide. LC 79-90111. (Illus.). 315p. 1979. Repr. of 1968 ed. 19.95 (ISBN 0-933852-03-7). Nautical & Aviation.

*Hinshaw, Arned L. Heartbreak Ridge: Korea, 1951. 163p. 1989. 19.95 (ISBN 0-275-93217-6, C3217). Pracger.

Hoyt, Edwin P. On to the Yalu. LC 84-40240. 348p. 1984 19.95 (ISBN 0-8128-2977-8); pap. 3.95 (ISBN 0-8128-8243-1). Scrbrough Hse.

*Huston, James A. Guns & Butter, Powder & Rice: U. S. Army Logistics in the Korean War. LC 87-43351. (Illus.). 496p. 1989. 65.00x (ISBN 0-941664-87-2). Susquehanna U Pr.

Langley, Michael. Inchon Landing: MacArthur's Last Triumph. LC 78-20688, 1979. write for info. (ISBN 0-8129-0821-X). Times Bks.

Marshall, S.L. Pork Chop Hill. 256p. 1986. pap. 3.95 (ISBN 0-515-08732-7). Jove Pubns.

KOREAN WAR, 1950-1953— FICTION

Michener, James A. Bridges at Toko-Ri. (gr. 10 up). 1953. 16.95 (ISBN 0-394-41780-1). Random.

KOREAN WAR, 1950-1953— NAVAL OPERATIONS

Cagle, Malcolm W. & Manson, Frank A. The Sea War In Korea. LC 79-6104. (Navies & Men Ser.). (Illus.). 1980. Repr. of 1957 ed. lib. bdg. 37.50x (ISBN 0-405-13033-3). Ayer Co. Pubs.

Hallion, Richard P. The Naval Air War in Korea. 432p. 1988. pap. 3.95 (ISBN 0-8217-2267-0). Zebra.

Langley, Michael. Inchon Landing: MacArthur's Last Triumph. LC 78-20688. 1979. write for info. (ISBN 0-8129-0821-X). Times Bks.

KOREAN WAR, 1950-1953— PERSONAL NARRATIVES, AMERICAN

Brainard, Morgan. Men in Low Cut Shoes. (Illus.). 176p. 1986. 11.95 (ISBN 0-89962-474-X). Todd & Honeywell.

Clark, Mark. From the Danube to the Yalu. (Military Classics Ser.: Bk. 2). (Illus.). 400p. 1988. 14.60 (ISBN 0-8306-4001-0, 4000) TAB Bks.

Griffin, Bobby. The Search. pap. 1.75 (ISBN 0-686-12739-0). Grace-Pub Co.

*Thompson, James. True Colors: One Thousand Four Days as a Prisoner of War. LC 88-39295. 1988. 19.95 (ISBN 0-87949-282-1). Ashley Bks.

Thornton, John W. & Thornton, John W., Jr. Believed To Be Alive. LC 81-78444. 320p. 1981. 14.95 (ISBN 0-8397-1064-X). Eriksson.

Walker, Wilbert L. We Are Men: Memoris of W. W. II & the Korean War. LC 72-81006. 129p. 1972. 9.00 (ISBN 0-935428-01-1). Heritage Pr.

KOREAN WAR, 1950-1953—PRISONERS AND PRISONS

Kinkead, Eugene. In Every War but One. LC 81-7014. 219p. 1982. Repr. of 1959 ed. lib. bdg. 35.00x (ISBN 0-313-23113-3, KIEW). Greenwood.

ˇThompson, James, True Colors: One Thousand Four Days as a Prisoner of War. LC 88-39295. 1988. 19. 95 (ISBN 0-87949-282-1). Ashley Bks.

Thornton, John W. & Thornton, John W., Jr. Believed to Be Alive LC 81-7844. 320p. 1981. 14.95 (ISBN 0-8397-1064-X). Eriksson.

White, William L. The Capitives of Korea: An Unofficial White Paper on the Treatment of War Prisoners; Our Treatment of Theirs: Their Treatment of Ours. LC 78-14347. 1979. Repr. of 1957 ed. lib. bdg. 35.00x (ISBN 0-313-20631-7, WHCK). Greenwood.

KOREAN WAR, 1950-1953—REGIMENTAL HISTORIES

Appleman, Roy E. East of Chosin: Entrapment & Breakout in Korea, 1950. LC 86-22184. (Military History Ser.: No. 2). (Illus.). 416p. 1987. 28.50 (ISBN 0-89096-283-9). Tex A&M Univ Pr.

Brainard, Morgan. Men in Low Cut Shoes, (Illus.). 176p. 1985. 11.95 (ISBN 0-89962-474-X). Todd & Honeywell.

ˇMarshall, S.L. Pork Chop Hill: The American Fighting Man in Action: Korea, Spring 1953. (Combat Arms Ser.). (Illus.). 313p. 1986. Repr. 19. 95 (ISBN 0-89839-090-7). Battery Pr.

Robertson, William G. Counterattack on the Naktong 1950. LC 86-2637. (Leavenworth Papers: No. 13). (Illus.). 149p. (Orig.). 1985. pap. 7.00 (S/N 008-020-01079-1). USGPO.

KOREANS IN CANADA

Lehrer, Brian. The Korean Americans. (The Peoples of North America Ser.). (Illus.). 112p. (gr. 5 up). 1988. lib. bdg. 17.95 (ISBN 0-87754-888-9). Chelsea Hse.

KOREANS IN FOREIGN COUNTRIES

Choy, Bong-Youn. Koreans in America. LC 79-9791. 376p. 1979. 26.95x (ISBN 0-88229-352-4). Nelson-Hall.

Dae-Sook Suh, ed. Koreans in the Soviet Union. LC 86-72108. (Papers from the center for Korean Studies: No. 12). 138p. (Orig.). 1987. 17.50; pap. 13.50 (ISBN 0-8248-1155-0). UH Manoa CKS.

Hahn, Byungchai C. A Case Study: How Twenty-One Koreans Perceive America. (TWEC World Education Monographs). 15p. 1978. 2.00 I N Thut World Educ Ctr.

Hurgh, Won Moo & Kim, Kwang Chung. Korean Immigrants LC 82-48466. 280p. 1984. 29.50 (ISBN 0-8386-3145-2). Fairleigh Dickinson.

Hurh, Won M. Comparative Study of Korean Immigrants in the United States: A Typological Approach. LC 76-55959. 1977. soft bdg. 10.95 (ISBN 0-88247-439-1). R&E Pubs.

Hyun, Peter. Man Sei! The Making of a Korean American. LC 86-11314. (Illus.). 186p. 1986. 17.50 (ISBN 0-8248-1041-4). UH Pr.

Hyung-Chan Kim & Patterson, Wayne. The Koreans in America. LC 77-73741. (In America Bks.). (Illus.). 64p. (gr. 5 up). 1977. PLB 8.95 (ISBN 0-8225-0230-5). Lerner Pubns.

Kim, Hyung-Chan. The Korean's in America. LC 74-13732. (Ethnic Chronology Ser.: No. 16). 147p. (gr. 9-12). 1974. text ed. 8.50 (ISBN 0-379-00513-1). Oceana.

Kim, Illsoo. New Urban Immigrants: The Korean Community in New York. LC 80-8556. 352p. 1981. 39.50 (ISBN 0-691-09355-5). Princeton U Pr.

Kim, Sangho J. A Study of the Korean Church & Her People in Chicago, Illinois. LC 75-18129. 1975. soft bdg. 10.95 (ISBN 0-88247-357-3). R & Pubs.

Lee, Changsoo & DeVos, George. Koreans in Japan: Ethnic Conflict & Accommodation. LC 80-6053. (ILlus.). 448p. 1981. 47.50x (ISBN 0-520-0428-1). U of Cal Pr.

Lee, Don C. Acculturation of Korean Residents in Georgia. LC 75-18126. 1975. soft bdg. 12.95 (ISBN 0-88247-360-3). R & E Pubs.

Min, Pyong G. Ethnic Business Enterprise: The Case of Korean Small Business in Atlanta. 200p. 1988. 19. 95 (ISBN 0-934733-15-5); pap. 14.95 (ISBN 0-934733-14-7). Ctr Migration.

Mitchell, Richard H. The Korean Minority in Japan. (Center for Japanese Studies, UC Berkeley: No. 2). 1967. 40.00x (ISBN 0-520-00870-7). U of Cal Pr.

Shim, Steve S. Korean Immigrant Churches Today in Southern California. LC 76-24724. 1977. soft cover 11.95 (ISBN 0-88247-426-X). R & Pubs.

Suh, Dae-Sook. Koreans in the Soviet Union. LC 86-72108. (Occasional Paper: No. 12). 154p. 1987. text ed. 17.00x (ISBN 0-8248-1126-7, Pub. by the Center for Korean Studies); pap. text ed. 13.00 UH Pr.

Weiner, Michael. The Origins of the Korean Community in Japan. LC 86-27548. (Studies on the East Asia). 172p. 1989. text ed. 45.00 (ISBN 0-391-03494-4). Humanities.

Wilkinson, H. Sook. Birth Is More Than Once: The Inner World of Adopted Korean Children. LC 85-62489. 73p. (Orig.). 1985. pap. 7.95 (ISBN 0-9615674-0-6). Sunrise Vent.

KOREANS IN THE UNITED STATES

ˇKang, Tai S. Korean-American Elderly: Access to Resources & Adjustments to Life Changes-An Exchange Approach. (Council on International Studies & Programs Special Studies: No. 151). 190p. 1986. pap. text ed. 15.00x (ISBN 0-924197-02-1, 151). SUNYB Coun Intl Studies.

Lehrer, Brian. The Korean Americans. (The Peoples of North America Ser.). (Illus.). 112p. (gr. 5 up). 1988. lib. bdg. 17.95 (ISBN 0-87754-888-9). Chelsea Hse.

ˇLight, Ivan & Bonacich, Edna. Immigrant Entrepreneurs: Koreans in Los Angeles, 1965-1982. 1988. 45.00 (ISBN 0-520-06146-2). U of Cal Pr.

ˇMacMillan, Dianne & Freeman, Dorothy. My Best Friend Mee-Yung Kim: Meeting a Korean-American Family, Steltenpohl, Jane, ed. (My Best Friends Ser.). (Illus.). 48p. (gr. 3-5. 1989. lib. bdg. 9.98 (ISBN 0-671-65691-0). Messner.

Mangiafico, Luciano. Contemporary American Immigrants: Patterns of Filipino, Korean, & Chinese Settlement in the United States. LC 87-17752. 229p. 1988. lib. bdg. 35.95 (ISBN 0-275-92726-1, C2726). Praeger.

Patterson, Wayne. The Korean Frontier in America: Immigration to Hawaii, 1896-1910. LC 88-1163. (Illus.). 320p. 1988. text ed. 30.00x (ISBN 0-8248-1090-2). UH Pr.

INDEX